PENGUIN BOOKS

A TREASURY OF GREAT AMERICAN SCANDALS

Michael Farquhar is the author of *A Treasury of Royal Scandals: The Shocking True Stories of History's Wickedest, Weirdest, Most Wanton Kings, Queens, Tsars, Popes, and Emperors.* A writer and editor at the *Washington Post* specializing in history, he is coauthor of *The Century: History As It Happened on the Front Page of the Capital's Newspaper.* His work has been published in the *Chicago Sun-Times, Chicago Tribune, Dallas Morning News, Reader's Digest,* and Discovery Online.

A Treasury of Great American Scandals

Tantalizing True Tales of Historic Misbehavior by the Founding Fathers and Others Who Let Freedom Swing

★

Michael Farquhar

PENGUIN BOOKS

PENGUIN BOOKS
Published by the Penguin Group
Penguin Group (USA), 375 Hudson Street, New York, New York 10014, U.S.A.
Penguin Books Ltd, 80 Strand, London WC2R 0RL, England
Penguin Books Australia Ltd, 250 Camberwell Road, Camberwell,
Victoria 3124, Australia
Penguin Books Canada Ltd, 10 Alcorn Avenue, Toronto, Ontario, Canada M4V 3B2
Penguin Books India (P) Ltd, 11 Community Centre, Panchsheel Park,
New Delhi-110 017, India
Penguin Books (N.Z.) Ltd, Cnr Rosedale and Airborne Roads, Albany,
Auckland, New Zealand
Penguin Books (South Africa) (Pty) Ltd, 24 Sturdee Avenue,
Rosebank, Johannesburg 2196, South Africa

Penguin Books Ltd, Registered Offices: 80 Strand, London WC2R 0RL, England

First published in Penguin Books 2003

5 7 9 10 8 6

Illustration credits:
Page ii: T. Patterson Clark. xii, 34, 132, 228, 270: The Granger Collection, New York. 112: David Levine. Courtesy of Kathy Hayes Associates. 168: From *Herblock: A Cartoonist's Life* (Times Books, 1998). Courtesy of The Herb Block Foundation.

LIBRARY OF CONGRESS CATALOGING-IN-PUBLICATION DATA:
Farquhar, Michael.
A treasury of great American scandals : tantalizing true tales of historic misbehavior by the founding fathers and others who let freedom swing / Michael Farquhar.
p. cm.
Includes bibliographical references.
ISBN 0-14-200192-9
1. Scandals—United States—History—Anecdotes. 2. United States—History—Anecdotes. 3. United States—Politics and government—Anecdotes. 4. Statesmen—United States—Bibliography—Anecdotes. 5. Politicians—United States—Biography—Anecdotes. I. Title.

E179.F3 2003
973'.09'9—dc21 2003044457

Printed in the United States of America
Set in Bembo with Horley Old Style Bold and OPTI Powell
Designed by Kathryn Parise

This is dedicated to my aunt and uncle,
Mary Jane and Bill Foote,
with love and gratitude for
all their support and enthusiasm.

Contents

★ *Part II* ★
Cold Wars

★ *Part III* ★
Hail to the Chaff

⋆ *Part IV* ⋆
Congressional Follies

⋆ *Part V* ⋆
Cruel Campaigns

⋆ *Part VI* ⋆
The American Hall of Shame

⋆ *Part VII* ⋆

Murder, Madness, and Just Plain Strange Episodes

229

⋆ *Part VIII* ⋆

Remains to Be Seen

271

Introduction

America the beautiful has scored incredibly well in the great pageant of history, but there have been a few stumbles along the way. That's okay. Sometimes the blunders are the best part of the show. Many less than stellar interludes in the American experience are included in this collection, but nothing after 1980—not a peep about DNA-stained dresses, for example, or astrologically influenced First Ladies. History needs a little time to percolate, after all. Besides, the first three centuries of American scandal should put a little perspective on the relatively minor sins of recent memory.

Certainly the worst episodes of our national past, from Indian degradation to slavery, deserve serious treatment—but in other books. Here the concentration is on individuals, rather than institutions, behaving badly. And though many movie stars, career criminals, and business tycoons have contributed their share to the stew pot of scandal, the people in and around government have consistently added the most spice. Consequently, the focus of this treasury is on them. Their foibles and failures, while sometimes tarnishing the ideals we hold dear, nevertheless provide the dirt in which we so often delight.

Benjamin Franklin back when he still liked his son.

Part I

Family Ties That Bind . . . And Gag

The American family has always been the nation's most precious asset—not only the very foundation of society and source of all values, but a cozy refuge from a cold and uncaring world. *Or not.* For members of many prominent families, home and hearth were pure hell, made miserable by a variety of ghastly relatives. What follows is a look at some of the most dysfunctional families in U.S. history.

★

1

Prepare for a Shock

Differing political ideologies have caused plenty of generational rifts over the ages, though few as profound as the one that developed between Benjamin Franklin and his only son, William. The Founding Father proved to be a harsh and vengeful parent.

The relationship didn't start out poorly. As a matter of fact, father and son made a pretty good team. William helped his dad with his *Poor Richard's Almanack,* served by his side defending the Pennsylvania frontier against Indian raids, and acted as his secretary, travel companion, and confidant. Moreover, he was his partner in science—though only in the sense that a drooling dog was partner to Pavlov. As Benjamin Franklin was preparing to conduct his daring experiment to draw lightning from the clouds with a kite and key, he assigned William the job of racing around a cow pasture with the infernal contraption, as the heavens flashed and roared. Ben sat in the safety of a shepherd's shed.

Few today know William ever existed, let alone that he contributed to his father's work. This obscurity may be due to the fact that Benjamin Franklin excised most references to his son from the final draft of his autobiography. The first draft had in fact been addressed

"Dear Son" and contained details of their twenty-five-year relationship as partners and friends. This version was temporarily shelved, however, and by the time the elder Franklin resumed work on it twelve years later, he had come to regard William as a bitter enemy.

It all began with the unrest in the colonies over British rule. William Franklin had risen through the ranks to become a royal governor of the New Jersey colony and considered himself a loyal son of the mother country. The idea of revolting against England was abhorrent to him. He believed the fate of the American colonies was intrinsically linked with Britain and that "this unnatural contest" pursued by his father and other American radicals would result in nothing but a horribly destructive civil war. His stance was rooted not in political expediency or material gain, but in a deep conviction that was shared by numerous Americans, including relatives of John Adams, John Hancock, and George Washington. As the revolutionary zeal increased in America, William remained firm and loyal in his commitment to king and country.

The final break between father and son came with the Declaration of Independence, and Governor William Franklin could no longer be tolerated by the new nation. His father arranged for his arrest and imprisonment. And a horrible confinement it was. Removed from his residence in New Jersey, William was taken to Connecticut, where he was eventually housed in a solitary cell with a floor covered in old straw matted from the waste of previous occupants. He was denied writing paper, clean clothes, and bathing or even toilet facilities. Benjamin Franklin absolutely forbade William's son, who was in his care, any contact with his imprisoned father. Urging him to abandon William, Benjamin tempted his grandson with a trip to France, which the boy accepted. "I have rescued a valuable young man from the danger of being a Tory," a satisfied Franklin wrote.

During his three-year confinement, William lost his hair, his teeth, his health, and his wife, who died. When she was on her deathbed, George Washington was moved enough to write Congress advocating William's request for one last meeting with her. His "situation is distressing and must interest all our feelings," Washington wrote. "Humanity and generosity plead powerfully in favor of his application." Ben Franklin did not weigh in with his preference, however, and the request was denied. Franklin, meanwhile, kept the interests of other prisoners close to his heart. Writing at least thirteen letters to his friend David Hartley in the British Parliament, he begged him to help alleviate "all the horrors of imprisonment" for his captive countrymen. He hadn't spoken a word to his son in years.

Nine months after the Revolutionary War ended, and nearly a decade since they last had contact, William got word that his father, then in Paris, would be willing to receive a letter from him. On July 22, 1784, he wrote, "Dear and Honoured Father: Ever since the termination of the unhappy contest between Great Britain and America, I have been anxious to write to you and to endeavor to revive that affectionate intercourse and connection which, till commencement of the late troubles, had been the pride and happiness of my life." William wrote that he was not sure his father wanted to hear from him because of "the decided and active part I took in opposition to the measures you thought proper." But he was making no apologies, and in fact made reference to "the cruel sufferings, scandalous neglects, and ill treatment which we poor Loyalists have in general experienced"—though he did not lay any blame for this on his dad. Regarding his activities during the war, William wrote, "I can with confidence appeal not only to you but to my God that I have uniformly acted from a strong sense of what I conceived my duty to my king and regard to my country required. If I have been mistaken, I cannot help it. It is an error of judgment that the maturest reflection I am capable of cannot rectify, and I verily believe, were the same circumstances to occur again tomorrow, my conduct would be exactly similar to what it was."

Three weeks later, William received a reply from his father. It wasn't exactly conciliatory. Benjamin wrote that he was "glad to find you desire to revive the affectionate intercourse that formerly existed between us. It would be very agreeable to me. Indeed, nothing has ever hurt me so much and affected me with such keen sensibilities as to find myself deserted in my old age by my only son; and not only deserted, but to find him taking up arms against me in a cause wherein my good fame, fortune and life were all at stake." As for William's principles, the father was unmoved. "You conceived, you say, that your duty to your King and your regard to your country required this. I ought not to blame you for differing in sentiments with me in public affairs. We are men, all subject to errors. Our opinions are not in our power. They are formed and governed much by circumstances that are often as inexplicable as they are irresistible. Your situation was such that few would have censored your remaining neuter, though there are natural duties which precede political ones, and cannot be extinguished by them. This is a disagreeable subject: I drop it."

Ben Franklin made it clear in his letter that he was not yet ready to see his son, who had been exiled to Britain, where he worked tirelessly for the concerns of Loyalists in America. But a year later they did meet for the last time, to settle financial accounts. Benjamin, nearing eighty and on his way back to America for the last time, "brought all the warmth of a real estate settlement" to the encounter, writes historian Willard Sterne Randall. Father insisted that son sign over deeds to his American property in exchange for the forgiveness of debts owed him. William soon realized Benjamin was making him pay for clothes and pocket money going back to his childhood. The rest of the time designated for the reunion was spent largely apart as Ben met with old friends from England. On the final day, the father slipped away on a States-bound ship, never saying good-bye to his son.

2

Mother Mary, Quite Contrary

George Washington's mother's tombstone reads, with understated dignity: "Mary, the Mother of Washington." A more fitting epitaph might have been "Mary, the Bother of Washington." The Grandma of Our Country proved more aggravating to son George than his false teeth. Mary Ball Washington spent her life in a struggle to keep her son at her disposal. She begrudged him his successes because they kept him, and his money, away from home. Her denigration of his accomplishments led to speculation during the American Revolution that Mrs. Washington was actually a closet Royalist trying to undermine the cause of independence.

Though there is ample evidence that Washington was generous to his mother and that she lived quite comfortably, she never ceased digging deeper into his pockets while loudly complaining of his financial neglect. She seemed to delight in humiliating him as publicly as possible. In 1781, Washington was mortified when he received a letter from Benjamin Harrison, the speaker of the Virginia House of Delegates, advising him of a movement in the House—in response to Mary Washington's cries of poverty—to have the state come to her financial rescue. The great Revolutionary commander was forced to make an excruciating public defense of his treatment of his mom. “Before I left Virginia, I answered all her calls for money, and, since that period, have directed my steward to do the same,” he wrote back. “Whence her distress can arise, therefore, I know not, never having received any complaint. . . . Confident I am that she has not a child that would not divide the last sixpence to relieve her from real distress. This she has been repeatedly assured of by me; and all of us, I am certain, would feel much hurt at having our mother a pensioner.”

In 1787, when his mother was suffering from breast cancer, Washington tried to persuade her to move in with one of her children—just not him. He did extend a tepid invitation for her to come and live at his Mount Vernon estate, but warned that she wouldn’t like it there. The house, he wrote discouragingly, was like “a well resorted tavern,” always filled with strangers. Their presence would require her to dress each day for company, appear publicly in “dishabille,” or remain a prisoner in her room. “The first you’ld not like. The 2nd, I should not like. And the 3rd, more than probably, would not be pleasing to either of us,” he wrote. George must have been relieved when his mom declined the halfhearted offer and stubbornly insisted on remaining independent.

3

Foundering Father

There are two types of fathers. The first instills self-confidence in his children by offering praise when merited and withholding criticism when possible. The second is John Quincy Adams. Adams's two eldest sons committed the unpardonable sin of being merely ordinary, decent guys. Father J.Q. was appalled. His father had been the second president of the United States. He himself was perhaps the greatest secretary of state in the nation's history, as well as its sixth president. His youngest son, Charles, emerged as a great statesman and scholar. But life for George and John Adams was a series of misguided dreams, base disappointments, and episodes of fragile mental health—conditions of which their father was brutally intolerant.

"I am a man of reserved, cold, austere and forbidding manners," John Quincy once said of himself. "I have not the pliability to reform it." His keen insight into himself was particularly apt when it came to his troubled sons. He hovered over their lives like a jealous god, instilling in them not respect so much as terror. Freud would have loved this: Adams's oldest son, George, was sixteen and on his way to Harvard when he described a dream. While receiving flirtatious encouragement from a young lady, "I saw the form of my father visible to me above, his eye fixed upon me." The amorous feelings toward the girl "relapsed into the most cold indifference," while the father's voice "rang at my ear—'Remember, George, who you are and what you are doing.'" Upon awakening, George "sank into a gloomy torpor"—a state that characterized most of his life.

The deep disappointment John Quincy felt in his sons, and never hesitated to share with them, began in earnest while they attended Harvard. Suffice it to say there were no valedictorians in the bunch. Even Charles, who would later become one of the nation's most successful diplomats, was not spared his father's wrath during this period. "I had hoped that at least one of my sons would be ambitious to excel," the elder Adams said. Instead, "the blast of mediocrity" was demeaning the family name. He forbade the boys to come home until their class standings improved, letting them know unequivocally they were in disgrace because of the "mortification" they brought him, "mingled with disgust." He warned, "I would feel nothing but sorrow and shame in your presence."

The only thing that would remove the blight, he pronounced, was each son ranking in the top six of his class, a number he chose arbitrarily and amended at random. Later, he magnanimously allowed that he'd be satisfied if they were in the top ten. He wanted achievements comparable "with that which your grandfather and your father held." Rank, however, soon became irrelevant. Middle son John and more than fifty other Harvard students were expelled on the eve of their graduation for staging a rebellion in protest of the school's denial of a popular classmate's diploma. The errant son was never forgiven.

George, desperate to make his own way in the world, failed miserably at almost everything he tried, from various business endeavors to a stint in the Massachusetts legislature. If the seriously depressed man hadn't fully grasped that he was a failure, his dad was always there to remind him. John Quincy badgered George constantly with threats and even public humiliation. He threw in a little guilt, too. Did George not know, his father inquired once in a letter, "how much of the comfort of my future life depends upon your conduct?"

Embarking on an all-out effort to steer George in the direction he wanted, John Quincy announced he would be returning to Massachusetts at the end of his presidential term in 1829 to take total control over his lost son's life. George, dreading the prospect, particularly as he realized that his parents would discover and condemn the illegitimate child he had conceived with a servant, flung himself into Long Island Sound and drowned.

4

I Now Pronounce You Miserable

Sam Houston, the hero of San Jacinto, was already a well-respected statesman when he married beautiful Eliza Allen in 1829. The marriage was not a good one. It lasted only eleven weeks, and its collapse nearly destroyed his career.

Raised on the Tennessee frontier, Houston was inspired early by the epic tales of *The Iliad*. He quit school at age sixteen and went to live for years among the Cherokee Indians. He fought the Creeks with distinction during the War of 1812, sustaining severe wounds, then became a major general in the Tennessee militia. He also served two terms in Congress and was elected governor. Despite all this, Houston's hero and mentor, Andrew Jackson—soon to become the seventh president—felt Sam's future career would be impeded if he remained a hard-livin' bachelor. Plain folks did not care much for playboys. Something of a matchmaker, Old Hickory insisted that his protégé settle down to the steadying influence of a wife and family.

Governor Houston obediently set his sights on Eliza, twenty, daughter of a Tennessee aristocrat. The two were married in a candlelight ceremony at the Allens' home on January 22, 1829. The public loved this marriage; it was proof at last that their fiery governor was a civilized man. The guests marveled at the beautiful bride, who gazed lovingly upon the handsome groom sixteen years her senior. The newlyweds then spent the night in a specially prepared honeymoon suite. What exactly happened that night is unknown. But it was not good, not good at all. The next day Eliza dutifully accompanied her husband to Nashville as Tennessee's new First Lady. Traveling on horseback, the couple stopped for the night at the home of Martha Martin. The next morning Eliza stood at a window watching her new husband in a snowball fight with the Martin children. Martha Martin remarked jovially that Eliza should go out and help the governor, as the children seemed to be getting the best of him. She later recalled Eliza's reaction. "Looking seriously at me, Mrs. Houston said: 'I wish they would kill him.' I looked up, astonished to hear such a remark from a bride of not yet forty-eight hours, when she repeated in the same voice, 'Yes, I wish from the bottom of my heart that they would kill him.'"

What had happened? Theories abound. One rumor handed down over the years has it that the worldly and promiscuous Houston tried to persuade the sheltered and virginal Eliza to participate in some of the exotic sexual positions he had picked up from the Cherokee and at various New Orleans bordellos. But biographer Marshall De Bruhl offers the most plausible explanation: Eliza was most likely revolted by the sight of her new husband's body, which was marred by the festering wounds he had suffered fighting the Creek Indians. An arrow had pierced his upper thigh, causing enormous damage, while two lead rifle balls had become embedded in his shoulder. The gunshot wounds never healed properly, covering his shoulder with great purple and red scars. Contemporary biographer C. Edwards Lester noted that "no surgical skill has ever been able to close up [the thigh] wound. It has discharged every day for thirty years."

In less than three months, Eliza left Nashville and went home. Houston was faced with total ruin. The public saw this sudden breakup as a betrayal. Was their governor some beast whose appetites drove a chaste young woman from his bed? Was he a debaucher? In several Tennessee towns, he was burned in effigy. Determined to reason with his wife, Houston rode to the Allen plantation and demanded to see her. An aunt of Eliza's witnessed him on his knees and in tears, begging "with all his dramatic force" for her to come back to him. Eliza refused, and the dejected man returned to Nashville.

The failed marriage forced his resignation as governor, after which he spiraled into an exile of hard drinking and aimless wandering. Some reported seeing him reeling through the streets, dressed only in a calfskin. In 1832, though, he wandered into the republic of Texas, where he went on to become its first president, a renowned patriot, a military hero, and defender of the Union. Twice more he married, with substantially greater success: He fathered eight children. But to his dying day, he never disclosed what terrible thing had happened on his first wedding night. Nor did Eliza.

5

Dishonor Thy Mother

Few who have studied the life of Mary Todd Lincoln would dispute that she could be, at times, a roaring pain in the rear. Haughty and high-strung, this nineteenth-century First Lady alienated half the people she encountered. "This woman was to me a terror," said William H. Herndon, describing Mrs. Lincoln as "imperious, proud, aristocratic . . . and bitter."

Abraham Lincoln himself recognized that some people had a strong aversion to his wife. In one letter he wrote her while he was serving in Washington as a congressman from Illinois and living in a local boardinghouse, he sent "the love in the house with whom you were on decided good terms—the others say nothing." And though Honest Abe was devoted to his wife, she sometimes drove him nuts as well. Her lavish tastes and obsessive spending were always unpleasant issues between them, as were her occasional fits of fury. During one such episode early in their marriage, Mary Lincoln was seen chasing her husband down the street with a butcher knife. On another occasion, an officer recorded her rage when she was inadvertently left out of a military review toward the end of the Civil War: "Mrs. Lincoln repeatedly attacked her husband in the presence of officers. . . . He bore it as Christ might have done with an expression of pain and sadness that cut one to the heart, but with supreme calmness and dignity. He called her mother, with his old-time plainness. He pleaded with eyes and tones, till she turned on him like a tigress and then he walked away hiding that noble ugly face so that we might not catch the full expression of its misery."

Mary Lincoln's histrionic tendencies grew more pronounced as she aged, but considering the horrors she faced in her life—the assassination of her husband and the untimely deaths of three children among them—her sometimes bizarre behavior was understandable. It certainly did not merit the cruel fate to which her only surviving son consigned her.

Rigid and uptight, Robert Lincoln was nothing like his more homespun dad, especially when it came to Mary Lincoln. While the president had indulged her many quirks, including her attempts to commune with her dead children through mediums, Robert was appalled by his mom. It wasn't so much that she smothered him or fought with his wife. It wasn't even her sometimes embarrassing eccentricities, though they did mortify him. It was her spending. Mary Lincoln was extravagant to the extreme, and Robert did not like that at all. Judging by the way he went about having her committed, a cynic might say he feared for his inheritance.

It was an ambush. On the morning of May 19, 1875, three men arrived unexpectedly at the Chicago hotel where Mrs. Lincoln had taken a room. They told her that she would have to accompany them immediately to the local courthouse, where a jury was waiting to judge her sanity. One of the men was Leonard Swett, a Chicago lawyer who had nominated her husband for president in 1860. Now he was representing her son, who had charged her with lunacy. The two other men were uniformed officers, there to use force if necessary.

"Your friends, with great unanimity, have come to the conclusion that the troubles you have been called to pass through have been too much and have produced mental illness," Swett told her. Astonished, Mrs. Lincoln replied, "If you mean to say I am crazy—I am much obliged to you but I am absolutely able to take care of myself.

Where is my son Robert?" At this point the poor woman had no idea that her son Robert had orchestrated the ordeal she was now facing. She would find out soon enough when he was presented as the star witness against her.

Swett informed Mrs. Lincoln that six doctors had already diagnosed insanity, and that it would be best if she came along quietly. Of course, not having been personally examined by any of these doctors, she protested. "They know nothing of me," she said. "What does this mean?" It meant that Robert Lincoln had hired the doctors to testify against his mother. They were part of a long roster of witnesses he had assembled and paid off to help make his case, and they were now waiting at the courthouse to pass judgment on the famous widow.

Realizing that Mrs. Lincoln would not easily be coaxed out of her room, Swett grew firmer. "I told her there were two carriages downstairs," he recounted, "one of them was mine and the other belonged to the officers, and unless she yielded to me I either had to seize her forcibly myself or turn her over to the officers, who might handcuff her if necessary and certainly would take her to court." Upset and frightened, Mary Lincoln lashed out at Swett, advising him that he ought to attend to his own wife, a longtime invalid, and leave her alone. "I have heard some stories on that subject about [your wife]," she snapped, "and you my husband's friend, you would take me and lock me up in an asylum." Then, according to Swett, she threw up her hands and tearfully "prayed to the Lord and called upon her husband to release her and drive me away." Finally, Mrs. Lincoln yielded and agreed to accompany Swett peacefully. She did, however, refuse any of his assistance in getting into the carriage. "I ride with you from compulsion," she said, "but I beg you not to touch me."

Arriving at the courthouse a few moments later, the former First Lady was ushered into a courtroom packed with people eager to witness the unfolding spectacle. But the proceedings were briefly delayed when Isaac Arnold, another Chicago lawyer and friend of Lincoln's, suddenly declined to serve as Mrs. Lincoln's defense attorney. He had been retained by Robert's camp as a reliable old boy who would not thwart their weak case by mounting an effective defense of the client they had assigned to him. Outraged by his defection, Swett confronted Arnold. "You will put into her head that she can get some mischievous lawyer to make and defend her," he hissed. "Do your duty." Although the reason for Arnold's decision to withdraw from the case remains clouded—perhaps a pang of conscience?—he eventually came around, and the case against Mary Lincoln proceeded in this kangaroo court.

Seventeen witnesses were produced by the prosecution, including the expert doctors who had never examined Mrs. Lincoln, but who had concluded she was fit for the asylum after hearing her symptoms described to them by Robert Lincoln and his lawyers. The court also heard from various hotel employees, including one housekeeper who proffered the damning testimony that "Mrs. Lincoln's manner was nervous and excitable," and a waiter who testified that she appeared "carelessly dressed and repeated 'I am afraid, I am afraid.'" A number of salesclerks also were produced to show how dangerously extravagant she was. One of them described her efforts to "beat down" the price he was charging for gloves and handkerchiefs, and concluded she was "crazy." Finally there was Robert Lincoln himself. "I have no doubt my mother is insane," he told the court. "She has long been a source of great anxiety to me. She has no home and no reason to make those purchases."

The defense rested without ever raising an objection or offering a witness of its own. Robert Lincoln would not have stood for that. While the jury retired to consider the evidence, he approached his mother and tried to take her hand. Rejecting the transparent gesture, Mary Lincoln made her only statement of the day: "Oh, Robert, to think that my son would do this to me." Ten minutes later, the all-male jury was back to deliver their verdict: insane.

The day after her trial, Mary Lincoln was sent to Bellevue Place, a private asylum outside Chicago. She would spend all her time there trying to get out, while Robert worked every bit as hard to keep her in. He was furious when his maternal aunt Elizabeth offered Mary sanctuary in her Springfield home. He also complained loudly of "an extraordinary interference" by Mrs. Lincoln's two greatest advocates, Judge James B. Bradwell and his wife, Myra. The couple, whom Robert condemned as "pests and nuisances," engineered her release through a public campaign and the threat of an open hearing that would show the world just how sane she really was.

Three months after entering Bellevue Place, Mary Lincoln was released. But by order of the court that had convicted her, Robert still had control over her movements and possessions for at least one year, a fact that rankled his mother no end. "To her proud spirit it is very galling awaiting the time when right of person and property will be restored to her," Robert's aunt Elizabeth wrote to him. The son had no intention of allowing more spending sprees, however, and kept a tight grip on his mother's purse. It was only after she successfully petitioned the court that her money was released to her. In a letter to her "monster of mankind son," brimming with resentment and lacking even a cordial salutation, Mary Lincoln demanded the return of everything she had ever given him:

> Do not fail to send me without *the least* delay, *all* my paintings . . . also other articles your wife appropriated and which are *well known* to you, must be sent, without a day's delay. Two lawyers and myself have just been together and their list coincides with my own and will be published in a few days. . . . Send me my laces, my diamonds, my jewelry. . . . I am now in constant receipt of letters, from my friends denouncing you in the bitterest terms. . . . Two prominent clergymen have written me, since I saw you, and mention in their letters, that they think it advisable to offer prayers for you in Church, on account of your wickedness against me and High Heaven. . . . Send me all that I have written for, you have tried your game of robbery long enough.

The letter was one of the last communications from a wronged mother to her treacherous son. They never reconciled.

6

A Short, Ugly Story

In 1875 James Stephen Hogg, the first native-born Texan to become the state's governor, named his daughter Ima.

Enough said.

7

With This Ring, I Thee Dread

President Harding's father perfectly captured the essence of his son when he declared, "Warren, it's a good thing you weren't born a girl because you'd be in the family way all the time. You can't say *No*." It was the twenty-ninth president's fatal flaw. His keen desire to please his friends, coupled with a chronic aversion to conflict, produced one of the most scandal-plagued administrations in American history, as Harding's poker-playing pals used their positions to plunder the government.[1] Yet it was in his personal life that Harding's debilitating weakness had its most withering effects.

He was twenty-five when he married Florence Mabel Kling DeWolfe, a shrill, dowdy harridan who had pursued him relentlessly. A thirty-year-old divorcée, she was tall and mannish, and the handsome, patrician Harding never liked her. Once, when he was arriving in town by train, he saw her on the platform and tried to sneak off the other side. She spotted him, however, and shouted in her flat Ohio burr, "You needn't try to run away, Wurr'n Harding. I see

1. See Part VI, Chapter 6.

your big feet." A stronger man would have kept walking. Wurr'n got worn down.

It was a miserable marriage in which he submitted feebly to her domination. His grudging nickname for her was "the Duchess." Her shrewish ways literally sickened him, driving him to seek refuge several times in Michigan's famed Battle Creek Sanitarium, J. P. Kellogg's crackpot resort featuring enema therapy. Inarguably, however, it was the Duchess who was largely responsible for his success. She oversaw the circulation of his Marion, Ohio, newspaper with crisp efficiency, increasing its revenues, and zealously plotted his unlikely political ascent. After his election in 1920 she reportedly said to him, "Well, Wurr'n Harding, I got you the presidency. What are you going to do with it?"

Making his own contribution to this unhappy union, Harding engaged in two extended affairs. His first mistress was Carrie Phillips, wife of a longtime friend. The brazen Carrie would often strut down the street in front of the Hardings' Ohio home, to the outrage of the scorned wife. A professor from Ohio Wesleyan University happened to be visiting on one such occasion and later recalled what happened: Carrie was standing on the front lawn talking to Harding, who was on the front porch. "Suddenly, Mrs. Harding appeared. A feather duster came sailing out at Mrs. Phillips, then a wastebasket. Mrs. Phillips did not retreat. Next came a piano stool, one of those old, four-legged things with a swivel seat by which it could be lowered or raised. Not until then was there a retreat. She tossed him a kiss and left quietly."

The affair ended badly when Carrie demanded marriage shortly before Harding was elected president. Possessing all his love letters, she threatened him with blackmail, even though he had already given her a Cadillac and offered her $5,000 a year. Campaign manager Albert Lasker sought to avoid scandal by paying her $20,000 and an all-expenses-paid trip around the world with her husband under the condition that they leave before the election.

Overlapping the Phillips affair was another with Nan Britton, who had developed a crush on Harding as an Ohio teenager. She was twenty and still a virgin when they first made love. Their affair continued after he became president in 1921. When Nan visited the White

House, they would sneak off to a five-by-five-foot coat closet and squeeze in some sex. Once they were nearly busted by the Duchess. Five minutes after they entered the tiny space, Florence showed up, arms flailing and fire in her eyes, demanding that the Secret Service agent posted at the door get out of her way. When he refused, she ran around the corner to enter the closet through an anteroom. The agent banged loudly on the door to alert the president, who slipped Nan away. Harding had just enough time to slide behind his desk and pretend to be working when the Duchess burst in. Eventually, Nan gave birth to Harding's baby and published a lurid account of their affair.

Though the theory that Florence Harding secretly poisoned her husband in the middle of his first and only term has been largely discredited (he died of heart failure), she certainly must have felt the urge. And death, no doubt, was a blessed relief for him.

8

Smother-in-Law

If Eleanor Roosevelt had any inkling just how monstrous her new mother-in-law would be, she may very well have begged new husband, Franklin, to make their European honeymoon permanent. The young bride was facing a formidable lady who liked control, especially over her only child. Sara Delano Roosevelt was so domineering that she even moved near Harvard so she could keep an eye on Franklin while he studied there. Needless to say, she didn't relish the prospect of sharing her precious son with another woman. "Franklin gave me quite a startling announcement," she wrote in her journal after hearing he had proposed to his distant cousin Eleanor in 1903.

"I know what pain I must have caused you," Franklin wrote his mother, "and you know I wouldn't do it if I really could have helped it." Eleanor, too, tried to be consoling about the announcement Sara was treating like a cancer diagnosis. "I know just how you feel and how hard it must be," she wrote the woman who would torment her for years to come, "but I do so want you to learn to love me a little."

In an effort to placate the threatened matriarch, the young couple agreed to her demand that they keep the engagement a secret for one year, during which time, Sara hoped, the romance might cool. To that end, she took her son on a cruise to distract him from his intended, and even tried to arrange a job for him out of the country. Poor Eleanor had no clue about her future mother-in-law's machinations and wrote Franklin upon his return from the cruise: "I knew your Mother would hate to have you leave her, dear, but don't let her feel that the last trip with you is over. We three must take them together in the future . . . and though I know three will never be the same to her, still someday I hope that she really will love me and I would be very glad if I thought she was even the least bit reconciled to me now."

Wishful thinking!

Eleanor Roosevelt's letters of the period reflect the shy, awkward, somewhat needy young woman she was at the time—far from the powerful liberal icon she would become. Orphaned since she was just nine years old, the sad little girl grew up desperate for love and acceptance, a condition Sara Roosevelt recognized and of which she took full advantage. When it became clear to her that she would not be able to stop the marriage, she determined to dominate it instead. Her daughter-in-law, reluctant to upset the old lady, offered little resistance. She even took to parroting Sara's narrow and bigoted opinions in a vain effort to please her. "[Eleanor] had already lived through so much unhappiness," a cousin later remarked to *Eleanor and Franklin* author Joseph P. Lash, "and then to have married a man with a mother like [Sara]."

Mrs. Roosevelt helped get the marriage off to a nice healthy start when she built the couple a home in New York City—directly adjoining the one she had built for herself. To make it easier for her to pop in any time she pleased, Sara had all four floors of the twin houses conveniently open up to one another. "You were never quite sure when she would appear, day or night," Eleanor later said of the suffocating arrangement. And if living right next to her son and his wife wasn't stifling enough, Sara felt free to take charge of their household as well, leaving Eleanor with nothing to do but sulk. One time Franklin found her weeping and asked what was the matter. "I said I did not like to live in a house which was not in any way mine," she later recalled, "one that I had done nothing about and which did not represent the way I wanted to live." Having grown up under Sara's strong thumb, Franklin saw nothing odd about the living arrangement and was bewildered by his wife's tears.

The already untenable situation grew worse when Eleanor and Franklin started to have children. For Sara, it meant a new generation of lives she could order and control. "I was your real mother," she later told her grandchildren, "Eleanor merely bore you." In the quest to become the adored focus of the children's lives, Sara acquiesced to their every whim and habitually countermanded all parental discipline. "We chicks quickly learned that the best way to circumvent Pa and Mummy when we wanted something they wouldn't give us was to appeal to Granny," James Roosevelt wrote.

Good old Granny was particularly helpful when Franklin became paralyzed with polio in 1921. She resented all the aid and support her son received from his friend and political supporter Louis Howe, whom she saw as an outsider usurping her exclusive domain. When "that ugly, dirty little man," as she described Howe, moved in with the Roosevelts to better assist them, Sara seized on the opportunity to pit her fifteen-year-old granddaughter Anna against Eleanor, who had invited him to stay. Howe was given Anna's bedroom, leaving her to sleep in a smaller cubicle. Sara quietly stoked Anna's adolescent fury over the setup. "I agreed completely with Granny that I was being discriminated against," Anna later remarked, ignoring the fact that Eleanor was sleeping on a small cot at the time to make more room for her sick husband's care and treatment. "Granny's needling finally took root," Anna continued. "At her instigation, I went to Mother one evening and demanded a switch in rooms. A sorely tired and harassed mother was naturally anything but sympathetic; in fact she was very stern with her recalcitrant daughter."[1]

Sara's constant interference added enormously to Eleanor's stress, but it characterized their relationship for years. "That old lady with

1. The "recalcitrant" daughter later caused her mother even more grief when Eleanor discovered Anna had been complicit in Franklin's affair with Lucy Mercer Rutherfurd. Indeed, all six of the Roosevelt children—with nineteen marriages between them—were quite a handful.

all her charm and distinction and kindliness hides a primitive jealousy of her daughter-in-law which is sometimes startling in its crudity," wrote Eleanor's close friend Caroline Phillips. Sara rarely missed an opportunity to criticize Eleanor, whether over her choice of friends, the way she dressed, her care of Franklin, or the way she raised children. The barbs were often covered with a veneer of sweetness, which made them all the more annoying, and continued until Sara's death in 1940. Eleanor, who was by that time a well-seasoned First Lady, had grown increasingly stronger and more confident—and much less willing to take any guff from her mother-in-law.

"What ironical things happen in life and how foolish it all seems," Eleanor wrote a friend after Sara's death. "I looked at my mother-in-law's face after she was dead and understood so many things I'd never seen before. It is dreadful to have lived so close to someone for thirty-six years and feel no deep affection or sense of loss."

9

One Bad Apple Tree

"My mother is a nothing," John F. Kennedy reportedly said once of family matriarch Rose Fitzgerald Kennedy. Ungenerous as this assessment may sound, it bears a certain truth. For when it came to shaping the destinies of the Kennedy children, especially the sons, Rose's influence was mostly incidental. It was Joseph P. Kennedy who, in the words of his wife, served as "the architect of our lives." With his wealth, power, and all-consuming ambition, he built the political careers of his sons. But he laid the foundation with his own corruption.

Joe Kennedy wasn't a terrible father in the sense that he beat or abused his children. On the contrary, he was devoted to them and deeply involved in their lives—when he wasn't out womanizing or away making his millions. The problem was that he wanted to mold his sons to be men in his own image, extensions of his own ego. In this he was remarkably successful, yet with his own moral compass so hopelessly off kilter, it was a terrible disservice.

"Daddy was always very competitive," recalled Eunice Kennedy Shriver. "The thing he always kept telling us was that coming in second was just no good." Winning was the paramount virtue to Joe

Kennedy. He had achieved great success and fortune, often through ruthlessness and cunning, and he wanted his children to be winners as well. "Not once in more than two hundred letters did he put forward any ultimate moral principles for his children to contemplate," writes historian Doris Kearns Goodwin. "On the contrary, he stressed to his children the importance of winning at any cost and the pleasures of coming in first. As his own heroes were not poets or artists but men of action, he took it for granted that his children too wanted public success, and he confined himself to advising them how they could get it. All too often, his understanding about their desires and his practical advice were fruits of his experience and his dreams, not necessarily theirs."

Kennedy's daughters-in-law had him to thank for the influence he had on their philandering husbands. He was himself an inveterate adulterer who, in his later years, practically had his sons pimping for him when he wanted a date. One of the most famous of all his paramours was the actress Gloria Swanson, whom he had met in 1927 during his stint as a Hollywood mogul. Kennedy made little effort to hide the affair. Swanson was, after all, a major sex symbol, and bedding her certainly stroked his vanity. He never hesitated to bring Gloria home to meet his children, and once even cruised across the Atlantic with her *and* his wife. "If [Rose Kennedy] suspected me of having relations not quite proper with her husband, or resented me for it, she never gave any indication of it," Swanson wrote. "In fact, at those times during the voyage when Joe Kennedy behaved in an alarmingly possessive or oversolicitous fashion toward me, Rose joined right in and supported him." The arrangement was odd enough for Swanson to wonder: "Was she a fool . . . or a saint? Or just a better actress than I was?"

Joe Kennedy dishonored his wife with his chronic womanizing, but Rose seems to have tolerated the situation well enough to simply ignore it. Perhaps a far greater disservice was his complete disregard for her feelings about the welfare of their mentally retarded daughter, Rosemary. He made a profound, and ultimately devastating, decision about the young woman's very existence without ever bothering to consult with his wife: He had her lobotomized when her behavior started to become uncontrollable as she reached adulthood. "He thought it would help her," Rose Kennedy told Doris Kearns Goodwin with some bitterness, "but it made her go all the way back. It erased all those years of effort I had put into her. All along I continued to believe that she could have lived her life as a Kennedy girl, just a little slower. But then it was all gone in a matter of minutes."

What Joe Kennedy taught his children, and showed them by example, was how to be just like Joe Kennedy. He passed down to them not only his low opinion of women, including their mother, but all his other biases and prejudices as well. Eldest son Joe Jr., for example, nicely reflected his father's fierce anti-Semitism in a 1934 letter he wrote home while traveling through Hitler's Germany. The increasing oppression of Germany's Jews, young Joe concluded, was justified by their own behavior. "[The Jews] were at the heads of all big business, in law, etc.," he wrote. "It is all to their credit for them to get so far, but their methods have been quite unscrupulous. . . . As far as the brutality is concerned, it must have been necessary to use some, to secure the whole-hearted support of the people, which was necessary to put through this present program. . . . As you know, [Hitler] has passed the sterilization law which I think is a good thing. I don't know how the Church feels about it but it will do away with many of the disgusting specimens of men who inhabit this earth." Sentiments sure to make Pops proud.

After making his fortune in banking, stock manipulation, and, as has been alleged, bootlegging, Joe Kennedy entered the political arena as a means of enhancing his power and prestige. His public career ended disastrously, however. As U.S. ambassador to Great Britain on the eve of World War II, Kennedy became an outspoken defeatist, going as far as to declare that democracy was dead in England. With his inglorious departure from center stage, the ambassador—as he insisted he be called for the rest of his life—foisted his ambitions onto his sons.

"I got Jack into politics," the ambassador later boasted; "I was the one. I told him [elder brother] Joe was dead and that it was therefore his responsibility to run for Congress. He didn't want to. He felt he didn't have the ability. . . . But I told him he had to." Jack Kennedy wasn't pushed into the political arena because of the great services his father felt he could offer the nation. The motive was far more cynical than that: It was to enhance the Kennedy brand name. "We're going to sell Jack like soap flakes," the ambassador once said, underscoring just how inconsequential true political ideals were when it came to winning.

Utilizing all his substantial resources, Joe Kennedy ultimately propelled one son to the White House, another to the attorney general's office, and a third to the U.S. Senate. It didn't matter much that Ted Kennedy, barely old enough to qualify for the Senate, had never held elected office before. It was all for the greater glory of Joe Kennedy. However, the ambassador, having reached the pinnacle of success through his sons, did not have long to savor his victories. He suffered a massive stroke at the end of 1961 and for the next eight years watched in helpless silence as his dreams collapsed with the assassinations of two sons and the crowning blow to the Kennedy dynasty, Chappaquiddick. He died in 1969, yet his legacy lives on, without a hint of irony, at the Joseph P. and Rose F. Kennedy Institute of *Ethics* (emphasis, of course, added) at Georgetown University.

10

Oh, Brother!

Presidential siblings have always provided a steady source of embarrassment for their more prominent brothers. Thomas Jefferson was forever chagrined by the inanities of his younger brother, Randolph. There are indications that Randy was rather dimwitted and something of a buffoon. Tom had to keep an eagle eye on Randolph's financial affairs lest he bankrupt himself through sheer stupidity. The greatest indictment of Randolph Jefferson comes from the gently self-effacing recollections of a Monticello slave named Issac: "[Randolph] was one mighty simple man—used to come out among the black people, play the fiddle and dance half the night; hadn't much more sense than Issac."

Ulysses S. Grant's administration was nearly done in by the shenanigans of the president's younger brother, Orvil, a thief and scoundrel of the first order. Orvil and Grant's secretary of war, William Belknap, lined their pockets with kickbacks from the sale of lucrative trading post franchises on the Western frontier. Since army regulations required soldiers to patronize the posts, a franchise was a valuable commodity with a guaranteed clientele. Annual payments to Grant and Belknap, however, forced traders to charge outrageously high prices for goods; even General George Armstrong Custer felt the pinch. Custer caused a huge sensation when he testified against

Belknap and implicated Orvil Grant during a Senate investigation that clinched Grant's as the most corrupt administration to that date.

Lyndon Johnson did his darnedest to avoid being shamed by his unpredictable brother, Sam Houston Johnson, but his efforts ultimately backfired. Like many siblings of the successful, Sam Houston lived in his brother's shadow. LBJ even had him living at the White House during his administration so he could keep an eye on him and control the fallout from his famous fondness for drink. Sam came to refer to the president's home as "the penitentiary": While being driven up the driveway he would hold his wrists together as if cuffed and shout, "Back to my cell." For a time LBJ was successful in reining in his brother, keeping his profile so low with busywork that people started calling him "Silent Sam." The silence, however, was soon to be shattered. Lyndon Johnson was said to have been deeply embarrassed by Sam's book, *My Brother, Lyndon,* which was released soon after the president's inglorious departure from the White House in 1969. Sam's portrait of his brother was hardly flattering. "I've always said that anyone who worked for my brother for at least a month deserved the Purple Heart," he wrote. The estrangement between the brothers lasted until LBJ's death in 1973.

If uncouth behavior really is an unconscious form of sibling rivalry, Billy Carter—the mother of all embarrassing brothers—had to have been waging war. This hillbilly cartoon of a character, however, never failed to entertain. Whether holding court in front of his Plains, Georgia, gas station, or making one of his numerous, and well-paid, public appearances—like judging and participating in a world championship belly flop competition—he was ever dependable as a goofy foil. Like when he was seen urinating in public while waiting at the airport for a delegation of Libyans he was hosting. Indeed the Libyan relationship was Billy Carter's crowning glory, especially when he accepted a $220,000 loan for representing the outlaw nation's interests, and got a federal investigation aimed at him just in time for Jimmy's reelection campaign. The president always said he was loath to interfere in his brother's business, possibly because Billy had already announced what he'd do if big brother ever did: "I'd tell him to kiss my ass."

Vice President Aaron Burr resolves his issues with Alexander Hamilton.

Part II

Cold Wars

Hatfield vs. McCoy may be the most famous American feud, but it was by no means an aberration. We the people have made bickering among ourselves a treasured pastime, especially the most prominent among us. The winding path of U.S. history is strewn with great spats—some lethal, others just plain old nasty.

★

1

Feuding Founding Fathers

Busy as they were building a new nation, the Founding Fathers always managed to squeeze in enough time to tear one another apart. In this mode, they came off looking more like squabbling fishwives—hurling insults and nursing petty resentments—than a brotherhood united in the quest for freedom. John Adams, "the crankiest Founding Father," as historian Jack D. Warren calls him, was involved in many of these sometimes vicious quarrels. He seems to have had a gripe with just about all of his esteemed colleagues, including George Washington, under whom he served as the nation's first vice president.[1]

"The rushing and dashing and roaring of the word Washington, Washington, Washington," Adams wrote resentfully, "like the waters at Passaic or the tremendous cataract of Niagara, deafens stuns astonishes and bedizzards, all who are within hearing."

It wasn't that Adams disliked Washington—he actually admired

1. Adams's status as vice president was part of his problem with George Washington, who kept him largely out of the loop—a trend that continued through many subsequent administrations. "I am vice president," Adams maintained; "in this I am nothing."

him in some ways—but all the laudatory attention he received, especially after his death in 1799, drove Adams nuts. "The feasts and funerals in honor of Washington," he complained, "is as corrupt a system as that by which saints were canonized and cardinals, popes, and whole hierarchical systems created." That his fellow Federalists idolized Washington galled Adams, who declared that they "have done themselves and their country invaluable injury by making Washington their military, political, religious and even moral Pope, and ascribing everything to him."

The roots of Adams's resentment of "the superstitious veneration that is sometimes paid to Genl Washington" lay in part with his own diminishing reputation. After his defeat in the presidential election of 1800, he was obsessed by what historian Joseph Ellis calls "a frantic and uncontrollable craving for personal vindication, a lust for fame," and "an acute awareness that history would not do him justice." To Adams, it just wasn't fair that Washington was getting all the credit for fathering the new nation. Many leaders, including himself, played key roles in the revolution, he insisted, complaining that it "offended against eternal justice to give to one, as the People do, the Merits of so many." Besides, Washington wasn't so great to begin with. In a letter to Benjamin Rush, Adams listed the "talents" to which Washington owed "his immense elevation above his fellows," noting sardonically that none of these talents involved "reading, thinking, or writing":

1. An handsome face. That this is a talent, I can prove by the authority of a thousand instances in all ages. . . .
2. A tall stature, like the Hebrew sovereign chosen because he was taller by the head than the other Jews.
3. An elegant form.
4. Graceful attitudes and movements.
5. A large, imposing fortune consisting of a great landed estate left him by his father and brother, besides a large jointure with his lady. . . .
6. Washington was a Virginian. This is equivalent to five talents. Virginian geese are all swans. Not a bairn in Scotland is more national, not a lad upon the Highlands is more

clannish, than every Virginian I have ever known. . . . The Philadelphia and New Yorkers, who are local and partial enough to themselves, are meek and modest in comparison with Virginian Old Dominionism. Washington, of course, was extolled without bounds.

7. Washington was preceded by favorable anecdotes.
8. He possessed the gift of silence. . . . This I esteem as one of the most precious talents.
9. He had great self-command.
10. Whenever he lost his temper, as he sometimes did, either love or fear in those about him induced them to conceal his weakness from the world.

If Adams was jealous of George Washington, he absolutely despised Benjamin Franklin, no slouch himself when it came to cultivating enemies—including his own son.[2] Adams called Franklin "the old Conjurer," dismissing him as a phony who managed to fool people with trite philosophies and contrived charm. Franklin didn't think much of Adams, either: "He means well for his country, is always an honest man, often a wise one, but sometimes and in some things, absolutely out of his senses."

Oddly enough, the two Founding Fathers had gotten along relatively well while serving together in the Second Continental Congress. Adams even wrote to his wife, Abigail, that Franklin was a "great and good Man," if a tad overrated as a leader. Trouble only began later, in 1778, when Adams joined Franklin in Paris as part of a three-man commission seeking to buttress France's support for the American war against Britain. Their first mistake was living together, and even sharing a bed—a sure way of transforming quirks of personality into glaring annoyances. Franklin's shameless flirtations with the ladies of Paris shocked Adams's Puritan sensibilities, as did his lackadaisical approach to work. (Ben was not one to follow his own

2. See Part I, Chapter 1.

aphorisms such as "Early to bed, early to rise. . . .") It probably didn't help matters that Franklin was revered in France while Adams's arrival barely made a ripple. A bruised ego no doubt informed the newcomer's assertion that Franklin had "a Monopoly of Reputation here [in France], and an Indecencey in displaying it."

The relationship was further strained when Congress dissolved the commission less than a year after Adams arrived in France. With no new assignment, Adams was despondent and determined to return home. He was booked to sail on the American frigate *Alliance,* but just as he was about to depart, Franklin informed him that the naval hero John Paul Jones needed the ship and that he would have to stay in France for a few more months. Adams, who didn't much care for Jones either, felt slighted—sacrificed, he believed, to Jones's ambition. His resentment was soon replaced by the nagging suspicion that Franklin was deliberately upsetting his travel plans to prevent his telling "some dangerous Truths" at home, presumably that Franklin was in cahoots with a French merchant trading with America, and that he was profiting at the public's expense. "Does the old Conjurer dread my voice in Congress?" Adams wrote in his diary. "He had some Reason for he has often heard it there, a Terror to evil doers."

Adams did eventually make it home on another ship, but it wasn't long before he was back in France, appointed by Congress as minister plenipotentiary to negotiate an end to the War of Independence. Needless to say, he did not move back in with Ben. He didn't even tell his former housemate the exact details of his appointment, lest Franklin find a way to sabotage it. Though they always maintained a cordial façade, the animosity between the two men intensified over their conflicting approaches in dealing with France, now America's indispensable ally in the war with Britain. Adams thought Franklin was too acquiescent with the French, too fearful of upsetting them. Franklin, he charged, believed "affairs in Europe ought to be under one direction, and that the French ought to be the center." For his own part, Franklin thought Adams too strident in pursuing American interests. "Decency and Delicacy," he said, were vital in securing greater assistance from France. Adams, he felt, lacked both.

French foreign minister Charles Gravier Vergennes, a snob of the highest order, preferred Franklin's more deferential style and quickly grew tired of Adams's bold entreaties on behalf of the United States. After receiving a letter from Adams calling for French naval support, Vergennes cut off communications completely, announcing that henceforth he would deal only with Franklin. "The King [Louis XVI]," he disdainfully informed Adams, "[does] not stand in need of your solicitation to direct his attention to the interests of the United States." Vergennes also sent a packet of Adams's pushy letters to Franklin with a note saying, "The King expects that you will lay the whole before Congress."

This Franklin did with apparent relish, adding his own note of condemnation. "Mr. Adams has given extreme offense to the court here," Franklin wrote to Congress. "Having nothing else wherewith to employ himself, he seems to have endeavored to supply what he may suppose my negotiations defective in. He thinks, as he tells me himself, that America has been too free in expressions of gratitude to France; for that she is more obliged to us than we to her; and that we should show spirit in our applications. I apprehend that he mistakes his ground."

Adams never forgave Franklin for this wholly unnecessary public slam, and later he expressed his contempt in a letter to Robert Livingston: "Sir, I must say, that I can lay no stress upon the Opinion of this unintelligible Politician [Franklin]. If I was in Congress, and this gentleman and the Marble Mercury in the Garden of Versailles were in Nomination for an Embassy, I would not hesitate to give my Vote for the Statue, upon the principle that it would do no harm."

★

John Adams may not have made many friends among the other Founding Fathers, but he did consider Thomas Jefferson a pal—particularly since the Sage of Monticello, eight years younger, always managed to give Adams his propers. Jefferson knew just how to stroke his colleague's prickly ego and leave him purring like a placated cat.

"Spent the evening with Mr. Jefferson, whom I love to be with," Adams effused in his diary, one of many such entries during the period they spent together as American ministers in Paris. Even Abigail Adams, always a hawk when it came to her husband's interests, was drawn in by Jefferson, "one of the choice ones of the earth," as she described him.

With Jefferson, however, nothing was ever quite as it appeared on the surface. Sure, he admired Adams in some ways, but the homage he paid to the older man's face was not always in keeping with what he had to say behind his back. In one letter to James Madison, for example, Jefferson likened Adams to a poisonous weed: "He hates Franklin, he hates [John] Jay, he hates the French, he hates the English. To whom will he adhere? His vanity is a lineament in his character which had entirely escaped me. His want of taste I had observed. Notwithstanding all this he has a sound head on substantive points, and I think he has integrity. I am glad therefore that he is of the commission [in Paris] and expect he will be useful in it. His dislike of all parties, and all men, by balancing his prejudices, may give the same fair play to his reason as would be a general benevolence of temper. At any rate honesty may be expected even from poisonous weeds."

Adams, of course, only saw the side of Jefferson that Jefferson wanted him to see, and was completely enamored of it. "Jefferson is an excellent hand," he gushed in a letter to Elbridge Gerry after Jefferson joined him in Paris. "You could not have sent better." To Henry Knox, Adams wrote, "You can scarcely have heard a character[ization] too high of my friend and colleague, Mr. Jefferson, either in point of power or virtues. . . . I only fear that his unquenchable thirst for knowledge may injure his health." For a man of Adams's temperament, this unrestrained praise was highly unusual, especially compared to what he had to say about that "old Conjurer" Franklin, or any of the other Founding Fathers he felt had done him wrong. It was obvious that Jefferson's outward deference went a long way with a man feeling as chronically unappreciated as Adams did.

The two men worked harmoniously together as commissioners

in Paris and were sad to part company after Adams was appointed the first American minister to Great Britain in 1785. "I shall part with Mr. Jefferson with great regret," Adams wrote, while Jefferson sent tender sentiments to Adams in London: "The departure of your family has left me in the dumps. My afternoons hang heavily on me." The two maintained a friendly correspondence back and forth between London and Paris, and at one point took a two-month tour together of the English countryside, after which Jefferson even praised Adams in private. It was an idyll in their relationship that was not to last.

The French Revolution that began in the summer of 1789 was celebrated by Jefferson, recently returned from France and serving as George Washington's secretary of state, as an epic fulmination of Republican ideals. Adams, now vice president, was skeptical of the revolution's excesses. "Everything will be pulled down. So much seems certain," he wrote. "But what will be built up? Are there any principles of political architecture? . . . Will the struggle in Europe be anything other than a change in imposters?"

Jefferson "deplored" Adams's failure to embrace the revolution in France, viewing it as an embarrassing betrayal of all they had worked for in America. Adams believed Jefferson was becoming a fanatic. Though the two remained cordial members of Washington's cabinet, their differing views on the events in France represented an emerging factionalism in American politics that would soon make them enemies.

The growing alienation between Adams and Jefferson was made excruciatingly public in 1791 when Jefferson sent an early copy of Thomas Paine's *The Rights of Man* to a Philadelphia printer with a note endorsing it as the answer to "the political heresies that have sprung up among us." The printer included Jefferson's words on the title page, and it was obvious that the "political heresies" of which he spoke belonged to Adams for his cautious stance on the French Revolution. In a letter to George Washington, Jefferson acknowledged that he was indeed referring to Adams, but claimed to be "mortified" at "the indiscretion of a printer" in making his position public. He was, he said, loath to offend his "friend Mr. Adams, for whom, as one of the most honest and disinterested men alive, I have cordial esteem"—despite "his apostasy to hereditary monarchy."

Jefferson's endorsement in *The Rights of Man* made Adams the object of ridicule in many newspapers as an avowed monarchist dismayed by the march of freedom in France. It was a charge that would plague him for the rest of his political career, and one for which he blamed Jefferson. To Adams, his old friend had become almost as radical as the violent extremists in France. While Jefferson reveled in the execution of Louis XVI, writing that "the spectre of royalty [would now be] broken in pieces, in every part of the globe," Adams was horrified. "Mankind," he wrote, "will in time discover that unbridled majorities are as tyrannical and cruel as unlimited despots"—a position borne out in France by the ensuing Reign of Terror.

The unleashing of opposing political parties, largely brought on by the events in France, eventually drove Jefferson out of George Washington's administration early in 1794. Adams was not sorry to see him go. "Jefferson went off yesterday," he wrote on January 6, "and a good riddance of bad ware." Though Jefferson was temporarily out of the picture, this was not the end of his simmering conflict with Adams. Both entered the presidential race of 1796. Adams narrowly won, but Jefferson, as runner-up, would be his vice president.[3] Perhaps unaware just how far politics had driven them apart, Adams expected Jefferson would be a loyal, nonpartisan vice president. How wrong he was.

France, now at war with Great Britain, was still the great, divisive issue. The United States was officially neutral in the European conflict, but its shipping was under constant assault by France in an effort to cripple American commerce with Britain. The Adams administration wanted peace with France, but not at any price. The president advocated negotiation, but he strengthened defenses as well. Jefferson, leading the Republican opposition, believed Britain should

3. In those days, there were no running mates. The person with the second most votes became the vice president.

be defeated in the war and sought to undermine the president's perceived anti-French policies. In a private meeting with Philippe-Henry-Joseph de Letombe, the French chargé d'affaires, Jefferson said America was "penetrated with gratitude to France" and would "never forget that it owes its liberation to France." According to Letombe, Jefferson also had a few choice words for President Adams, describing him as "vain, irritable, stubborn, endowed with excessive self-love, and still suffering pique at the preference accorded Franklin over him in Paris." So much for loyalty.

Adams was able to avert a war with France, one of the great accomplishments of his administration, but Jefferson's enmity was unrelenting. He secretly encouraged, and even helped finance, Republican propagandist James Callender's scurrilous attacks on the president. Callender called Adams a "repulsive pedant," a "gross hypocrite," and "in his private life, one of the most egregious fools upon the continent." The president, he wrote, was "that strange compound of ignorance and ferocity, of deceit and weakness," a "hideous hermaphroditical character which has neither the force and firmness of a man, nor the gentleness and sensibility of a woman."

Adams and Jefferson were once again in opposition during the presidential campaign of 1800, one of the most vicious in American history.[4] Jefferson won this time, but Adams did not leave office without a last slap at his successor, making a rash of last-minute judicial appointments certain to rankle Jefferson. In this he was most successful. "I can say with truth that one act of Mr. Adams's life, and only one, ever gave me a moment's personal displeasure," the new president later wrote to Abigail Adams. "I did consider his last appointments to office as personally unkind. . . . It seemed but common justice to leave the successor free to act by instruments of his own choice." Adams did not bother to attend Jefferson's inauguration, opting instead to leave Washington early that morning. Except for one brief bit of business after Jefferson took office, there was no communication between the once friendly Founding Fathers for more than a decade. It was a bitter silence.

4. See Part V, Chapter 1.

But then something amazing happened in 1812. Adams and Jefferson, both now in retirement, began what historian David McCullough calls "one of the most extraordinary correspondences in American history—indeed, in the English language." As the two great men discoursed over the years on philosophy, literature, and their own shared history, a terrible rift was healed. "Mr. Jefferson and I have grown old and retired from public life," Adams said in 1820. "So we are upon our ancient terms of goodwill." They died on the same day, July 4, 1826.

The clash between Founding Fathers Alexander Hamilton and Aaron Burr did not end quite so peacefully.

2

Showdown at Weehawken

Alexander Hamilton was as much a hater as John Adams ever was. Not surprisingly, the two despised one another. Hamilton even wrote a scathing attack on Adams, a fellow Federalist, while Adams was running for a second presidential term in 1800.[1] Hamilton also had an active dislike for other Founding Fathers, such as Thomas Jefferson and James Madison, but his hatred for Aaron Burr bordered on the pathological. The simmering tensions between them would end tragically.

Although Hamilton and Burr maintained a superficial friendship—socializing together and occasionally teaming up as cocounsel on a number of civil and criminal cases in New York—Hamilton seemed bent on destroying his "friend" politically from the time Burr was elected to the U.S. Senate in 1791, if not before.

"[Burr] is unprincipled, both as a public and private man," Hamilton wrote in 1792 in his first recorded attack on the future vice president. "He is determined, as I conceive, to make his way to

1. See Part V, Chapter 1.

the head of the popular party," meaning the Republican party, "and to climb *per fas aut nefas* ["by fair means or foul"] to the highest honors of the State, and as much higher as circumstances may permit. Embarrassed, as I understand, in his circumstances, with an extravagant family, bold, enterprising, and intriguing, I am mistaken if it not be his object to play the game of confusion, and I feel it to be a religious duty to oppose his career." Less than a week later, Hamilton was again railing against Burr, writing that he "as a public man . . . is one of the worst sort . . . secretly turning liberty into ridicule. . . . In a word, if we have an embryo-Caesar in the United States, 'tis Burr."[2]

Clearly Hamilton did not think too highly of Burr, but did his animosity go beyond politics? Historians have long speculated on other factors behind Hamilton's vitriol. Some have theorized that a romantic rivalry existed, with both men often competing for the same woman. (Hamilton and Burr were both unapologetic adulterers. Hamilton, in fact, even stepped out with his own sister-in-law, and was forced to make a public account of another affair he had with Maria Reynolds.) Other historians think Hamilton saw unflattering aspects of himself in Burr, and loathed him as a result. Hamilton himself maintained that his distaste was purely political. "With *Burr* I have always been personally well," he wrote, a bit disingenuously, as if it were perfectly reasonable for a guy to call his pal the "Catiline[3] of America," as well as a man of "an irregular ambition" and "prodigal cupidity."

Whatever the cause of Hamilton's animosity, his criticisms of Burr were relentless. He was particularly venomous during the election of 1800, when Burr was running for president. (He lost by a hair to Thomas Jefferson in one of the most contested presidential elections in U.S. history, and, as runner-up, became vice president instead. John Adams, the incumbent, came in third.) "Adieu to the

2. Hamilton may have had a point, given Aaron Burr's potentially treasonous imperial ambitions. (See Part VI, Chapter 2.)

3. Catiline was a notorious political conspirator in ancient Rome.

Federal Troy if they once introduce this Grecian Horse into their Citadel," Hamilton warned fellow Federalists inclined toward Burr. In another letter, one of many during this period of uncertainty as to who would be the next president, he wrote, "Burr loves nothing but himself." He followed this with another diatribe the next day, Christmas Eve: "[Burr] is sanguine enough to hope everything—daring enough to attempt everything—wicked enough to scruple nothing." So much for the holiday spirit.

For years, Aaron Burr seems to have ignored, or at least forgiven, Hamilton's invective, but that all changed in 1804, when Burr was running for governor of New York. He lost miserably, thanks in no small part to Hamilton's efforts against him. During the campaign, a letter appeared in the Albany *Register,* a newspaper unfriendly to Burr. Though it wasn't written by Hamilton, the letter attributed to him the declaration that, among other things, Burr was "a dangerous man . . . who ought not to be trusted." When the letter writer, Dr. Charles D. Cooper, was challenged on this in another letter by General Philip Schuyler, Hamilton's father-in-law, Cooper defended his position and stated, "I could detail to you a still more despicable opinion which General Hamilton has expressed of Mr. Burr."

No one knows to this day just what "still more despicable opinion" Hamilton might have expressed, though some have ventured that he accused Burr of incest with his own daughter. In any event, Burr decided it needed clarification and called Hamilton out on it. He insisted on "the necessity of a prompt and unqualified acknowledgment or denial of the use of any expressions which could warrant the assertions of Dr. Cooper." Hamilton's response was quick but evasive. He wrote that having "maturely reflected on the subject," he could not, "without manifest impropriety, make the avowal or disavowal you seem to think necessary." He continued by saying "that the phrase 'still more despicable' admits of infinite shades, from very light to very dark. How am I to judge of the degree intended?"

Letters between Hamilton and Burr continued back and forth, resolving nothing and moving them ever closer to their fateful encounter. That came on a muggy Wednesday morning, July 11, 1804.

Aaron Burr, the vice president of the United States, stood facing his opponent, Alexander Hamilton, one of the nation's preeminent statesmen, on a wooded palisade overlooking the Hudson River in Weehawken, New Jersey. They were preparing to settle their dispute the way gentlemen had for centuries—in ritualized mortal combat, each man seeking to kill or maim the other in the "court of the last resort."

Hamilton had spent the evening before the duel preparing for his very possible death at the hand of a far superior marksman. While settling his affairs, he penned a reasoned, five-point account of why he wished to avoid the ritual, citing his moral opposition to the practice of dueling and the detrimental effect his death would have on his family and creditors. He also noted that he bore no personal animosity, just political, toward Burr and concluded, "I shall hazard much and can possibly gain nothing." Yet there he stood, at the very same spot on which his beloved son Philip had been killed in a duel several years before, holding the same pistol. Like Burr, he was accompanied by a second, whose prescribed role it was to ensure that the duel was fought honestly and fairly, to negotiate its terms, and, if necessary, shoot a principal who didn't fight by the rigidly prescribed rules.

Perfect decorum was displayed at Weehawken. When Burr and his second, William Van Ness, saw Hamilton approaching the site with his second, Nathaniel Pendleton, they straightened, removed their hats, and saluted politely. Anything else would have been considered ungentlemanly. The seconds made their arrangements, measuring the distance between combatants, casting lots for choice of position, and carefully loading the pistols in each other's presence. Then Burr and Hamilton took their assigned places. The instant the agreed-upon second called "Present!" Burr pulled his trigger. Hamilton drew up convulsively, spun to the left, and pitched forward on his face. At the same time his arm jerked upward, and his pistol discharged in the air. The bullet clipped a twig off a branch high over Burr's head.

While Hamilton lay mortally wounded (he died the next day), his opponent was quickly ushered from the site. Burr had survived the encounter and received the satisfaction he sought, but he faced murder indictments in New York and New Jersey. He also faced the scorn of a nation horrified by Hamilton's violent demise. Burr's political career was ruined, giving Hamilton in death that which he had expended so much energy trying to accomplish in life.

3

Giving the Devil His Duel

Affairs of honor must be conducted cooly, courteously and steadily, as a contrary course serves but to aggravate difficulties, and leads to results harsh, passionate and discreditable to men of true and deliberate courage.

—Code Duello, 1777

That Hamilton and Burr, two of the most prominent men in the nation, would engage in such deadly and seemingly pointless recourse is stunning, yet their duel was hardly an isolated event. Dueling usually evokes images of vaguely foppish European aristocrats sputtering insults, slapping one another in the face with embroidered gloves, and then drawing swords. America presumably had bid farewell to such conceits. Yet deadly duels were frequently fought throughout the country—from before its independence to well after the Civil War—by some of its most esteemed citizens. Future presidents, members of Congress, judges and journalists, governors and generals often found themselves on bloody fields of honor, settling real and perceived attacks on their dignity. Indeed, both Burr and Hamilton had been engaged in other duels, as had many of those close to them. Hamilton, for instance, once nearly dueled with future president James Monroe. (Ironically enough, it was Aaron Burr who stepped in and defused that situation.)

This violent method of conflict resolution had its formal origins 1,500 years ago in medieval Europe, where disputes were often adjudicated by a process called "Ordeal." A defendant, for example, might have to walk over hot coals. If he was innocent, the theory went, God would spare him the agony of burned and blistered feet. Obviously, the usual verdict was guilty. Out of this tradition emerged trial by single combat, based again on the presumption that God would reward the righteous with victory. Although trials by combat declined by the middle of the seventeenth century, ritualized private dueling rose up to replace them.

Dueling became enormously popular over the centuries, especially in Ireland, where it was a sport as well as a means of settling disputes. The Code Duello, developed there in 1777, became the set of rules that would govern nearly all American duels. The code originally contained twenty-six provisions for all aspects of dignified and formal combat. Firing in the air or purposely missing an opponent, for instance, were strictly prohibited and seen as "children's play . . . dishonorable on one side or the other." Of course, dueling had been formalized since the sixteenth century and spread to the New World before the establishment of the Code Duello. In fact, the first recorded duel took place soon after the Pilgrims arrived. But Americans eagerly adopted the code, adding measures such as posting, a humiliating ordeal in which a man who refused a challenge might be called something like an "unprincipled villain, a cur, a coward and a poltroon" in newspapers and other conspicuous public places. Americans also tended to favor pistols over swords, and many a well-heeled man owned an elaborately decorated set.

From Dodge City to the Dueling Green of New Orleans, Americans enthusiastically killed one another with class. Nowhere was this more true than at the Bladensburg Dueling Ground just over the Washington, D.C., border. Here, on what became known as "The Dark and Bloody Grounds," more than fifty duels were fought during the first half of the nineteenth century. One of the most famous victims was the naval hero Stephen Decatur. Hailed as the conqueror of the Barbary pirates, the man who famously proclaimed, "My country, may she always be right, but my country right or wrong," was at the height of his fame when he was shot down by an embittered fellow officer, James Barron, in 1820.

Barron's antagonism toward Decatur had a long history, stretching back thirteen years. Barron had been in command of the frigate *Chesapeake* when it encountered the British ship *Leopold* outside the Virginia capes. Britain was then in the habit of boarding American ships and taking, or impressing, sailors they claimed were British citizens. Barron's ship was so unprepared for defense that he was compelled to haul down its colors, submit his vessel to search, and allow several of his seamen to be impressed—all without the firing of a single cannon. The encounter outraged America and was one of the events leading up to the War of 1812. Barron was court-martialed and suspended from the service in a degrading process presided over by Decatur. During the next several years, lengthy and rancorous letters were exchanged between the two men. For example, Barron wrote Decatur, "I am informed that you have tauntingly and boastfully observed that you would cheerfully meet me in the field [of honor], and hoped that I would act like a man," to which Decatur responded, "I never invited you to the field, nor have I expressed a hope that you would call me out. . . . I stated that if you made the call I would meet you; but that, on all scores, I should be much better pleased to have nothing to do with you." Yes, angry men once talked like this.

Barron wrote back: "It is true that you have never given me a direct, formal, and written invitation to meet you in the field, such as one gentleman of honor *ought* to send another. But if your own admissions, that you would meet me if I wished it, do not amount to a challenge, then I can not comprehend the object or import of such declarations." Decatur returned the volley: "I do not consider it essential to my reputation that I should notice any thing which may come from you. . . . If we fight, it must be at your seeking, and you must take all the risk and all the inconvenience which usually attend the challenger in such cases."

Barron did at last issue a challenge and Decatur accepted, but meeting on "fair and equal grounds" would prove difficult. Decatur was known as a superior marksman, while Barron had a handicap particularly troublesome in dueling: He was extremely nearsighted. Pistols at eight paces were finally agreed upon with the additional provision, in deference to Barron's myopia, that each party would take deliberate aim at the other before the count.

Barron, Decatur, and their seconds met at the Bladensburg Dueling Ground on the morning of March 22, 1820. After they had taken their positions, Barron addressed Decatur: "Sir, I hope, on meeting in another world, we shall be better friends than in this." Decatur, who reportedly intended only to wound Barron, responded, "I have never been your enemy, sir." After the call, the shots were fired at almost the same time. Both men fell, and each believed himself to be dying. Lying in pools of blood, their heads not ten feet apart, they addressed each other. "I am mortally wounded; at least I believe so," Decatur said. "I wish I had fallen in the service of my country." Making his peace, Barron begged for forgiveness. "I freely forgive you my death," Decatur told him, "though not those who have stimulated you to seek my life." Decatur was taken back to his Washington home, where he succumbed to his injury later that night. Barron, like Burr before him, lived to face the wrath of a nation plunged into grief over a fallen hero.

★

A year before the Barron-Decatur duel, Bladensburg's "Dark and Bloody Grounds" was the sight of the fatal showdown between General Armistead T. Mason, former U.S. senator from Virginia, and his cousin, Colonel John M. M'Carty of the same state. Mason had questioned M'Carty's right to vote at the Leesburg polls, an affront that so incensed M'Carty he instantly challenged his cousin to a duel. His challenge, however, prescribed the terms and conditions for their fight, which was heretical to the Code Duello. The code specifically stated that only the challenged party had the right to place conditions on the fight. Mason, therefore, declined, but advised his cousin he would gladly accept a proper dueling offer. M'Carty ignored him and posted Mason as a coward. Indignant, Mason now challenged M'Carty, but he was summarily dismissed due to his original refusal. Seething at the rebuke, Mason nevertheless took his friends' advice and let the matter drop—that is, until some months later a future U.S. president convinced him otherwise.

Andrew Jackson, notorious dueling aficionado,[1] bluntly told Mason he should throw down the gauntlet again. Duly inspired by Old Hickory, Mason fired off a note to his rival: "I have resigned my commission for the special and sole purpose of fighting you [dueling was against army regulations] and I am now free to accept or send a challenge and to fight a duel." Mason then instructed his seconds to present the note to M'Carty and offer a challenge: "Agree to any terms that he may propose, and to any distance—to three feet, his pretended favorite distance—or three inches, should his impetuous and rash courage prefer it. To any specifics of firearms—pistols, muskets, or rifles—agree at once." M'Carty still refused him, however, once again citing Mason's original cowardice. It was only when Mason's seconds threatened to slap him with a shameful posting that he changed his mind.

Perhaps inspired by Mason's obvious determination for bloodshed, or maybe fearing it, M'Carty proposed they settle their squabble once and for all by leaping off the dome of the U.S. Capitol. Rejected by Mason's seconds as unsanctioned by the code, as well as patently insane, M'Carty then proposed they blow themselves to bits atop a gunpowder keg. M'Carty obviously wasn't clear on the concept of this dueling thing. According to newspapers of the time, M'Carty at last heroically—or desperately—suggested they fight with muskets, charged with buckshot, at ten feet. Doubtless this proposal too would prove fatal to both participants, but Mason's seconds, recalling their man's instructions, accepted. It was later modified to twelve feet with a single ball.

The two cousins met at the dueling ground on the morning of February 6, 1819. Though it was snowing violently, M'Carty was stripped to his shirt with his sleeves rolled up, while Mason wore a

1. See the next chapter.

large overcoat. Presented with their weapons, they were given the count and warned not to shoot before one or after three. In accordance with the Code Duello, the seconds were instructed to shoot the opposing party immediately for firing too soon or too late. With the muzzles of their weapons nearly touching, the men fired simultaneously. Mason fell dead, his aim apparently thrown off by his heavy coat. M'Carty's shoulder was shattered as Mason's ball entered his wrist and tore up through his arm. The surrounding shrubbery was reportedly decorated for days with grisly ornaments of shredded flesh and clothing. Mason's seconds were able to report publicly "that the affair, although fatally, was honorably terminated."

★

The same could not be said of the 1836 duel between two congressmen, Jesse Bynum of North Carolina and Daniel Jenifer of Maryland. It was a pathetic spectacle. Jenifer had denounced in the House the course of President Jackson's party, which caused Bynum to leap to his feet and proclaim, "It is ungentlemanly of you to say so." Jenifer, wounded, insisted Bynum retract his statement. "I won't take it back!" the defiant Bynum retorted. "I repeat it!" And so off they were to Bladensburg, with fellow congressmen serving as seconds and witnesses.

Both men stood on the field, ten feet apart, boasting of their marksmanship. The first shots were fired. Neither was hit. Same result with the second, third, and fourth shots. "When they gonna fight?" Jenifer's hackman reportedly asked an attending surgeon. "Why, don't you see they have already fired four times?" the surgeon replied. "Oh," said the hackman, "I thought they was jus' practicin'."

Before the sixth shot, Bynum's pistol discharged, probably accidentally. One of Jenifer's seconds immediately aimed his pistol at Bynum preparing to shoot him down in accordance with the code. "Don't shoot!" Jenifer ordered before taking his own shot and missing. The pitiful match, after six missed shots, was at last, mercifully, called a draw.

4

Overreaction Jackson

Andrew Jackson was one of dueling's most ardent enthusiasts. This may have had something to do with the marked homicidal tendencies he exhibited throughout much of his career, coupled with a hair-trigger temper and an overheated sense of personal honor. Sources vary as to exactly how many ritual combats Old Hickory participated in, either as a principal or second, but the frequency is by all accounts astonishing. And though Jackson was spared death on the field of honor, he was left full of lead for the rest of his life.

Perhaps his most notable duel was fought in 1806 with a well-connected Tennessee lawyer named Charles Dickinson. It was this conflict, which arose out of horse racing debts, that left the future president with a bullet permanently embedded near his heart, and his reputation shot as well. Dickinson had publicly declared Jackson to be "a poltroon and a coward," which, given the general's allergy to even the slightest insult, immediately resulted in a challenge. Dickinson accepted and the two agreed to an encounter in Logan County, Kentucky, just over the Tennessee border. They would face each other at a distance of twenty-four feet.

Clearly the better shot of the two—in fact, one of the best in Tennessee—Dickinson made merry on his journey to the Kentucky dueling ground with a large group of friends, confident that he would win. He delighted his companions with his quick wit and demonstrations of his shooting skills. After severing a string with a bullet shot from a distance of twenty-four feet, Dickinson left the pieces with an innkeeper on the way. "If General Jackson comes along this road, show him *that!*" he gloated. Jackson, by contrast, was all business, plotting strategy with his companions, knowing he was at a disadvantage. They decided that since Dickinson was the better shot, it would be best to let him fire first. That way, assuming he lived, Jackson could take careful aim back at Dickinson and not be thrown off his mark by trying to draw and fire faster.

Arriving at the chosen site, the parties took their positions. At the order to fire, Dickinson quickly raised his pistol and shot Jackson in the chest. But the general did not fall. Instead, he stood his place, clutching at his chest with teeth clenched. "Great God!" a horrified Dickinson cried. "Have I missed him?" Stunned, he was ordered back to his mark. Jackson was now free to shoot him at his leisure. Slowly and deliberately he raised his pistol, took aim, and squeezed the trigger. Nothing happened. The pistol hammer had stopped at half cock. In what could have only been an agonizing wait for Dickinson, Jackson slowly drew back the hammer, aimed again, and fired. The bullet ripped through Dickinson's body and he bled to death. "I'd have hit him," Jackson quipped, dismissing his own injury, "if he had shot me through the brain."

★

Despite all the criticism of the cold-blooded way in which Jackson had killed Dickinson, that encounter at least met all the stringent contemporary requirements for civilized quarreling. Not all of Jackson's fights did. Seven years after killing Charles Dickinson by the rules, he was badly wounded in what was a gutter brawl by comparison. It all started when a junior officer named William Carroll asked Jackson to serve as his second in a duel he was to fight with one Jesse

Benton. Jackson, at age forty-six, wisely demurred. "Why, Captain Carroll, I am not the man for such an affair," he wrote. "I am too old. The time has been when I should have gone out with pleasure; but, at my time of life, it would be extremely injudicious. You must get a man nearer to your own age." But Carroll persisted, and Jackson eventually agreed.

The duel between Carroll and Benton was a ridiculous affair, with Benton taking a squatting position as he wheeled around to shoot at Carroll. In the process, he caught a bullet in his behind, along with a sharp reprimand from Jackson for his disgraceful technique. Thomas Hart Benton, Jesse's brother and an aide-de-camp to Jackson, was away in Washington working on the general's affairs when the duel occurred. Upon returning to Tennessee and learning of his brother's humiliation, Thomas Hart Benton threatened revenge. Word of his anger and threats soon reached Jackson, who wrote Benton asking if what was being said was true. Benton responded with four points, the first of which Old Hickory may have very well agreed with: "That it was very poor business in a man of your age and standing to be conducting a duel about nothing between young men who had no harm against each other, and that you would have done yourself more honor by advising them to reserve their courage for the public enemy."

Whether or not Jackson agreed with the points, the issue still remained as to whether Benton wanted a duel or not. "I have not threatened to challenge you," Benton wrote. "On the contrary I have said that I would not do so; and I say so still. At the same time, the terror of your pistols is not to seal my lips. What I believe to be true, I shall speak; and if for this I am called to account, it must ever be so."

So, although there was no official challenge, Benton continued to bad-mouth Jackson all over Tennessee. This infuriated the general, whose reputation was only just beginning to recover from the Dickinson affair. He swore he would horsewhip Benton the next time he saw him. That opportunity came in Nashville, where Jackson and the Benton brothers were staying for a time. Making their way to the post office soon after arriving in Nashville, the general and his companions walked deliberately past the inn where the Bentons had rooms. This was a fairly clear indication that they were spoiling for a fight. Thomas Benton stood out front, "looking daggers" at them, as Jackson's companion John Coffee noted. "Do you see that fellow?" Coffee asked Jackson in a hushed tone. "Oh yes," the general replied, "I have my eye on him." For some reason, though, Jackson did not attack. Instead, he and his group proceeded to the post office, picked up their mail, and headed back in the same direction.

Now both Bentons were standing outside the inn. As Jackson came abreast of Thomas Benton, the future president suddenly wheeled on him, brandished a whip, and yelled, "Now, you damned rascal, I am going to punish you. Defend yourself!" With that, Benton reached into his pocket as if going for his gun. Jackson then drew out his own gun and forced his adversary back inside the inn. As this was happening, Jesse Benton slipped away and took another position inside. As his brother was being forced in, Jesse fired at Jackson, shattering the general's arm and shoulder. Jackson fired at Thomas as he fell, but his shot missed.

Racing in from the street, John Coffee immediately saw his friend lying prostrate in a pool of blood and fired at Thomas Benton. Missing, he then tried to club him with his pistol, but Benton retreated, falling out of the building backward down a flight of stairs. Another of Jackson's companions, his nephew Stockley Hays, tried to run Jesse Benton through with his sword cane, but the weapon hit a button and broke. As the two men wrestled on the ground, Hays resorted to stabbing Jesse Benton repeatedly in the arms with a dirk. The crowd pulled them apart before Benton was in a position to shoot Hays.

As the melee came to end, Jackson was carried away to the Nashville Inn. He was bleeding profusely, saturating two mattresses. A physician in attendance suggested amputating the shattered limb, but Jackson wouldn't hear of it. "I'll keep my arm," he ordered before drifting into unconsciousness. The bullet remained with him for the next twenty years, along with the one lodged near his heart. The Bentons, meanwhile, were loudly denouncing Jackson as a failed assassin. Coming across a small sword the general had dropped in the encounter, Thomas Hart Benton snapped it in two while shouting insults about Jackson. He then paraded the pieces across the public square. Yet despite his bravado, Benton was well aware of the true danger he now faced from Jackson and his outraged associates: "I am literally in hell here," he wrote; "the meanest wretches under heaven to contend with—are at work on me. . . . I am in the middle of hell, and see no alternative but to kill or be killed; for I will not crouch to Jackson; and the fact that I and my brother defeated him and his tribe, and broke his small sword in the public square, will for ever rankle in his bosom and make him thirst for vengeance. My life is in danger . . . for it is a settled plan to turn out puppy after puppy to bully me, and when I have got into a scrape, to have me killed somehow in the scuffle."

Benton's fears turned out to be baseless. He was spared the wrath of Old Hickory. In fact, the two later became political allies when they were both elected to the U.S. Senate. Jesse Benton, on the other hand, cursed Jackson to his grave.

★

Andrew Jackson proved himself a violent foe when it came to defending his own honor but went nearly insane with rage if anyone dared besmirch the good name of his wife, Rachael. He had fallen in love with the pipe-smoking frontier woman while she was separated from her first husband, Lewis Robards. That marriage had been a disaster, and Rachael moved away to Natchez in Spanish Florida. Jackson accompanied her there, ostensibly to protect her on the dangerous journey south. Rachael was eventually divorced from Robards, although the legality of the divorce was later called into question, making Rachael a possible bigamist when she married Jackson in 1791. Such marital limbo made her a target for many of Jackson's political enemies, including the first governor of Tennessee, John Sevier.

After a series of political clashes, Sevier verbally accosted Jackson, then a judge on the Tennessee Superior Court, outside the Knoxville courthouse in 1803. "I know of no great services you have rendered to the country except taking a trip to Natchez with another man's wife!" Sevier taunted. With that crack Jackson went berserk. "Great God!" he bellowed. "Do you mention *her* sacred name?" Pistols were immediately drawn and shots fired, but neither man was hit and they were quickly separated. Jackson was still enraged, however, and challenged Sevier to a formal duel. When the governor hedged, Jackson posted him in the Tennessee *Gazette:* "Know ye that I, Andrew Jackson, do pronounce, publish, and declare to the world, that his excellency John Sevier . . . is a base coward and poltroon. He will basely insult, but has not the courage to repair."

When the two did eventually meet on the field of honor, they immediately started shouting insults and profanities at one another. Jackson rushed forward with a raised stick, threatening to cane Sevier, who drew his sword. This sudden movement frightened the governor's horse, which trotted away with his pistols in the saddle bag. Jackson took full advantage of the situation, drawing his own pistol as Sevier ducked for cover behind a tree. This was not how gentlemen were supposed to fight! Seeing his father's peril, Sevier's son drew his own pistol on Jackson, while Jackson's second drew on the son. At a stalemate, and realizing how foolish the whole scene had become, the parties withdrew. They were alive, but enemies still. Rachael, meanwhile, would endure far more abuse when her husband later ran for president, and she died just before he took office.[1]

1. See Part V, Chapter 2.

5

"The Eaton Malaria"

Andrew Jackson was every bit as chivalrous as he was murderous. With the untimely death of his wife still a raw wound, he came to the defense of another woman's honor soon after being elected president in 1828. Though no duels were fought and no blood was shed over Margaret "Peggy" Eaton's reputation, the issue nevertheless had devastating consequences. In the two years that it dominated the new Jackson administration, "the Eaton malaria," as Secretary of State Martin Van Buren called it, contributed to a serious rupture in the president's family relationships, the dissolution of his entire cabinet, and, perhaps most significantly, a bitter and permanent breach between Jackson and his vice president, John C. Calhoun.

Jackson had come to know the young woman who was at the center of these messy conflicts earlier in his career as a senator from Tennessee. He lived in her father's boarding house while working in Washington and came to dote on her, treating her almost like a daughter. Yet while Jackson found Peggy to be a delight, others in Washington weren't so enamored. They saw her as brash and opinionated, a woman who stepped way too far outside the bounds of what was considered proper female behavior.

The gossip about her was vicious, and it only grew worse when president-elect Jackson appointed her husband, Senator John Eaton of Tennessee, to his cabinet as secretary of war. People whispered that Peggy had been sleeping with Eaton while still married to her first husband, John Timberlake, and that she carried his child. The affair, it was said, caused Timberlake such despair that he slit his own throat while out to sea with the U.S. Navy. Peggy maintained that she was always faithful to Timberlake, and that it was asthma that killed him. Andrew Jackson was one of the few who believed her. "I had rather have live vermin on my back than the tongue of one of these Washington women on my reputation," he once said to Peggy sympathetically.

The ugly chatter about Peggy Eaton had ramifications beyond a bunch of society hens clucking with disapproval. Though women of the era had little power in most arenas, they ruled supreme when it came to maintaining community morals and standards. If they decided someone was unfit for polite society, that person was ostracized without appeal. Men were expected to honor the women's decisions and snub whomever they were told to snub. Peggy Eaton had been declared unworthy of Washington society and thus was eminently snubable. The rejection of his wife would make John Eaton's position in Jackson's cabinet difficult. "The great objection to this gentleman is his wife, whom, it is said, is *not* as *she* should be," wrote James Gallatin, son of Thomas Jefferson's secretary of the treasury Albert Gallatin.

But what made the Eaton affair as incendiary as it became was Andrew Jackson's belief that the attacks on Peggy were actually political daggers being thrust at him—a conspiracy to make John Eaton's position in the cabinet untenable, thus destabilizing his administration and undermining his decisions. Gallant as he was in defending Peggy Eaton, Old Hickory was ultimately fighting for himself. And as those on the wrong end of his pistol knew, he could be a savage fighter.

Nathan Towson, a hero of the War of 1812 and a leader of Washington society, discovered just how determined Jackson could be when he questioned the president-elect's choice of John Eaton for secretary of war. "Mr. Eaton is an old personal friend of mine," Jackson told Towson. "He is a man of talents and experience, and one in whom his state, as well as myself, have every confidence. I cannot see, therefore, why there should be any objection to him."

"There is none, I believe, personally, to *him*," Towson replied, "but there are great objections made to his wife."

"And pray, Colonel," Jackson said with rising irritation, "what will his wife have to do with the duties of the War Department?"

"Not much, perhaps," answered Towson, "but she is a person with whom the ladies of this city do not associate. She is not, and probably never will be, received into society here, and if Mr. Eaton shall be made a member of the cabinet, it may become a source of annoyance to both you and him."

Jackson was now boiling: "Colonel, do you suppose that I have been sent here by the people to consult the ladies of Washington as to the proper persons to compose my cabinet? In the selection of its members I shall consult my own judgment, looking to the great and paramount interests of the whole country, and not to the accommodation of society and drawing rooms of this or any other city. Mr. Eaton will certainly be one of my constitutional advisors." With that, the tense conversation concluded, and Towson was ushered out of Jackson's office.

If Andrew Jackson's determination to stand by the designated secretary of war and his wife was fierce, so was the opposition to Peggy Eaton. Her sound snubbing at Jackson's inauguration set the tone for what was to come. Few of the cabinet wives, led by Vice President Calhoun's wife, Floride, deigned speak to her or even acknowledge her presence. The women's lead was dutifully followed by their husbands, enraging the new president all the more. The people who were supposed to be on his side were boldly defying him by their open rejection of Peggy Eaton. Even his niece Emily Donelson, who was to stand in for his late wife as official hostess, joined in the anti-Eaton movement—as did her husband, Andrew Donelson, who was also Jackson's nephew and private secretary. Both lived at the Executive Mansion (as the White House was then known) with the president, making for a rather tense household.

Postmaster General William Barry was one of the only cabinet members, along with Secretary of State Van Buren, who refused to reject Peggy Eaton. He firmly believed that the organized movement against her was not the result of anything she had done but rather a snobbish reaction to the elevation of an innkeeper's daughter to the status of cabinet wife. "This has touched the pride of the self-constituted great," Barry wrote, "awakened the jealousy of the malignant and envious, and led to the basest calumny."

Jackson was of the same mind and made it his mission—to the exclusion of all the other issues facing his new administration—to vindicate Peggy Eaton. He sought out and interrogated her accusers, collected evidence in her defense, and threatened and cajoled those who remained recalcitrant. His tireless efforts, however, did nothing but cause more whispers. "God knows we did not make him president . . . to work the miracle of making Mrs. E an honest woman," wrote Alexander Hamilton's son James.

At one point, the president gathered his cabinet before him and presented the evidence he had collected on behalf of Mrs. Eaton. When he turned to one of the gossip spreaders, Reverend Ezra Stiles Ely, whom he had invited to the meeting to retract what he had been saying, Ely hedged. Now Jackson was furious. "She is as chaste as a virgin!" he sputtered in frustration. The cabinet remained unconvinced, and Peggy Eaton remained *persona non grata*.

Seething, Jackson soon threatened to force the resignation of any in his cabinet who refused Mrs. Eaton's company. Secretary of the Treasury Samuel D. Ingham was surprised at his boss's vehemence but unwavering in his anti-Peggy position. Even the president of the United States, Ingham argued, could not dictate with whom he and his family would socialize. Tempering his stance somewhat, Jackson called Ingham and the other dissenting cabinet members, Secretary of the Navy John Branch and Attorney General John M. Berrien, into his office. "I do not claim the right to interfere in any manner in the domestic relations or personal intercourse of any member of my cabinet," he told them, "nor have I ever in any manner attempted it." But, he continued, the mistreatment of Mrs. Eaton adversely affected her husband, which was unacceptable. "I will not part with Major Eaton from my cabinet, and those of my cabinet who cannot harmonize with him had better withdraw for harmony I must and will have."

Harmony remained elusive, however, and Branch, Berrien, and Ingham soon found themselves out of a job. One publication likened the forced resignations from Jackson's cabinet to "the reign of Louis XV when Ministers were appointed and dismissed at a woman's nod, and the interests of the nation were tied to her apron string."

★

Never short on paranoia, President Jackson became increasingly convinced that Vice President John Calhoun was quietly working to undermine him through the Eaton affair and other matters, while at the same time maneuvering to succeed him as president. Even though the vice president and his wife had been at home in South Carolina during much of the administration's first year, Jackson had not failed to notice that Mrs. Calhoun had led the snubbing of Mrs. Eaton at the inauguration. He was sure something sinister was at work.

Jackson and Calhoun had strongly opposing views on the role of government. The vice president was a proponent of a state's right to nullify federal laws not in its best interests. The president, while a believer in states' rights, saw this concept as a dangerous threat to the stability of the union. Their differences on the nullification issue became glaringly public at a Washington dinner in 1830 when President Jackson exclaimed in a toast, "Our Union; it must be preserved," while staring right at Calhoun. The vice president then responded with a toast of his own: "The Union. Next to our liberty, the most dear."

As the relationship between president and vice president disintegrated, an issue from the past was revived to polarize them further. Back in 1818, when General Jackson was still basking in the glory of his victory over the British at New Orleans during the War of 1812, he led an unauthorized invasion into Spanish Florida in pursuit of the Seminole Indians. In the process, he seized territory and executed two British subjects—again, without authorization. Calhoun, who was then secretary of war under President James Monroe, wanted to punish Jackson for his insolence. The general, however, was unaware of this, believing instead that Calhoun was his defender in the matter. It was only later, when President Jackson started growing suspicious of Calhoun, that he listened to information coming to him about Calhoun's actual role in the Seminole matter. Livid, the president confronted the vice president with the information he had obtained. "I had a right to believe you were my sincere friend," Jackson wrote, "and, until now, never expected to have occasion to say to you, in the language of Caesar, *Et tu Brute.*"

When it came to the Eaton affair, Calhoun maintained it was purely a social issue, and that Peggy Eaton was being justly ostracized by his wife and others on sound moral principles. "Happily for our country, this important censorship is too high and too pure to be influenced by any political considerations whatever," the vice president wrote, applauding "the great victory that has been achieved in favor of the morals of the country, by the high minded independence and virtue of the ladies of Washington."

It was his political rival, Secretary of State Martin Van Buren, whom Calhoun believed was whispering poison into the president's ear in an effort to curry favor and take Calhoun's place as Jackson's chosen successor. Van Buren had been openly and actively supportive of Mrs. Eaton, a sure way to Jackson's favor, and even paved the way for the clearance of the rest of the president's cabinet by offering his own resignation. The Red Fox, as Van Buren was sometimes called, had maneuvered well in the Eaton matter and would be well rewarded. "It is odd enough," noted Daniel Webster, "but too evident to be doubted, that the consequences of this dispute in the social and fashionable world is producing great political effects, and may very probably determine who shall be successor to the present chief magistrate." Webster was remarkably prescient in his observation. Now distrusted and despised by Jackson, Calhoun would resign the vice presidency and return to the Senate—his hopes for the highest office destroyed—while Van Buren stepped right in as vice president, and eventually as president in 1837.

★

Just as "the Eaton malaria" had splintered the president and vice president, along with most of the cabinet, it opened deep fissures within Jackson's own family as well. His niece and nephew, Emily and Andrew Donelson, served not only as his hostess and secretary respectively, but also as companions to the widowed president. Much to his horror, though, the Donelsons decided to follow Washington society in their treatment of Peggy Eaton. Jackson was convinced that they had become enemy operators of Calhoun and the rest. "That my Nephew and Nece [sic] should permit themselves to be held up as the instruments, and *tools,* of such wickedness, is truly mortifying to me," the president fumed in a letter. He even contemplated firing Andrew Donelson as his secretary. "I Know I can live as well without them, as they can without me, and I will govern my Household, or I will have *none.*"

The Donelsons were sent to an unofficial exile in Tennessee, and the president was left to shuffle around the Executive Mansion all alone. Lonely as he was, he was not about to budge on the Eaton issue. "Better to put up with the separation for a short time," he wrote, "than to come on and introduce again those scenes here that has cost me so much pain, which first and last has almost destroyed me, and this too produced by my dearest friends [the Donelsons], uniting with and pursuing the advice of my worst enemies."

The Eaton scandal, which dominated his administration for more than two years, so exhausted the president that he longed to lie in a grave next to his beloved wife, Rachael. "I only wish if it pleased the will of providence, that I was by her side," he wrote, "free from all the deception and depravity of this wicked world. Then my mind would not be corroded by the treachery of false friends, or the slanders of professed ones." Relief only came after the mass resignations from his cabinet and the departure of the Eatons from Washington. (Eaton had joined Van Buren in tendering his resignation, thus allowing Jackson to save face while clearing the way for the ouster of the anti-Eaton cabinet members.) As President Jackson tried to put the whole Eaton mess behind him and start fresh, a new toast became popular in Washington: "To the next cabinet—may they all be bachelors—or leave their wives at home."

The storm had passed, but Washington had not seen the last of the woman at the center of the hurricane. Peggy Eaton eventually came back to the capital, and after the death of her husband in 1856, set tongues wagging once again when she married, at age fifty-nine, a nineteen-year-old Italian dance instructer named Antonio Buchignani. The marriage seemed to be a happy one, at least until Buchignani ran off to Italy with all her money as well as her granddaughter. Left in poverty, Peggy nevertheless remained a fixture in Washington—a curious remnant of an earlier era when the issue of one woman's reputation was almost enough to destroy a presidency.

Peggy O'Neale Timberlake Eaton Buchignani died in 1879 at a home for destitute women. She was buried in the capital's Oak Hill Cemetery next to John Eaton. A newspaper commenting on her death and on the irony of the situation editorialized: "Doubtless among the dead populating the terraces [of the cemetery] are some of her assailants [from the cabinet days] and cordially as they may have hated her, they are now her neighbors."

6

A Not So Civil War

As war was raging between the American North and South, a behind-the-scenes struggle erupted between President Abraham Lincoln and his general, George McClellan. Both leaders were firmly entrenched in their respective positions, but the markedly different styles in which they approached their conflict showed just what kind of men they really were. Lincoln, facing enormous pressure over Union setbacks and defeats early in the Civil War, grew increasingly frustrated by McClellan's hesitation to confront the enemy—what he called the general's chronic case of "the slows." Yet despite his serious concerns, the president tried to motivate McClellan with respectful suggestions and gentle cajoling, often deferring to his superior military experience. It didn't work. McClellan treated his commander-in-chief with barely disguised contempt, ignoring his orders and requests, and calling him, among other things, "an idiot" and "nothing more than a well-meaning baboon."

McClellan's total lack of regard for the president was glaringly demonstrated one evening late in 1861 when Lincoln came to his home to discuss strategy. McClellan was not in, so Lincoln decided to sit and wait. The general eventually returned, but ignored a porter's announcement that the president was there to see him and went straight up to his room. After about half an hour had passed, Lincoln sent up a message that he was still waiting. He was told, on McClellan's orders, that the general had retired for the evening and would not be receiving company. The president chose not to react to the gross affront, saying, "It was better at this time not to be making points of etiquette and personal dignity." Yet despite his forbearance on this occasion, Lincoln's patience with his general was fraying rapidly.

It snapped early the next year after a particularly humiliating debacle near Harper's Ferry, Virginia, when canal boats McClellan had ordered as anchors for a temporary bridge across the Potomac River proved too large to fit through the locks of the Chesapeake and Ohio Canal. "Why in tarnation . . . couldn't [McClellan] have known whether a boat would go through that lock, before he spent a million of dollars getting them there?" President Lincoln exploded. "I am no engineer, but it seems to me that if I wished to know whether a boat would go through a . . . lock, common sense would teach me to go and measure it. I am almost despairing at these results. Everything seems to fail." Lincoln concluded his rant by articulating the ultimate source of his frustration with McClellan: "The general impression is daily gaining ground that the General does not intend to do anything." He had a point there.

Things had seemed so promising when George McClellan, at thirty-four, was appointed head of the Army of the Potomac after the stunning Union defeat at the first battle of Bull Run at the beginning of the Civil War. Charged with defending Washington and building a force that would help crush the Confederacy, he was hailed as the "Savior of the Republic" and called "the Young Napoleon." The handsome young general cut a dashing figure astride his mount, reviewing troops that would come to adore him. (Lincoln, in contrast, looked "like a scare-crow on horseback," as an observer once described him riding next to McClellan.)

"I find myself in a new & strange position here," the general wrote his wife. "By some operation of magic I seem to have become *the* power of the land." Unfortunately McClellan actually seems to have believed this, quickly showing himself to be utterly dismissive of his civilian superiors—especially the president. Furthermore, he thought God had ordained him to his position—a belief rarely conducive to collaboration and compromise—and refused to discuss his strategies and agenda. At one council meeting, for example, he pronounced that "no General fit to command an army will ever submit his plans to the judgment of such an assembly . . . there are many here entirely incompetent to pass judgment upon them."

Lincoln might not have minded McClellan's obstinate refusals to reveal his plans if he thought he actually had any. While the newly appointed general had done a fine job fortifying the capital and reorganizing and strengthening the Army of the Potomac, he seemed to lose momentum after that. And this is what concerned the president most. He wanted his general to take the offense against rebel forces in Manassas, Virginia, but McClellan always had an excuse for delay: His men were not yet strong enough to fight, or they would be facing Confederate forces of far greater numbers and strength. A frustrated Lincoln noted wryly at one point that if General McClellan was not going to use his army, he "would like to *borrow* it, provided he could see how it could be made to do something."

Finally the president demanded action; he ordered McClellan to advance on Manassas, site of the disastrous Union defeat at the first battle of Bull Run. McClellan objected, of course, but he did offer a detailed plan of his own—at last. He proposed attacking the Confederate capital of Richmond, Virginia, from the eastern waterways. Lincoln had grave reservations about the plan, particularly the potential exposure Washington would face with its defenders engaged further south, but he reluctantly agreed. To assuage his concerns about the defense of Washington, however, the president held back about one-quarter of the troops McClellan intended to use in the Richmond campaign. The general was outraged. "It is the most infamous thing that history has recorded," he wrote his wife with more than a touch a drama. "The idea of depriving a general of 35,000 troops when actually under fire!" He later claimed his entire plan was paralyzed by the president's decision. "It compelled the adoption of another, a different and less effective plan of campaign,"

McClellan later wrote in a self-justifying report on his tenure as commander of the Army of the Potomac. "It made rapid and brilliant operations impossible," he continued. "It was a fatal error."

To Lincoln, the reduction in troops was just another excuse McClellan used so as not to have to confront the enemy, and the president just wasn't buying it. He reminded his general that even after a portion of his troops were held back, he still had 100,000 at his command. "I think you better break the enemies' line . . . at once," Lincoln demanded. Indignant, McClellan wrote his wife: "I was much tempted to reply that he had better come and do it himself."

Though Lincoln was clearly dissatisfied with McClellan's "sluggishness of action," as he told his friend Orville Hickman Browning, he wrote his general a letter intended to soothe his tender feelings and implore action. Only the Confederates benefitted by delay, he noted. "And, once more let me tell you, it is indispensable to *you* that you strike a blow. *I* am powerless to help this." Lincoln added a note of admonition in an otherwise conciliatory letter: "You will do me the justice to remember I always insisted, the going down the [Chesapeake] Bay in search of a field, instead of fighting at or near Manassas, was only shifting, and not surmounting, a difficulty—that we would find the same enemy, and the same, or equal, intrenchments [*sic*], at either place." The president then concluded, "I beg to assure you that I have never written you, or spoken to you, in greater kindness of feeling than now, nor with fuller purpose to sustain you. . . . *But you must act.*"

McClellan didn't bother to reply. He was unrepentant about the ultimate failure of his campaign to capture Richmond, blaming, once again, the refusal of Washington to provide the necessary troops. Lincoln thought otherwise. "If by magic [I] could reinforce McClelland [*sic*] with 100,000 men today," he remarked, "he would be in ecstasy of it, thank [me] for it, and tell me that he could go to Richmond tomorrow, but that when tomorrow came he would telegraph that he had certain information that the enemy had 400,000 men, and that he could not advance without reinforcements."

After the Richmond debacle, McClellan sat at Harrison's Landing on the James River, stewing and immobile. A master of self-delusion, he saw the hand of God in the losses he had accumulated. "If I had succeeded in taking Richmond now," he wrote, "the fanatics of the North might have been too powerful & reunion [with the South] impossible." And of course he continued to believe President Lincoln had it in for him. "I am confident that he would relieve me tomorrow, if he dared do so," McClellan wrote his wife. "His cowardice alone prevents it. I can never regard him with other feelings than those of thorough contempt—for his mind, heart & morality."

In a tiff, McClellan refused an order to get back to the vicinity of Washington and assist in General John Pope's Army of Virginia advance on Manassas. His refusal contributed to another demoralizing Union loss at the second battle of Bull Run in late August 1862. The president was devastated. "I am almost ready to say . . . that God wills this contest," he wrote, "and wills that it shall not yet end." Lincoln was forced to abandon the idea of an aggressive war against the Confederacy and return to a defensive posture. For this he needed McClellan, the man he called "the chief alarmist and grand marplot of the Army." Though the president was weary of his general's "weak, whiney, vague and incorrect despatches" and considered his failure to join Pope unforgivable, he knew McClellan was a superb organizer and the only one who could revive the army's shattered spirits. "I must have McClellan to reorganize the Army and bring it out of chaos," he said, over the vigorous protests of his cabinet advisors. "We must use what tools we have," he told them. Nevertheless, a final clash between Lincoln and McClellan was looming large.

It came after the battle of Antietam. Although McClellan managed to repel Confederate General Robert E. Lee's advance across the Potomac into Maryland, it was a squandered victory—and a lucky one, too. Ezra A. Carman, an Antietam veteran and the author of the most detailed tactical study of the battle, noted that "more errors were committed by the Union commander than in any other battle of the war." For Lincoln, McClellan's greatest sin was allowing Lee's forces to slip back across the Potomac largely intact. The president believed an opportunity to crush the Confederates had been wasted, and was incensed that McClellan was not pursuing Lee into Virginia.

The general, however, was quite satisfied with himself after Antietam, "knowing that God had in his mercy a second time made me the instrument of saving the nation." While the enemy was left as strong as ever, as the general himself acknowledged, he was still pleased: "I have shown that I can fight battles & *win* them!" Yet after this particular battle the general was pooped, and when it came to his failure to pursue the retreating rebels, he called upon the arsenal of excuses he had used so often in the past. "The real truth is that my army is not yet fit to advance," he claimed. "These people [in Washington] don't know what an army requires & therefore act stupidly."

The frustration in Washington over McClellan's failure to give chase was growing daily. "It requires the lever of Archimedes to move this inert mass," General Halleck remarked. "I have tried my best, but without success." When McClellan complained that his cavalry force was too exhausted to move, Lincoln sent a reply dripping with acid: "Will you pardon me for asking what the horses of your army have done since the battle of Antietam that fatigue anything?" The president's stinging telegram made McClellan "mad as a March hare," as he told his wife. "It was one of those dirty little flings that I can't get used to when they are not merited." And yet he still did not move against the enemy.

President Lincoln, in a final effort to get the general off his rear, wrote McClellan that it was imperative that he overcome his chronic reluctance to fight once and for all. Was he not being overcautious when he assumed his army could not do what the enemy was constantly doing?—that is, moving—the president wondered. "Should you not claim to be his equal in prowess, and act upon the claim?" The advance into Virginia that the president proposed "is all easy if our troops march as well as the enemy; and it is unmanly to say they can not do it." McClellan got the message, or so it seemed, and began crossing the Potomac with the bulk of his army. But he wasn't happy about it and had to be continuously prodded by Washington.

"If you could know the mean & dirty character of the dispatches you would boil over with anger," McClellan whined to his wife. "Whenever there is a chance of a wretched inuendo [*sic*]—there it comes. But the good of the country requires me to submit to all this from men whom I know to be greatly my inferiors socially, intellectually & morally! There never was a truer epithet applied to a certain individual [Lincoln] than that of the 'Gorilla.'"

Ignoring the "Gorilla"'s order to move swiftly to get between Lee and his destination of Richmond, McClellan instead proceeded with extreme caution, taking eleven days to cover the first thirty-five miles. It was no trouble at all for the Confederate army—who marched twice as fast, taking half the time—to cross McClellan's line of advance. Lincoln had seen it coming. "I began to fear he was playing false—that he did not want to hurt the enemy," the president said later. "I saw how he could intercept the enemy on the way to Richmond. I determined to make that the test. If he let them get away, I would remove him." And so he did. On November 5, 1862, General George B. McClellan, "the Young Napoleon," got the boot.

7

When "Mush" Came to Shove

The friendship between Theodore Roosevelt and William Howard Taft was not one of equals. Think of the coolest kid on the playground allowing the fat kid with no friends to tag along with him. Then imagine the cool kid's chagrin upon discovering the fat kid has a mind of his own and is no longer willing to play follow the leader. Such was the Roosevelt-Taft dynamic, and it resulted in a bitter breach.

Secretary of War Taft, having no real political base of his own, was content to serve President Roosevelt and unconditionally support his progressive agenda. His loyalty was rewarded when Roosevelt tapped him as his successor. The president had promised the nation that he would not seek a third term of office and needed a compliant replacement to carry on his policies. Taft, the amiable yes-man, seemed a natural choice. He was, said Henry Adams, "a fat mush," apparently easy to manipulate. But appearances deceived.

The president had considered a number of potential successors before reluctantly settling on Taft. Having picked his replacement, Roosevelt went to work to ensure Taft's nomination at the Republican convention. His efforts were well rewarded. By the time the convention opened on June 16, 1908, Taft already had 563 delegates, considerably more than the 491 needed to nominate. But despite the numbers, there was someone else the conventioneers wanted more than Taft—Roosevelt himself. The mere mention of his name brought about thunderous cheers and a chant of "Four, four, four years more!" Taft's worried supporters ordered the band to play "The Star-Spangled Banner," but it wasn't enough to stifle the spontaneous demonstration. It went on for forty-nine minutes as Roosevelt listened in on the telephone from the White House with obvious glee. He was "in as gay a humor as I have ever seen him," observed his aide, Archie Butt.

Over at the War Department, meanwhile, Taft's ambitious wife, Helen, listening to the same demonstration, was decidedly less pleased. She was downright irritated, in fact, convinced that the president was actually going to allow himself to be nominated again. The cheers for Roosevelt stopped only when Henry Cabot Lodge announced to the delegates that the president's decision not to run a third time was "final and irrevocable. . . . Anyone who attempts to use his name as a candidate for the presidency impugns both him and his good faith."

The next day, Helen Taft listened tensely as her husband was nominated. A rather contrived and feeble cheer followed. "I only want it to last more than forty-nine minutes," she said of the demonstration. "I want to get even for the scare that Roosevelt cheer . . . gave me yesterday." Alas, despite the best efforts of Taft's campaign managers to keep it going, the applause petered out after only twenty-five minutes.

Roosevelt pronounced himself "*dee*-lighted!" with Taft's nomination, and though he did not actively campaign for him (in an era when it was considered unseemly for a president to do so), he was an avid supporter from the sidelines as well as a virtual dispensary of advice. There were lots of things to remember, the president told Taft, but above all, "you big, generous, high-minded fellow, you must *always* smile, for your nature shines out so transparently when you smile." Though Taft was a plodding, unenthusiastic campaigner—he hated "buttering people up" and being "exposed to all sorts of criticism and curious inquisitiveness"—he did what he had to do. And he kept with the progressive Roosevelt program. "I agree heartily and earnestly with the policies which have become known as the Roosevelt policies," he declared.

After a decisive win over the Democratic candidate, William Jennings Bryan, President-elect Taft told a crowd that his administration would be a "worthy successor to that of Theodore Roosevelt." But William Howard Taft was no Theodore Roosevelt. He was far more conservative. "With his reverence for legalisms," writes Nathan Miller in his biography of Roosevelt, "[Taft] believed a president should be less of an activist and should observe the law more strictly than Roosevelt had done." That the man Roosevelt believed to be his political clone should show himself otherwise shattered a friendship and opened in its place a fierce political rivalry.

The breach grew slowly at first. In a letter to Roosevelt, President-elect Taft wrote, "You and my brother Charley made that possible which in all probability would not have occurred otherwise." Roosevelt was stunned to read his efforts on Taft's behalf mentioned in the same sentence as Taft's deep-pocketed brother, as if they were comparable. It was like saying, Roosevelt later observed, that "Abraham Lincoln and the bond seller Jay Cooke saved the Union."

Taft's cabinet announcements were a further blow. Before the election, he had indicated that he would keep any member of Roosevelt's cabinet who wished to stay. "Tell the boys I have been working with that I want to continue with all of them," he had said. But after his election, Taft decided that the cabinet would be more loyal to the outgoing president, and was determined to replace them with his own people. Roosevelt, who was planning an extended African safari after leaving office, accepted the decision with equanimity, although underneath he was surprised and hurt. "Ha ha!" he wrote jovially to Taft at the end of the year. "*You* are making up your Cabinet. *I* in a lighthearted way have spent the morning testing the rifles for my African trip. Life has its compensations."

The apparent good cheer masked Roosevelt's growing apprehensions about his successor. "He's all right," the president said to a newsman during his last day in office. "He means well and he'll do his best. But he's weak. They'll get around him." To emphasize the point, Roosevelt pushed his weight against the newsman's shoulder. "They'll—they'll lean against him." Roosevelt was already disillusioned by some of Taft's emerging policies, and the tension between the two friends was obvious as they prepared to change places. "It can be truthfully said," wrote White House chief usher Ike Hoover, "that there has seldom been such bitterness between an incoming and outgoing administration. This applies to the entire families."

Poor weather forced the inauguration of William Howard Taft inside the Capitol, a dreary foreboding of what was to come in the new administration. Taft simply lacked the Roosevelt magic. Certainly he was decent and honest, but he was lazy[1] and almost entirely devoid of his predecessor's political acumen and appeal. In allying himself with the conservative Old Guard in Congress, particularly Speaker of the House "Uncle Joe" Cannon, he alienated Roosevelt's progressive Republicans, or Insurgents, as they were called. Everyone in the Republican party wanted a piece of the new president, and Taft was ill-equipped to deal with them. He was, said Senator Jonathan Dolliver of Iowa, "a ponderous and amiable man completely surrounded by men who know exactly what they want." And his presidency was failing, hampered by Taft's inability to steer his own ship.

News of Taft's problems reached Roosevelt in Africa, distressing the former president who had placed so much faith in him. Particularly galling was Taft's handling of conservation, an area most dear to Roosevelt. The new president replaced Roosevelt's Interior secretary, James Garfield, with Richard A. Ballinger, a man known to favor the rapid exploitation of the nation's resources, and demanded the resignation of Gifford Pinchot, chief of the Forestry Service and a disciple of Roosevelt's conservation policies.

"I cannot believe it," Roosevelt wrote Pinchot from Africa. "I do not know any man in public life who has rendered quite the same service you have rendered." In a follow-up letter, Roosevelt emphasized that it would be "a very ungracious thing for an ex-President

1. See Part III, Chapter 8.

to criticize his successor; and yet I cannot as an honest man cease to battle for the principles [for] which you and I and Jim [Garfield] . . . and the rest of our associates stood." The Pinchot dismissal, in short, was another wedge driven between the new president and the old.

Shortly after returning home from his African trek and subsequent tour of Europe, Roosevelt received a letter from Taft. "It is now a year and three months since I assumed office," the president wrote, "and I have had a hard time—I do not know that I have had harder luck than other Presidents, but I do know that thus far I have succeeded far less than others. I have been conscientiously trying to carry out your policies but my method of doing so has not worked smoothly." Taft at least got that right, even if he significantly understated his plight. The Insurgents were in open rebellion. Roosevelt responded to Taft's letter, noting that he was "much concerned about some of the things I see and am told; but what I felt it best to do was to say absolutely nothing—and indeed to keep my mind open as I keep my mouth shut!"

Roosevelt had intended to stay far away from politics upon his return to the United States, but he was greeted with an emerging movement by Pinchot and other Insurgents to split from Taft and the conservative Republicans and form a third party with Roosevelt as the leader. "Back from Elba," became the rallying cry. But Roosevelt was not prepared to take this drastic a step, considering it political suicide as well as an opening for the Democrats to take the White House in 1912. He warned Pinchot to ease up on President Taft as he would most likely be the Republican candidate. "Taft has passed his nadir," he wrote, "and independently of outside pressure he will try to act with greater firmness, and to look at things more from . . . the interests of the people, and less from the standpoint of a technical lawyer." It was almost as if Roosevelt was trying to convince himself.

The former president had good cause to wish for Taft's success. He was, after all, directly responsible for his being in the White House. Taft's failure would be his failure. But all the wishes in the world could not alter Roosevelt's ultimate realization that his man was a flop and the major cause of a broken Republican party. "Taft is utterly hopeless," he said to a friend. "I think he would be beaten if nominated [in 1912], but in any event it would be a misfortune to have him in the president's chair for another term, for he has shown himself an entirely unfit President." The time had come, Roosevelt reluctantly concluded, to answer the call of the Insurgents and run again.

"My hat is in the ring!" the former president proclaimed in February 1912. "The fight is on and I am stripped to the buff." It was a brutal match, with the two former friends battering one another mercilessly. Roosevelt called his successor a "fathead" with "brains less than a guinea pig." Taft labled his onetime benefactor a "dangerous egotist" and "demagogue." "In every announcement he makes you would think he was the whole show," Taft taunted at one rally. "It is 'I, I, I.' If you feed that vanity and that egotism by giving him something Washington did not get, Jefferson did not get, and Grant could not get [meaning a third term], you are going to put him in office with a sense of his power that will be dangerous for this country."

Roosevelt's enormous popularity showed itself when he beat the president in nine state primaries, including Taft's home state of Ohio, and won 278 delegates to the incumbent's 48. Yet despite the popular will, the conservative Republicans, who controlled the party machinery, rammed through Taft's nomination at the convention in Chicago. Roosevelt's supporters, charging "fraud," "robbery," and "naked theft," stormed out of the convention, met with Roosevelt, and convinced him to run on an independent ticket. "If you wish me to make the fight, I will make it," Roosevelt declared at a rally of the newly formed Progressive, or "Bull Moose"[2] Party, "even if only one state should support me."

The third-party candidate knew he was in for a tough battle. "In strict confidence, my feeling is that the Democrats will probably win if they nominate a progressive candidate," he told a friend. His worst fears were realized when the Democrats nominated New Jersey gov-

2. The party got its nickname from an earlier declaration by Roosevelt to the press that he was "fit as a bull moose."

ernor Woodrow Wilson. The race was on, but it was between Roosevelt and Wilson. Poor Taft never had a prayer. In an era of reform, he and his conservative agenda were simply irrelevant. "Sometimes I think I might as well give up so far as being a candidate is concerned," Taft wrote plaintively. "There are so many people in the country who don't like me. Without knowing much about me, they don't like me."

With the Republican party split, Wilson won the election handily with 42 percent of the vote. Roosevelt pulled off the best third-party performance in history, finishing second with 27 percent of the popular vote. Taft carried only two states, Utah and Vermont. The ousted president, of whom Roosevelt later said, "He meant well, but he meant well feebly," achieved his ultimate dream nine years later when President Warren G. Harding appointed him chief justice of the U.S. Supreme Court. "I don't remember that I was ever President," Taft joyfully remarked on the occasion.

8

"I'd Rather Vote for Hitler"

As far as Theodore Roosevelt's children were concerned, the wrong Roosevelt eventually succeeded their late father to the White House in 1933. Franklin D. Roosevelt was a lightweight in their eyes—a distantly related upstart, and a Democrat to boot. It didn't matter that he had married their first cousin Eleanor,[1] strengthening his ties to their branch of the clan. He was still an outsider, an unfit one at that, whose rise to power was a gross usurpation of the political mantle they believed should have rested with them.

Alice Roosevelt Longworth, Theodore's acid-tongued daughter, often gave voice to the decades of ill will generated by the conflicting ambitions within the extended family. "There we were," she once said of her branch of the family, "*the* Roosevelts—hubris up to the eyebrows, *beyond* the eyebrows—and who should show up but *Nemesis* in the person of Franklin."

FDR grew up worshiping his distant kinsman Theodore, eagerly absorbing tales of his adventures in the American West and his military exploits with the Rough Riders. He also followed the great

1. Eleanor's father, Elliott, was Teddy Roosevelt's younger brother.

man's path when it came to charting his own future—attending Harvard, starting in politics in the New York state legislature, and becoming assistant secretary of the navy while the country was at war. But his close identification with the late president became a bit too much for Theodore Roosevelt's children when FDR was nominated as Ohio governor James Cox's running mate in the 1920 presidential race against Warren G. Harding. Franklin was quick to latch onto TR's legacy during the campaign, whistle-stopping through the West, which was proven Roosevelt territory, and slamming the Republican nominee by saying he couldn't help believing that Theodore Roosevelt, who had "invented the word 'pussy-footer,' would not have resisted the temptation to apply it to Mr. Harding." The tactic worked almost too well, with many people believing FDR was TR's son. "You're just like the old man!" people would shout at various stops. "I voted for your father!"

Theodore Roosevelt's brood believed the public's confusion was being cultivated deliberately by FDR and quickly mobilized against him. Ted, TR's eldest son and namesake—and his only legitimate heir, from the family's point of view—joined Harding's campaign and started trailing FDR to counter any impression that this obscure Roosevelt relative had any real connection to the late, great president. "He is a maverick," Ted said of Franklin. "He does not have the breed of our family." That included courage, Ted implied, noting that FDR had only gone to Europe as an observer for the Wilson administration during World War I, while all four of TR's sons had fought.

Ted's gadfly campaign seemed to be effective; at one point the *Chicago Tribune* echoed him by calling FDR "the one half of one percent Roosevelt." It was enough to prompt presidential candidate James Cox to confront Ted publicly: "It is a pitiable spectacle to see this son of a great sire shamelessly paraded before the public. Out of respect for the memory of his illustrious father someone ought to take this juvenile spokesman aside and in primer fashion make plain what really ought to be obvious." Ted and his siblings were vindicated by Harding's crushing victory against Cox and his running mate, Franklin.

None of the clan could be described as overly concerned about FDR's subsequent paralysis from polio, either. (Alice's husband, Nick Longworth, an Ohio congressman and future speaker of the House, cruelly called him the "denatured Roosevelt.") With Franklin apparently out of the way, it was now Ted's turn to claim his rightful place in the political arena. He started by moving to Washington in 1921 and taking over the post of assistant secretary of the navy that FDR had held during the previous Wilson administration. From there Ted decided to run for governor of New York in 1923. It was just about this time, however, that he was tarred by Teapot Dome, one of the worst scandals in the nation's history.[2] Although Ted was not personally involved, the scandal consumed him nonetheless.

FDR, adjusting to his paralysis and aiming for a return to politics, could not have been more delighted with his distant cousin's misfortune. Frances Perkins, his future secretary of labor, said that one of his leading characteristics during this time was the overwhelming desire "to outshine his cousin Ted." As there could be only one Roosevelt in the arena, Ted's troubles came almost as a gift. Franklin loved getting newspaper articles from his advisor, Louis Howe, chronicling the Teapot Dome mess, and Ted's perceived role in it as assistant secretary of the navy. "I'm sending you clippings from which you will see that little Ted appears to be down and out as a candidate for governor," Howe wrote, adding as a postscript: "The general position of the newspaper boys is [that] politically he is as dead as King Tut, for the moment at least."

Ted wasn't dead, but he was seriously wounded. Franklin, on the other hand, gloriously reclaimed the spotlight at the Democratic National Convention of 1924 when, despite his disability, he bravely walked up to the podium—with the help of his son James, and after hours of practice at home—and nominated New York governor Al Smith for president. It was a rapturous moment for FDR. And though Smith failed to get the nomination, he did run for reelection as New York's governor, dramatically decreasing Ted Roosevelt's

2. See Part VI, Chapter 6.

chances of winning that race. "They have certainly handed you a fight," Alice telegraphed her brother.

Despite his newly claimed political stature, and Louis Howe's urgings, FDR refused to campaign against Ted. His wife, Eleanor, had no such qualms. Though she was Ted's first cousin, she had long been treated by his family as a pathetic relation whom they occasionally allowed to bask in their collective glory. Growing up shy and awkward, she was tormented by Alice, who was later complicit in FDR's affair with Lucy Mercer, and who delighted audiences with her wicked imitations of Eleanor's protruding teeth and receding chin. So, the family ties Eleanor Roosevelt might have been severing by campaigning against Ted were already seriously frayed to begin with. Besides, Franklin was her husband, and her emerging political fortunes were entwined with his. Armed with the knowledge that a victory for Ted could compromise their own ambitions, Eleanor launched a ferocious attack on her cousin.

It began at the state Democratic convention when she seconded Al Smith's nomination for governor, caustically observing that by nominating Ted the Republicans "had done everything they could to help [Smith]." As Ted had done to FDR years earlier, Eleanor badgered her cousin at his campaign stops, trailing him in a car outfitted with a giant teapot spouting steam—a glaring reminder of the scandal that haunted Ted's campaign. She denounced him as "a personally nice young man," but a political weakling "whose public service record shows him willing to do the bidding of his friends."

To the family who had once dismissed Eleanor as a meek and insignificant orphan in their midst, her activism came as a stunning, and most unwelcome, surprise. "I just hate to see Eleanor let herself look as she does," her aunt Anna wrote after a visit by Eleanor and a couple of her feminist friends—"female impersonators," as Alice called them. "Though never handsome," Anna continued, "she always had to me a charming effect, but alas and lackaday! since politics have become her choicest interest, all her charm has disappeared, and the fact is emphasized by the companions she chooses to bring with her." Ted's wife wasn't happy about Eleanor's behavior either, particularly since they shared the same first and last names. People were bound to think Ted's own wife was campaigning against him. Yet no matter how much she upset her relatives, Eleanor plowed on, tasting power and savoring her cousin's eventual defeat in the New York governor's race.

In 1928, Franklin Roosevelt was elected governor of New York, the same office Ted had been denied four years earlier. Theodore Roosevelt's family was being eclipsed again, as Ted had to settle for an appointment by President Herbert Hoover as governor-general of Puerto Rico. One of Ted's nieces recalled a visit by FDR's family during his gubernatorial campaign, when the resentment was palpable: "We were *awful* to those Franklin children. And after the family left, we took the Franklin Delano Roosevelt buttons they left with us and stomped on them with glee!" It was about all they could do, as FDR was becoming an unstoppable force.

The stock market crash of 1929 and the economic chaos that followed spelled disaster for the Republican party, which was buried in the midterm elections of 1930, and for the Republican Roosevelts. For Franklin Roosevelt, though, it was a boom period. He was reelected governor by a huge margin, greatly increasing the likelihood that he would be the Democratic presidential nominee in 1932. "Well, as far as I can see, the ship went down with all on board," Ted wrote his mother from Puerto Rico about the Republican reversals. "Franklin now, I suppose, will run for the Presidency, and I am beginning to think of nasty things to say concerning him."

Anything Ted had to say would be an insignificant squeak amid the chorus calling for FDR. Although he was appointed to the more prestigious and visible post of governor-general of the Philippines, and still harbored hope for even greater things, Ted seemed to know that his time was passing. "I believe that the Governor Generalship of the Philippine Islands may well mark the end of my active career as a public servant," he wrote his mother from Manila. "Should it do so . . . I would like to feel that I had done the best that lay in me. I do not feel now that I have anything to be ashamed of [for] having gone into public life or that Father would feel other than that I have done well."

Ted submitted his resignation shortly after Franklin became president in 1933. A new party was in power, and Theodore Roosevelt Jr. did not belong. Asked by a newsman in Manila precisely what his relationship with the new president was, he responded wryly, "Fifth cousin about to be removed." The reversal of Ted's place in the world, and that of his family, was made all the more bitter when he discovered that his brother Kermit had defected to FDR. In an ingratiating letter to the president-elect, Kermit wrote, "I can say with absolute truth that, although I have been a Republican all my life, I am tremendously relieved and pleased that you were elected." Then, to seal the new alliance, Kermit joined FDR on a two-week Caribbean cruise aboard Vincent Astor's yacht.

The rest of the Theodore Roosevelt family maintained ranks and did what they could to make life miserable for their distant cousin in the White House. Alice often led the charge, offering a steady stream of cruel commentary for the benefit of Washington's conservative cave dwellers while perfecting her Eleanor imitation. Her visits to the White House were often unsettling, such as when she showed up dripping in gold jewelry right after FDR had taken the country off the gold standard. But the fact that she visited the White House at all, even if it was to torment its occupants, irked Ted. "I could not help feeling it was like behaving in like fashion to an enemy during war," he wrote his mother. "More so, for enemies generally only fight for territory, trade or some material possessions. These are fighting us for our form of government, our liberties, the future of our children. I did not expect Kermit to see—for that's his blind side. But I did expect [Alice] to see this, for she's acute and her life has been politics."

Ted's own assault on the Roosevelt administration was relentless. He charged FDR's New Deal programs with "making false promises to the needy," administering relief in such a way as "to leave a stench in the nostrils of decent people," and destroying the country "morally and spiritually and ruining it materially." In one 1935 speech he addressed the president directly: "You have been faithless. You have usurped the functions of Congress, hampered the freedom of the press. . . . You have urged Congress to pass laws you knew were unconstitutional. . . . You have broken your sacred oath taken on the Bible." It was harsh stuff, which Ted only intensified as he tried to subvert FDR's efforts to engage the United States in World War II (by the end of which both cousins would be dead). "Like you I am bitterly fearful of Franklin," Ted wrote his sister Alice. "I am confident he is itching to get in the situation, partly as a means of bolstering himself and partly merely because of megalomania."

Alice herself had not mellowed much over the course of FDR's first two terms. When asked her views on a third term, she snorted, "I'd rather vote for Hitler." After years of tolerating her ferocious wit, FDR was fed up. "I don't want anything to do with that damned woman again!" he roared. As invitations to the White House dried up, Alice seemed bemused by Franklin and Eleanor's reactions to her: "They might have said, 'Look here, you miserable woman, of course you feel upset because you hoped your brother Ted would finally achieve [the presidency] and now he hasn't. But, after all, here we are. Come if it amuses you!' But they took it all seriously. They took the meanness in the spirit in which it was meant."

9

General Dissatisfaction

Almost a century after Abraham Lincoln was forced to fire George McClellan, another president was confronted with another troublesome general. Harry Truman's problems with Douglas MacArthur were of a much different sort, however. While McClellan had been a newly promoted general afraid to make a move, MacArthur, the "American Caesar," was an old warrior with an aggressive agenda of his own. Unfortunately, it was in direct conflict with President Truman's. MacArthur never seemed to become reconciled to the fact that the president, a mere civilian, was his commander in chief; he treated him more like a pesky private. Truman, who had been subjected to the general's insulting behavior since taking office at the end of World War II, described him as "Mr. Prima Donna, Brass Hat," a "play actor and bunco man." MacArthur, he said, was a "supreme egotist" who thought himself "something of a god." Such was the state of the relationship when, in the summer of 1950, Communist forces from North Korea stormed into South Korea in an act of naked aggression.

President Truman responded with a commitment of U.S. forces, which was followed by United Nations forces. MacArthur was appointed chief of the U.N. Command, but he would not be an autonomous leader. Truman ordered full reports from him every day. "I practically had to telephone General MacArthur to get information from him [during World War II]," the president grumbled. Things would be different now, he insisted. Truman's direct involvement meant inevitable delays as MacArthur's messages were filtered through various channels before reaching the president, irking the general no end. "This is an outrage," he snapped. "When I was Chief of Staff I would get [President] Herbert Hoover off the can to talk to me. But here, not just the Chief of Staff of the Army delays, but the Secretary of the Army and the Secretary of Defense. They've got so much lead in there it's inexcusable."

If MacArthur resented having to wait to get to the president, he was even more annoyed by the orders coming from the White House—especially the one to "stay clear" of Chinese Nationalist leader Chiang Kai-shek. Communist forces under Mao Tse-tung had taken over China the year before South Korea was invaded, chasing Chiang's Nationalist forces off the Chinese mainland to the island of Formosa (now Taiwan). President Truman's one overriding concern in Korea was to avoid involving Red China and the Soviet Union in the conflict. Courting Chiang, he felt, might prompt such an intervention—and possibly lead to World War III. MacArthur, on the other hand, believed Chiang could be a valuable ally, if not an ideal one.

"If he has horns and a tail, so long as Chiang is anti-Communist, we should help him," MacArthur declared. "Rather than make things difficult, the State Department should assist him in his fight against the Communists—we can try to reform him later!" For Truman, it was bad enough that MacArthur had visited Formosa under his own initiative shortly after the invasion of South Korea, and was photographed kissing the hand of Madame Chiang. After that embarrassing episode, Truman sent Ambassador Averell Harriman to meet the general and set him straight. MacArthur gave assurances that he understood the president's policy, but less than a month later he publicly slammed it in a speech before the Veterans of Foreign Wars. "Nothing could be more fallacious," he pronounced, "than the threadbare argument by those who advocate appeasement and defeatism in the Pacific that if we defend Formosa we alienate continental Asia."

Truman was livid when he heard of MacArthur's meddling. This was rank insubordination worthy of dismissal, the president's advisors argued. Angry as he was, though, Truman was not prepared to relieve the general—yet. "It would have been difficult to avoid the appearance of demotion," he said later, "and I had no desire to hurt General MacArthur personally." Nevertheless, a fateful clash was coming.

In the meantime, things had not been going well in Korea. The North Korean invaders had penetrated deep into the South, with American casualties mounting in what *Time* magazine correspondent John Osborne called "an especially terrible war." MacArthur had a bold plan, though, one he declared would "crush and destroy the army of North Korea." He proposed making a surprise amphibious landing on the western coast of Korea at the port of Inchon, 200 miles north of where the enemy had pushed American and South Korean forces. The North Koreans, he promised, would be trapped in a deadly pincer. The plan was fraught with danger, and the president and the Joint Chiefs of Staff agreed to it only reluctantly. On September 15, 1950, the assault began. It was a stunning success that turned the tide of the war completely. Within two weeks the North Koreans were pushed back beyond the thirty-eighth parallel, which divided the two countries, and South Korea was reclaimed. If only MacArthur had stopped there.

Basking in the glow of victory, and perhaps intent on scoring a few political points, Truman flew to Wake Island in the Pacific to meet MacArthur for the first (and, as it turned out, last) time. By most accounts it was a cordial encounter, although the general was decidedly rude at times, refusing to salute his commander-in-chief, for example, and rebuffing his invitation to stay for lunch. While little of substance was discussed during the meeting, Truman did ask about the chances of Chinese or Soviet intervention in the war now that MacArthur's military objective was the destruction of the North Korean forces in their own territory.

MacArthur had in fact been given permission to cross the thirty-eighth parallel into North Korea after the success at Inchon, so long as Chinese or Soviet forces did not become involved and their borders with North Korea were kept off-limits to MacArthur's forces. In assuring the president that there was little chance of intervention, MacArthur, as historian Geoffrey Perret writes, "delivered up one of the fattest hostages to fortune ever seen in a century that has been filled with calamitous bad guesses." Sure enough, the Chinese did get involved.

MacArthur had practically invited them, ignoring the administration's restrictions against sending troops anywhere near the Chinese border. With only tepid resistance coming from Washington, he pushed far into North Korea, launching what he called one powerful "end-of-war" offensive that he said might get the troops "home in time for Christmas." Instead, it got thousands of them slaughtered. The Chinese responded to MacArthur's far northern push with a ferocious counterattack, sending down a horde of nearly 30,000 men who pushed MacArthur's forces back below the thirty-eighth parallel and well beyond.

Of those not killed in the retreat south, many died of hypothermia and pneumonia in the harsh Korean winter. President Truman was devastated. "His mouth drew tight," witnessed author John Hersey, "his cheeks flushed. For a moment, it almost seemed as if he would sob. Then in a voice that was incredibly calm and quiet, considering what could be read on his face—a voice of absolute courage—he said, 'This is the worst situation we have had yet. We'll just have to meet it as we've met all the rest.'" MacArthur, too, was reeling. "This command . . . ," he said, "is now faced with conditions beyond its control and its strength." But in their views on how to deal with the terrible setback, the general and the commander-in-chief were utterly opposed.

Truman was more determined than ever to avoid a greater conflagration. "There was no doubt in my mind," he later wrote, "that we should not allow the action in Korea to extend to a general war. All-out military action against China had to be avoided, if for no other reason than because it was a gigantic booby trap." MacArthur disagreed, of course, advocating a widening of the war by, among other things, bombing China. In addition, he warned that if another 200,000 troops were not immediately sent to Korea, either the U.N. Command would be annihilated or it would have to be evacuated. The administration's restrictions in dealing with China amounted to "an enormous handicap without precedent in military history," he told *U.S. News & World Report* in one of a series of face-saving public pronouncements.

The general's indiscretion enraged Truman. "I should have relieved General MacArthur then and there," he later wrote. Though the administration quickly issued a gag order on all military commanders and senior civil servants, it was clearly aimed at one man—Douglas MacArthur. But it would take a lot more than an order from Washington to shut this general up, especially as events in Korea started to improve again.

MacArthur had requested that Lieutenant General Matthew Ridgway be appointed to serve under him as commander of the Eighth Army after the death of General Walton Walker. Ridgway, one of the finest combat commanders of World War II, was a brilliant choice on MacArthur's part, although his great success in Korea would come to make MacArthur's gloomy forecasts of imminent disaster look ridiculous. Ridgway quickly rallied the battered and demoralized Eighth Army and led it to a succession of crushing victories over the Chinese, decimating their forces and pushing them back to the thirty-eighth parallel. MacArthur later tried to claim credit for Ridgway's outstanding performance, but "the mantle of military genius draped around him since Inchon was trailing in the mud," writes Geoffrey Perret. Ridgway was now *the* man in Korea, while MacArthur, as General Omar Bradley put it, had become "mainly a prima donna figurehead who had to be tolerated." Truman's tolerance, however, was rapidly eroding.

It didn't matter to MacArthur how successful Ridgway had been in hammering the Chinese. He still wanted to widen the war and reunite Korea. At one point he even made the almost insane suggestion that the Korean peninsula be severed from China's border by creating a radioactive desert of nuclear debris between them. The general was stunned, therefore, when the Truman administration took the great gains made by Ridgway as an opportunity to open peace talks with China. He was convinced that the president's nerves were at the breaking point, as he later wrote, "not only his nerves, but what was far more menacing in the Chief Executive of a country at war—his nerve." Settling with China now would be an outrage, he felt, keeping the situation in Korea more or less the same as it was before the North Korean invasion. This would be not a victory but a stinging insult to the thousands of men who had died fighting.

Rather than allow what he saw as a shameful capitulation to Communism, MacArthur determined to short-circuit the administration's peace feelers by issuing a direct threat to the Chinese on his own initiative. He called on them to admit defeat or face the risk of "a decision by the United Nations to depart from its tolerant efforts to contain the war to the area of Korea" by expanding military operations to China's coastal areas and interior bases, which "would doom Red China to the risk of imminent military collapse." In one subversive stroke, MacArthur had sabotaged Truman's peace efforts.

"I couldn't send a message to the Chinese after that," the president later said of MacArthur's brazen threat. "I was ready to kick him into the North China Sea. . . . I was never so put out in my life. . . . MacArthur thought he was the proconsul for the government of the United States and could do as he damned pleased." And yet Truman felt powerless to act. The country was firmly behind the famous general, and it would take another major misstep for the president to move against MacArthur. He wouldn't have to wait long.

House Minority Leader Joe Martin had given a speech early in 1951 calling for the use of Chiang Kai-shek's Nationalist troops in Korea and accusing Truman of a defeatist policy. "What are we in Korea for," he demanded, "to win or lose? . . . If we are not in Korea to win, then this administration should be indicted for the murder of American boys." Martin then sent a copy of his speech to MacArthur, who candidly responded in a letter that he heartily endorsed the speech. With no pretense of confidentiality, the general criticized, among other things, the Eurocentricism of American foreign policy, which was at the expense of the Far East. "If we lose this war to Communism," he wrote to Martin, "the fall of Europe is inevitable; win it, and Europe most probably would avoid war and yet preserve freedom." In the end, though, what galled MacArthur most was the prospect of how the Korean War was going to end. "There is no substitute for victory," he exclaimed. On April 5, Joe Martin read the text of MacArthur's letter on the House floor, claiming that the administration's misguided policy in Korea compelled him to do it.

That same evening Truman wrote in his diary: "This looks like the last straw. Rank insubordination." MacArthur had to go. The general seemed to know it, too. After meeting with one of his field officers, Edward Almond, he said, "I may not see you anymore, so goodbye, Ned." Confused, Almond asked him why. "I have become politically involved," MacArthur responded, "and may be relieved by the President."

The end came after several days of high level discussions within the Truman administration. The president knew he was in for "a great furor," but was willing to endure it. He signed the order relieving MacArthur of all his commands on April 10, 1951. Word leaked out, though, and the president was warned that if MacArthur heard about the order before it reached him, he might preempt it by resigning first. "The son of a bitch isn't going to resign on me," Truman fumed. "I want him fired!" The dismissal was announced in a hastily arranged press conference that night. MacArthur, who didn't find out until the next day, was almost the last to know.

"Publicly humiliated after fifty-two years in the Army," he reflected bitterly. Years later he wrote, "No office boy, no charwoman, no servant of any sort would have been dismissed with such callous disregard for the ordinary decencies." While MacArthur's dismissal perhaps could have been handled with more decency, Truman made no apologies for the deed itself: "The American people will come to understand that what I did had to be done."

10

LBJ vs. RFK

President Lyndon B. Johnson was seething. Paul Corbin, a member of the Democratic National Committee and a supporter of Attorney General Robert Kennedy, was orchestrating a movement to get his man on the ticket as Johnson's running mate in the upcoming 1964 New Hampshire primary. Johnson despised Kennedy and wanted Corbin's Bobby-for-veep campaign stopped cold. "We either make him desist or get rid of him," Johnson demanded, adding later through an intermediary that Kennedy himself should fire Corbin.

"Tell him to go to hell," the attorney general snorted upon hearing the president's order. Since very few would be willing to tell the president of the United States where he could stick his order, Kennedy had to face Johnson himself in a most unpleasant meeting at the Oval Office. "It was a bitter, mean conversation," Kennedy later recalled. "It was the meanest tone I'd ever heard." Indeed the president was in no mood for niceties, and bluntly gave notice that he wanted Corbin out of New Hampshire and off the DNC. "He was loyal to President [John F.] Kennedy; he'll be loyal to you," Johnson barked. "Get him out of there. Do you understand? I want you to get rid of him."

Johnson's deep animosity toward his attorney general, brother of the late president and inherited from that administration, was certainly mutual. "I don't want to have this kind of conversation with you," Kennedy said in response to Johnson's tirade. Corbin, he said, was harmless, and not his responsibility anyway. "He was appointed by President Kennedy, who thought he was good." This was just what Johnson, already self-conscious of the fact that his accidental presidency was due only to JFK's assassination, did *not* want to hear. "Do it," he demanded. "President Kennedy isn't president anymore. I am." Johnson's vitriol stunned and wounded Kennedy, who struggled to maintain his composure. "I know you're president," he said evenly, "and don't you ever talk to me like that again." With that, the attorney general stormed out of the White House in a white rage.

Unpleasant as it was, the scene between Johnson and Kennedy was just one episode in the epic feud that consumed both men for nearly a decade. To Johnson, Bobby Kennedy was a "snot-nosed little son-of-a-bitch," who sought to undermine him at every opportunity. Kennedy, on the other hand, felt nothing but contempt for Johnson, whom he viewed as a liar, a bully, and a pretender to the throne. "This man . . . ," he said, "is mean, bitter, vicious—an animal in many ways." As historian Jeff Shesol writes, the antagonism between the two men "spawned political turf battles across the United States. It divided constituencies [they] once shared and weakened their party by forcing its members to choose between them. It captivated the newly powerful media that portrayed every disagreement . . . as part of a prolonged battle for the presidency or a claim on the legacy of the fallen JFK. It helped propel one to the Senate and drive the other from the White House." And, Shesol might have added, it was as entertaining a clash of personalities as any in American history.

The tenor of the relationship between LBJ and RFK was established early on, late in 1959, when Kennedy, then acting as campaign manager for his brother Jack's nascent presidential bid, visited Johnson at his Texas ranch to find out if the powerful Senate majority leader had any presidential ambitions of his own. Johnson assured

Kennedy that he did not, and took his guest deer hunting. Upon spotting a deer, Kennedy fired his borrowed shotgun at the quarry. The gun's powerful recoil knocked him to the ground, cutting his forehead. Johnson seemed to revel in Kennedy's humiliation. "Son," he said, "you've got to learn to handle a gun like a man."

To the scrappy young man once considered the runt of the Kennedy litter, and whose parents feared he would grow up to be a sissy, Johnson's crack must have stung. But any shame Bobby Kennedy might have felt at the time was soon replaced by anger when he found out that Lyndon Johnson had lied to him and entered the presidential race. He was further inflamed when Johnson implied that his father, Joseph P. Kennedy, had been a Nazi appeaser while serving as ambassador to Great Britain at the dawn of World War II. "You Johnson people are running a stinking damned campaign and you're gonna get yours when the time comes!" he fumed at Johnson aide Bobby Baker. Kennedy would prove to be true to his word.

Johnson's presidential campaign had fizzled when Jack Kennedy began considering him as a possible running mate, despite the earlier mudslinging. What followed was an awkward dance. Would Kennedy actually offer Johnson the spot, and if so, would LBJ take it? On the morning of July 14, 1960, Jack Kennedy met with Johnson. Accounts vary as to the substance of the conversation, but from Bobby Kennedy's point of view, his brother was merely trying to gauge Johnson's feelings—to dangle the vice presidential prospect before him—and no firm decisions about a running mate had been made. He was horrified, therefore, when JFK returned from the meeting with the grim news that LBJ had interpreted his overtures as an actual offer and had accepted. Bobby later told his biographer Arthur Schlesinger that "the idea that [JFK would] offer him the nomination in hopes that he'd take [it] is not true. The reason he went down [to Johnson's suite at the Democratic National Convention in Los Angeles] . . . was because there were enough indications from others that [Johnson] wanted to be offered the nomination. But [JFK] never dreamt that there was a chance in the world that he would accept it."

It now fell to Bobby Kennedy to undo what he termed "the terrible mistake." His efforts at doing so only served to further alienate the two men.

Several meetings between the Kennedy and Johnson camps solved nothing, a situation further aggravated by the fact that Jack Kennedy had decided at one point that it would be unwise to try to remove Johnson once word leaked out to the convention that he would be on the ticket. Bobby Kennedy, apparently unaware of his brother's final decision, which had already been confirmed with Johnson, again visited LBJ's suite hoping to get him to withdraw. Wounded by the contradictions coming from the Kennedys, and believing them to be maliciously orchestrated by Bobby, Johnson refused to budge. LBJ, Bobby Kennedy later said, "is one of the greatest sad-looking people in the world. You know, he can turn that on. I thought he'd burst into tears. . . . He just shook, and tears came into his eyes, and he said, 'I want to be Vice President, and if [JFK] will have me, I'll join him in making a fight for it.' It was that kind of conversation." Kennedy wasn't privy to other conversations in which an outraged Johnson called him "that little shit-ass," among other epithets even more colorful. He was convinced that RFK had deliberately, and of his own initiative, set out to sabotage his political future.

After John F. Kennedy's narrow victory over Richard Nixon in 1960, Lyndon Johnson—like so many before him—was left impotent in the role of vice president. Robert Kennedy was determined to keep him that way. As attorney general and one of his brother's closest advisors, RFK was, in the words of the president, "the second most powerful man in the world." *U.S. News & World Report* proclaimed him to be "the number two man in Washington . . . second only to the president in power and influence." The attorney general rarely missed an opportunity to lord his status over the vice president, barging in on Johnson's private meetings with the president to address business he considered more important, or making a mockery of him among the political and media elite who gathered at his Hickory Hill estate.

On one occasion, President Kennedy had to leave a White House meeting with a group of civil rights leaders and asked LBJ to conclude the session for him. Johnson, rarely given much of a role in anything, seemed pleased to do so. Bobby Kennedy, also in attendance and itching to leave as well, instructed a staffer to tell the vice president to cut it short. The staffer was reluctant to perform such a potentially unpleasant task, however, and did nothing. Irate, Kennedy called him over again. "Didn't I tell you to tell the vice president to shut up?" he snapped. With that, the frightened staffer eased his way over to Johnson's chair and whispered to him the attorney general's order to wrap it up. Johnson glared up at him, but kept on talking—and talking, going on for another ten or fifteen minutes while Bobby Kennedy stewed.

On another occasion, the attorney general stormed into a meeting of the President's Committee on Equal Employment Opportunity, of which Johnson was chairman, and began bombarding committee members with questions about employment progress and other issues in Birmingham, Alabama. Johnson listened to Kennedy's barrage with growing impatience, finally interjecting the committee's position on many of the issues the attorney general was raising. Unsatisfied, Kennedy began lobbing questions at the vice president. "It was a brutal performance, very sharp," recalled one person in attendance. "It brought tensions between Johnson and Kennedy right out on the table, and very hard. Everybody was sweating under the armpits."

LBJ's hatred of RFK grew more intense every day, and he complained about him to anyone who would listen, including the president himself. His rantings about the attorney general's efforts to crush him were, in the words of his aide Bobby Baker, "border[ing] on the paranoiac," and his jealousy and resentment over RFK's access were nakedly apparent. "Every time they have a conference," he spouted off to an Associated Press writer, "don't tell me who is the top advisor. It isn't [Secretary of Defense Robert] McNamara, the chiefs of staff, or anybody else like that. Bobby is first in, last out. And Bobby is the guy he listens to." As far as Bobby was concerned, though, the vice president was responsible for his own place in the backseat. Johnson, he claimed, "wasn't very helpful at times that he might have been helpful. . . . He never gave any suggestions or ideas on policy." Even the president, always protective of Johnson's ego, grew "really irritated with him," Bobby maintained, testing him at times. "'I'm going to give him a chance . . . to go on the record as to how he stands,'" RFK said the president told him before meetings. "And he would never say how he stood on any matter! . . . And then he groused at people afterward."

The dynamic underlying all Johnson's "grousing" was forever altered on November 22, 1963, when President John F. Kennedy was assassinated. The once impotent vice president was now in charge. Bobby Kennedy would never forgive him for the boorish way (as he viewed it) he assumed power. "There were four or five matters," Bobby said later, "that arose during the period of November 22 to November 27 or so . . . which made me bitterer, unhappy at least, with Lyndon Johnson." One issue that particularly irked him was the way LBJ kept Air Force One—with the suddenly widowed First Lady on board with her dead husband's casket—waiting in Dallas with him until he was sworn in as president. Kennedy, it seems, thought Johnson a bit too eager to grab the reins of power.

Johnson, on the other hand, was very concerned about the proper, Constitutional transfer of the presidency, as well as the negative effect a vacuum of leadership might have on the nation. "What raced through my mind," he later recalled, "was that if they had shot our president driving down there, who would they shoot next? And what was going on in Washington? And when would the missiles be coming? I thought that it was a conspiracy."

Johnson, unsure of just what the Constitution required for the assumption of office, and also concerned about how his actions would be perceived by the grieving Kennedy family, called Bobby, as both the nation's top law enforcement official and as the new head of the Kennedy clan, to get his approval for swift action. "A lot of people down here think I should be sworn in right away," Johnson said in a phone call to the attorney general. "Do you have any objection to that?" Kennedy was silent on the line. "I didn't see what the rush was," he later said, noting that his brother had been dead only an hour, and that it might have been nice for the family if he could have returned to Washington as President Kennedy—"But I suppose that was all personal." Neither man appeared to realize that under the Constitution, Johnson automatically became president upon JFK's death.

After hanging up with Johnson, Bobby made some phone calls to answer LBJ's questions about the particulars of the swearing in, and then called him back with the details. He had acquiesced to Johnson's wishes, but what really galled him was later hearing that LBJ had squelched any criticism of the delay on Air Force One by claiming that the attorney general had actually *requested* that he take the oath of office immediately. Johnson, he said, was "simply incapable of telling the truth." So much for a smooth transition.

President Johnson needed Bobby Kennedy to remain as attorney general, mainly because he wanted to keep JFK's administration intact, and he knew RFK's departure would likely cause a flood of other resignations. But Bobby's willingness to stay put didn't mean that Johnson liked him any better. In fact, things between them only got worse. The new president felt that Bobby treated him as an imposter. And, suspicious and insecure though he was, he was right. Kennedy could barely disguise his contempt.

It was evident from the very first cabinet meeting of the new administration. Bobby was late. When he did sit down, it was "quite clear," noted Agriculture Secretary Orville Freeman, "that he could barely countenance Lyndon Johnson sitting in his brother's seat." Secretary of State Dean Rusk's declaration of loyalty on behalf of the cabinet did not sit well with the attorney general either. He scornfully called it "a nice little statement," adding that he was informed after the meeting how impressed LBJ was with Rusk because he was the only one who spoke up at the cabinet meeting. "So I thought . . . what he wanted is declarations of loyalty, fidelity from all of us." But Johnson knew he wasn't going to get this from RFK, in either word or deed, and was soon obsessing over what became known as "the Bobby problem."

Lyndon Johnson was president, but Robert Kennedy was the brother of a martyr and, in the eyes of some, his natural successor. This made him a threat, especially when people started discussing the possibility of RFK serving as LBJ's running mate in the upcoming election of 1964. "I don't want to go down in history as the guy to have the dog wagged by the tail, and have the Vice President elect me," Johnson said about the possibility of Kennedy running with him, "because that's what they're going to write. With Bobby on the ticket, I'd never know if I could be elected on my own." For his own part, RFK appeared delighted by all the trouble he was causing the president. "I think he's hysterical about how he's going to try to avoid having me or having to ask me. And that's what he spends most of his time on, from what I understand: figuring out how he's going to avoid me." And avoiding Bobby, the "little shit-ass," wasn't easy.

"Every day," Johnson later said, "as soon as I opened the papers or turned on the television, there was something about Bobby Kennedy; . . . about what a great Vice President he'd make. Somehow it just didn't seem fair. I'd given three years of loyal service to Jack Kennedy. During all that time I'd willingly stayed in the background; I knew that it was *his* Presidency, not mine. . . . And then Kennedy was killed and I became the custodian of his will. . . . But none of this seemed to register with Bobby Kennedy, who acted like *he* was the custodian of the Kennedy dream, some kind of rightful heir to the throne. It just didn't seem fair. I'd waited for my turn. Bobby should've waited for his. But the Kennedy people wanted it now."

Johnson eventually derailed any momentum to place RFK on the ticket by announcing to the press that he had "reached the conclusion that it would be inadvisable for me to recommend to the Convention any member of the Cabinet" for vice president. This, of course, included Bobby. "Now that damn albatross is off my neck," the president said privately, though he wasn't any more subtle about his feelings in public. Calling a select group of prominent reporters to the White House, Johnson gleefully recounted for them Kennedy's reaction to the news that he wouldn't be in the running: "When I got him in the Oval Office and told him it would be 'inadvisable' for him to be on the ticket as the Vice President–nominee, his face changed, and he started to swallow. He looked sick. His Adam's apple bounded up and down like a yo-yo." With that, the president audibly gulped in imitation of his nemesis, while mimicking his "funny voice."

Kennedy was not amused when he heard about the president's performance, accusing him of violating the trust of their private meeting. Johnson feigned innocence in the face of the attorney general's wrath, which infuriated Bobby even more. "He tells so many lies," Kennedy said in a familiar refrain, "that he convinces himself after a while he's telling the truth." Johnson was too pleased with having this "grandstanding little runt" out of the running to care much what RFK thought, but his relish at the turn of events was short-lived. Though he would no longer have to face the prospect of Bobby as his vice president, he would soon have to deal with him as a vocal foe in the U.S. Senate.

Kennedy had decided that working for LBJ again would be intolerable. He resigned his position as attorney general in 1964 and entered the New York Senate race. In a strange twist, RFK and LBJ became temporary allies in this endeavor. Johnson was wildly popular in New York and was expected to take the state in a landslide in the upcoming presidential election. Kennedy, however, was not so well received and desperately needed to be on the president's bandwagon. Johnson, no doubt enjoying having Bobby so beholden to him, gladly let him on. The pair traveled all over New York, looking "as close as twins," the *New York Times* reported. "You don't often find a man who has the understanding, the heart and the compassion that Bobby Kennedy has," the president gushed at one rally, while at another, RFK declared Johnson "already one of the great presidents of the United States. . . . I think of President Johnson with affection and appreciation." It was all a load of political bull, but it worked.

Bobby Kennedy won his seat, but he didn't bother to thank Lyndon Johnson, the man many considered crucial to his victory. "Bobby thanked the postmasters, he thanked the precinct captains, he thanked every two-bit person who helped in the campaign," recalled Johnson press aide Liz Carpenter. "But he didn't thank the President of the United States. He just couldn't choke it out of himself." The brief detente, orchestrated for the New York voters, was now over. Almost as soon as Bobby Kennedy settled into his new Senate seat, he launched his campaign against the administration of Lyndon Johnson.

Most of the president's policies were under siege, from the war on poverty to urban renewal. But it was Vietnam that most sharply divided RFK and LBJ, much as it did the rest of the nation. While Kennedy had supported a military presence during his brother's administration and beyond, he was becoming increasingly convinced that there would be no military solution. To Johnson, Vietnam, though a "little piss-ant country," was vital in the larger war against Communist expansion. "Knowing what I did of the policies of Moscow and Peking," he later said, "I was sure as a man could be that if we did not live up to our commitments in Southeast Asia and elsewhere, they would move to exploit the disarray in the United States and in the allies of the Free World."

Then there was what he imagined Bobby would be doing if Vietnam was lost, "out in front leading the fight against me, telling everyone that I had betrayed John Kennedy's commitment to South Vietnam. That I had let a democracy fall into the hands of the Communists. That I was a coward. A man without a spine. Oh, I could see it coming, all right."

As the war in Vietnam escalated, so did the differences between Johnson and Kennedy, each man creating separate orbits around themselves. "It was a galaxy with two suns," writes Jeff Shesol, "and as one shone more brilliantly the other dimmed." It was Johnson who was being eclipsed, his administration under increasing attack in the turmoil of the late 1960s, and he blamed it all on Bobby. His hatred and paranoia increased to such levels as to prompt occasional outbursts that were utterly irrational, such as when he claimed that

RFK put Martin Luther King on the Kennedy payroll "to rile up the Negroes. That is why we had the riots. After all I've done for the Negroes. They never would have *attacked me* if they hadn't been put up to it."

Kennedy, meanwhile, continued to speak out more forcefully against the war. "We have misconceived the nature of the war . . . ," he said in a speech after the Tet offensive in early 1968. "We have sought to resolve by military might a conflict whose issue depends upon the will and conviction of the South Vietnamese people. It is like sending a lion to halt an epidemic of jungle rot." It was time, he said, for the administration to "face the reality that a military victory is not in sight and that it will probably never come."

Kennedy's differences with Johnson became irreconcilable when he decided to run against him for the Democratic presidential nomination in 1968. It was a drastic step on RFK's part, one that effectively split the party, but that he felt was necessary. "My decision reflects no personal animosity or disrespect toward President Johnson," he said as he announced his candidacy. "I have often commended his efforts in health, in education, and in many areas, and I have the deepest sympathy for the burden that he carries today. But the issue is not personal. It is our profound differences over where we are heading and what we want to accomplish. . . . At stake is not simply the leadership of our party or even our country—it is our right to moral leadership on this planet."

Bobby was a little less lofty when it came to the actual campaign, taking swipes at the president that made it seem as if he were fighting in a barroom brawl rather than for the opportunity to provide "moral leadership." At one point, for example, he accused Johnson of "calling on the darker impulses of the American spirit. . . . Integrity, truth, honor, and all the rest seem like words to fill out speeches, rather than guiding principles."

The contest never got too nasty, though, mainly because it was over almost as soon as it started when Johnson announced to the stunned nation that he would not be seeking his party's nomination. Bobby, he said later, was no small factor in his decision: "The thing

I feared from the first day of my presidency was actually coming true. Robert Kennedy had openly announced his intention to reclaim the throne in memory of his brother. And the American people, swayed by the magic of the name, were dancing in the streets. The whole situation was unbearable for me."

Warren Harding: A satyr courting irrelevance.

Part III

Hail to the Chaff

Not all presidents can be great, nor can their scandals. History has relegated some chief executives to obscurity, their malfeasances remembered now as mere oddities. Ten of our less appreciated first citizens, as well as their eccentricities, are celebrated here. But not a word will be said about Millard Fillmore, who has become so famous for his obscurity that, strictly speaking, he no longer qualifies as obscure.

★

1

Zachary Taylor
(1849–1850)

The great statesman is the person who can balance principle and pragmatism, wrestle with great moral issues, and do what's right. Then there was Zachary Taylor. A slovenly soldier from Kentucky with sad eyes and a weary mien, the hero of the Mexican Wars arrived in the White House in 1849 to face the issue that would in twelve years rend the nation: slavery. It was increasingly apparent to an enlightened civilization that the forced bondage of a race of people was morally indefensible. Most other countries had outlawed the practice. Taylor understood that. He wanted the slave trade stopped. Unfortunately, he also owned slaves. Had paid a pretty penny for them, too. Taylor realized it would not look good for the president of the United States to keep slaves. The issue was simply too incendiary. So he came to a difficult, but firm, decision. He hid them in the White House attic.

2

Franklin Pierce

(1853–1857)

Franklin Pierce of New Hampshire may have been the first president elected because he had a great flack. Pierce was a close friend of the poet and novelist Nathaniel Hawthorne. As the 1852 campaign approached, Hawthorne wrote for his friend a riveting, lyrical biography that made him out to be a cross between St. Francis of Assisi and Alexander the Great, as opposed to what he was—a rather nice-looking loser. "Pierce was the best looking president the White House ever had," Harry Truman said of his distant predecessor, "but as president he ranks with Buchanan[1] and Calvin Coolidge."

Pierce was a small, weak man accused, perhaps unfairly, of battlefield cowardice in the war with Mexico. He was married to a complete loony-bird. Jane Pierce was a reclusive melancholic and a religious fanatic who dressed in black and spent all her time writing letters to her dead son. Not surprisingly, Franklin began to drink a little. Then he began to drink a lot. This became something of a problem. One day a Washington policeman reportedly arrested some babbling, slobbering sot for going amok on horseback on a public

1. See the next chapter.

street and running over a woman. He turned out to be the president of the United States. The charge was quickly dropped.

Pierce would ultimately die of cirrhosis of the liver. But mere dipsomania does not itself qualify him for enshrinement here. What best survives his undistinguished presidency are ten words, his legacy. National campaigns have made for some fabulously vicious political sloganry,[2] but none was as fabulous as the slogan the Whigs bestowed on the fourteenth president: "Franklin Pierce, the Hero of Many a Well-Fought Bottle."

2. See Part V.

3

James Buchanan
(1857–1861)

Historians have often dismissed James Buchanan as a do-nothing president who stood by idly as the nation careered toward civil war. Yet despite the utter failure of his administration, Buchanan may have distinguished himself after all—by being the country's first gay chief executive.

In an era before the concept of a different sexual orientation existed, let alone a public discussion (or even a scientific word for it), the behind-the-scenes snickering of Buchanan's contemporaries provides compelling but by no means complete evidence. It wasn't necessarily Buchanan's failure to marry (the only president not to do so) that got people talking. It was his relationship with Senator Rufus King of Alabama. The two were inseparable, living together for many years before King's death and Buchanan's elevation to the presidency. Andrew Jackson called Senator King "Miss Nancy," a common term of the era for effeminate though not necessarily gay men. Representative Aaron Brown of Tennessee referred to King as Buchanan's "better half" and "wife" in a letter to Mrs. James K. Polk. Brown mentioned possible rough sailing in the relationship, noting that King, whom he calls "Aunt Fancy" in the letter, "may now be seen every day, triged out in her best clothes & smirking about in hopes of securing better terms than with her former companion [Buchanan]."

Of course, wagging Washington tongues cannot be relied upon to establish anything for certain about Buchanan's sexuality, but his own words, and those of King, do add a touch of credibility to the gossip. When King was appointed minister to France by President Tyler in 1844, Buchanan seemed out of sorts and pining for his man. "I am now solitary and alone," he wrote a friend, "having no companion in the house with me. I have gone a wooing to several gentlemen, but have not succeeded with any of them. I feel that it is not good for a man to be alone; and should not be astonished to find myself married to some old maid who can nurse me when I am sick, provide good dinners for me when I am well, and not expect from me any very ardent or romantic affection."

King, who would briefly serve as Franklin Pierce's vice president before his death in 1853, seemed to miss Buchanan's company, too, writing: "I am selfish enough to hope you will not be able to procure an associate who will cause you to feel no regret at our separation." Again, there is no proof of a sexual relationship. Maybe Buchanan and King were just very good friends.

4

Andrew Johnson
(1865–1869)

Being president is an ego trip; some men let it go to their heads. Martin Van Buren strutted the White House like a self-important little fop. Tom Jefferson, for all his egalitarian posturing, raised a pinkie or two in his day. Presidents have tended to put on airs, but Andrew Johnson never lost touch with the little folk. Even the very little folk.

Johnson was an accidental president, a Tennessean chosen by Abraham Lincoln as a running mate to appease the South. With Lincoln's death, Johnson inherited a bleeding nation and a Congress determined to punish the defeated Confederacy and speed Reconstruction. By and by, Johnson's resistance to this, and his general pigheadedness, got him impeached. Never before was the resolve of the young nation so tested: Would its leaders corrupt the Constitution to achieve petty political ends? Everyone looked to Johnson for leadership, but Johnson remained holed up in the White House, sending emissaries to speak on his behalf. What was he doing in there? Theories abounded. Was he busy plotting a brilliant tactical strategy, remaining imperially above the fray? Was he busy secretly building alliances? As it turns out, he was busy going sweetly bonkers.

Historians report that in those waning days of his administration, Johnson developed a peculiar hobby. His daughter, Martha Patterson, had declared war on the mice that had made themselves at home in the White House; she imported cats, set traps, and spread poison. Johnson couldn't stand it. Possibly he felt for the rodents, hounded as he was by his own yowling predators. Spotting one of the unfortunate critters one night in his bedroom, the president took pity. He placed some flour by the fireplace, allowing the mice to "get their fill." That was just the beginning.

He would soon boast to a bewildered aide that he had finally won the confidence of "the little fellows," as he called the mice. The president began not only to feed them but to add "some water that they may quench their thirst." The president had become a mouse rancher! Anyway, it all turned out fine. The Senate failed to convict, and the presidency was saved—though it had been a close squeak.

5

Ulysses S. Grant

(1869–1877)

U. S. Grant was a war hero. A cigar smoker. A drinker. A killer. And something of a girlie man. It's the oddest thing. It has confounded historians. "Young Grant had a girl's primness of manner and modesty of conduct," biographer W. E. Woodward wrote. "There was a broad streak of the feminine in his personality. He was almost half-woman."

This is a somewhat uncharitable attitude, perhaps, but General Grant did indeed have a certain prissiness about him that minced and sashayed, in contrast to his battlefield swagger. He hated dirty jokes. In the field, he bathed in a closed tent so that not even his aides would see him naked. Foul language rattled him. As a cadet at West Point, Grant was mortified at a court-martial hearing when he had to repeat the offending words of a cadet who had called an officer a name. The name was "shit-pants," or some such.

It is perhaps unfair to poke fun at a man for exhibiting what in a more enlightened era might simply have been called sensitivity. What fault was it of Grant's that he lived in rugged times, among rugged men, in the rugged business of making war? Still, it bears mentioning that when President Grant was informed that his personal secretary was involved in a scheme to defraud the government of liquor tax revenue, he took the following executive action: He burst into tears.

6

Grover Cleveland

(1885–1889, 1893–1897)

Grover Cleveland was our second-fattest president, the only one elected to nonconsecutive terms, the only one who got married in the White House, and the only one who ever admitted to having an illegitimate child. Until John F. Kennedy, he was renowned for having the prettiest first lady. He was a good guy and a hard worker who might well have been a great president had anything at all important occurred during his tenure. Alas, it didn't, and so he is not particularly noteworthy, except for one item on his résumé that qualifies him for inclusion here.

Before getting to that, however, it is important to lay to rest for all time the scurrilous rumor, often reprinted, that when Cleveland had a law office in Buffalo he had a habit of relieving himself out the window and was once sued by a drenched passerby. This story is apparently apocryphal; it stays alive only because unscrupulous history writers keep gleefully repeating it.

Now, what did make Cleveland somewhat memorable was his rather commendable unwillingness to delegate responsibility. Many persons in high public office must make decisions of life and death, but they tend to do it from comfortably afar. Harry Truman did not fly the plane and drop the bomb. Abe Lincoln did not fire a musket at Gettysburg. But as sheriff of Erie County, New York, in the 1870s, Grover Cleveland assigned to himself the role of official hangman. Twice the future president of the United States stood on the gallows, affixed the noose, and personally yanked the trapdoor open.

With Cleveland, the buck really did stop there.

7

William McKinley (1897–1901)

William McKinley may not have been a captivating orator, or a skilled internationalist, or an inspired leader. He was so enslaved by public opinion that he permitted a newspaper to declare war on Cuba. The speaker of the House once said of McKinley that he kept his ear so close to the ground "it was full of grasshoppers." Still, he dearly loved his wife. No other president was as devoted a husband. It was a protectiveness bordering on obsession. Ida McKinley was a semi-invalid, subject to piercing headaches and frequent epileptic seizures. The condition left her something of a recluse, shut in her room for hours with nothing to do but knit. McKinley would abandon affairs of state to squire her around, taking her out for afternoon strolls. He even broke protocol by having her sit next to him during formal dinners.

It was at one of those dinners that McKinley performed a strange act that is evidence of either extreme solicitousness or almost breathtaking callousness, like a locker room joke involving a woman and a paper bag. You decide. William Howard Taft recalled sitting with the couple at that dinner and asking the president for a pencil so he could take notes. As McKinley reached into his pocket, "a peculiar hissing sound" came from Ida. She was apparently having an epileptic seizure. Her features began to contort. Without missing a beat, the president calmly dropped his napkin over her face and proceeded to hand over the pencil, as though nothing remotely out of the ordinary had occurred. A few moments of awkward conversation ensued. When Mrs. McKinley recovered, she removed the napkin and resumed dining.

8

William Howard Taft

(1909–1913)

There is nothing particularly noteworthy about the fact that William Howard Taft was the nation's fattest president. If that was all there was to it, he wouldn't merit inclusion here. As it happens, there was more. William Howard Taft was the nation's fattest president who could not stay awake. Big Bill's corpulence contributed to his habit of falling asleep at the most inopportune times—sitting in the front row at a state funeral, or riding in an open car during a New York campaign. It got to be quite an embarrassment.

Attending the opera one evening, Taft aide Archie Butt recalled agonizing over the slumbering president during the entire first act, hoping he would wake up before intermission so the audience would not see the president snoring through a command performance. Mercifully, he did. After one dinner for cabinet members, President Taft called for some music on the Victrola, but he fell asleep during the first selection. When he woke up he called for another tune, then dozed off again before the record was even put on. Attorney General George Wickersham then suggested the sextet from *Lucia di Lammermoor,* since "it will awake anyone but a dead man." When the song failed to rouse the slumbering president, Wickersham declared dourly, "He must be dead."

"I will make a conscientious effort to lose flesh," Taft once wrote his wife, Helen. "I am convinced that this undue drowsiness is due to the accumulation of flesh." He never did lose the weight. After he finished being the fattest president ever, he went on to become the fattest U.S. chief justice ever.

Taft did have a sense of humor about his avoirdupois, however. He encouraged the retelling of a story from his days as governor general of the Philippines. He had cabled Secretary of War Elihu Root from Manila. "Took long horseback ride today; feeling fine," was the message, to which Root immediately cabled back: "How is the horse?"

9

Woodrow Wilson
(1913–1921)

Woodrow Wilson is by no means an obscure president—far from it—but he is included here because there was a hidden side to him, one that he rarely revealed. To the world, Wilson projected an image of professorial gravity as he led the nation through World War I, but when courting his second wife, a Washington widow named Mrs. Edith Galt, he behaved more like a giddy teenager. The president's letters to his lady love dripped with sentiment.

"You are so vivid. . . . You are so beautiful!" he wrote. "I have learned what you are and my heart is wholly enthralled. You are my ideal companion. . . . You are my perfect *playmate,* with whom everything that is gay and mirthful and imaginative in me is at its best." In another, the president wrote, "How deep I have drunk of the sweet fountains of love that are in you . . . how full of life and every sweet perfection!" So enthralled was he that, after a date, a Secret Service agent recalled the president skipping along the streets of Washington and whistling a popular ditty, "Oh, you beautiful doll! You great big beautiful doll!"

The *Washington Post* inadvertently added an element of scandal to the relationship when it reported on the front page in 1915 that "the president spent much of the evening *entering* Mrs. Galt." It was a typographical error. The story was supposed to say that he was *entertaining* her.

Wilson's courtship also provided plenty of material for Washington's wags. "What did Mrs. Galt do when the president asked her to marry him?" went one popular joke of the day.

"She fell out of bed!"

10

John Tyler

(1841–1845)

Some ex-presidents retire to the golf course. Others write their memoirs, seek to rehabilitate their reputations, or go on the road and make expensive speeches. John Tyler went to work for an enemy government.

Tyler was the first accidental president, inheriting the office after the death of William Henry Harrison in 1841. (Harrison had made a long and tedious inauguration speech in the cold rain and was dead of pneumonia a month later.) After serving most of Harrison's term, and facing a threatened impeachment in the process, Tyler retired to his Virginia estate where he lived quietly until the dawn of the Civil War fifteen years later. Tyler took up the rebel cause, backed Virginia's secession from the Union, and was elected to the Confederate House of Representatives in 1861. Unfortunately, he died just before taking his seat, depriving him of the opportunity of being the only U.S. president to serve two different governments. And opposing ones at that.

Representative Brooks delivers his opinion of Senator Sumner's "Crimes Against Kansas" speech.

Part IV

Congressional Follies

If, as columnist Joseph Alsop once suggested, "the only way to look at a congressman is down," the view below in many instances would include a motley assortment of rascals and thieves, fools and philanderers. From a widely representative body like Congress, such detritus must inevitably spew. Some of it is regurgitated here.

★

1

Floor Fights

The first recorded clash between congressmen started with spit. In 1798, Representative Matthew Lyon of Vermont stalked across the House floor and hocked one right into the face of Connecticut's Roger Griswold for making fun of his Revolutionary War record. A resolution to expel "Spitting Lyon" failed, but Griswold got his own revenge. Two weeks after the loogie landed, he walked over to where Lyon was sitting and whacked him over the head with a large hickory cane. Stunned, Lyon struggled to his feet, grabbed some fire tongs, and started hitting Griswold back. The undignified brawl was quickly broken up, and the next day both men signed a pledge not to commit any act of violence upon each other from that day forward. It was a peaceful resolution, but a precedent had been set.

★

Some congressional quarrels became so heated that opponents routinely decided to settle their differences on "the field of honor," where many died or were severely wounded. One of the most notable duels took place between William Jordan Graves of Kentucky and Jonathan Cilley of Maine in 1838. Strangely enough, neither man had a problem with the other, but fought nonetheless because a provision in the Code Duello, the bible of dueling principles, required it. Cilley had made some critical remarks about Colonel James Watson Webb, a New York newspaper publisher, during a House debate. Webb was insulted and issued a challenge to Cilley through his second, Congressman Graves. Cilley refused to accept the challenge, however, arguing that under the Constitution he was not responsible outside the House for anything he said within it. Graves agreed that Cilley was legally correct, but issued him a challenge of his own because, according to the dueling code, Cilley's refusal of Webb's challenge constituted a grave insult to his second, Graves. These were touchy times indeed.

Cilley accepted Graves's challenge, though he apparently thought the whole matter absurd. As it happened, Graves chose Representative Henry Wise of Virginia, one of Cilley's most hardened enemies, as his second. If there was any chance the two sides might have settled their differences without bloodshed, Wise was quick to undermine it. It was he who was largely blamed for coaxing Graves forward. On the day before the duel, as Graves was practicing his shot, Wise reportedly clapped him on the shoulder and said, "Graves, you must kill that damned Yankee." And so he did, with a rifle blast through Cilley's femoral artery. That was after the third round of shots had been fired, the first two having missed. "I must have one more shot!" Graves had insisted, to which Cilley responded, "They must thirst mightily for my blood."

The fatal encounter caused a national uproar. The fallen congressman was just thirty-five and left behind a wife and three children. In the minds of many, Graves killed him in cold blood. The Washington correspondent for the New York *Evening Post* called the duel a "horrid and harrowing spectacle," and said Cilley had fallen a victim to "a false and bloody code in a wretched quarrel." Even former president Andrew Jackson, the dean of dueling, registered his horror. "I cannot write on the murderous death of poor Cilley," he wrote to President Martin Van Buren. "If Congress does not do something to wipe out the stain of the blood of murdered Cilley from its walls, it will raise a flame in the public mind against it, not easily to be quenched. Cilley was sacrificed." Congress did pass an antidueling act, but to little effect.

★

The practice of dueling eventually fell from favor as a means of settling disputes and satisfying honor, but the U.S. Capitol still remained quite a violent place. This was particularly true of the years leading up to the Civil War, when sectional differences over slavery and other issues intensified to a dangerous degree. Legislation was sometimes stalled as "belligerent Southrons glared fiercely at phlegmatic Yankees," one observer noted, and the House of Representatives "seethed like a boiling caldron." Congress in those days could have easily been mistaken for a Western saloon. "Every man on the floor of both Houses is armed with a revolver," reported Senator James Hammond of South Carolina, "some with two revolvers and a Bowie knife." Senator Benjamin Wade of Ohio even carried a sawed-off shotgun. When a pistol concealed in one House member's desk accidentally discharged, there were instantly "fully thirty or forty pistols in the air," recalled Representative William Holman of Indiana, who was present.

One of the most disturbing episodes that emerged from these troubled times was the brutal beating of Charles Sumner. On May 19, 1856, the abolitionist senator from Massachusetts delivered his famous "Crimes Against Kansas" speech in which he decried the efforts of Southerners to force slavery into that territory. Sumner's speech was brimming with overwrought rhetoric and oratorical bombast, with more than a few sharp digs at Andrew Pickens Butler, a proslavery senator from South Carolina. Butler, Sumner declared, "touches nothing which he does not disfigure with error. . . . He cannot open his mouth, but out there flies a blunder." As one of slavery's "maddest zealots," Butler raised himself "to eminence on this floor in championship of human wrongs."

And Sumner had even more to say. "The Senator from South Carolina," he continued, "has read many books of chivalry and believes himself a chivalrous knight. . . . Of course he has chosen a mistress to whom he has made his vows, and who, though ugly to others, is always lovely to him; though polluted in the sight of the world, is chaste in his sight. I mean the harlot, Slavery. For her, his tongue is always profuse in words. Let her be impeached in character, or proposition made to shut her out from the extension of her wantonness, and no extravagance of manner or hardihood of assertion is then too great for this Senator. The frenzy of Don Quixote, in behalf of his wench, Dulcinea del Toboso, is all surpassed."

Butler might have beaten up Sumner for his pomposity alone, but he wasn't actually present to hear the screed. His kinsman and fellow Carolinian, Representative Preston S. Brooks, was there, however, and he didn't appreciate Sumner's lofty insults one bit. Three days after the speech was delivered, Brooks quietly entered the Senate chamber and found Sumner working at his desk. "I have read your speech twice over carefully," Brooks announced. "It is a libel on South Carolina and Mr. Butler who is a relative of mine." Without warning, Brooks then started whacking Sumner with a cane until it splintered and his victim fell from his chair in a bloody heap.

Northern reaction to the assault was one of horror. "The crime is not merely against liberty but civilization," editorialized the Boston *Evening Transcript,* while the Albany *Evening Journal* noted that "For the first time has the extreme discipline of the Plantation been introduced into the Senate of the United States." In the South, though, Brooks was hailed as a hero. "Sumner was well and elegantly whipped," gloated the Charleston *Mercury,* "and he richly deserved it." Southerners sent Brooks commemorative canes, with HIT HIM AGAIN inscribed on them. It was all an ugly preview of the Civil War to come.

Sumner's injuries kept him out of the Senate for three years, and his empty chair became a symbol of the antislavery movement. Several weeks after the attack, a House investigation committee concluded that it was a breach of congressional privilege, and said in a report, "This act cannot be regarded by the committee otherwise than as an aggravated assault upon the inestimable right of freedom of speech guaranteed by the Constitution . . . and, if carried to its ultimate consequences, must result in anarchy and bring in its train all the evils of a reign of terror." As debate raged in the House over whether or not to expel Brooks, he decided to resign on his own. His exile was brief, however. He ran for office again, and was sworn in just two weeks after his resignation. Five months later, Brooks was dead of liver disease. Sumner, after his long convalescence, served in the Senate until 1874.

★

Of course, not all congressional brawls were physical. There were plenty of lacerating tongues to keep things lively, especially that of Senator John Randolph of Virginia. Though a childhood illness rendered him beardless and impotent, with a high-pitched voice, he was capable of knocking an opponent out cold with words alone. When one congressman, freshly elected to fill the vacancy left by the death of another, attacked Randolph, the senator remained uncharacteristically quiet. Several days later, though, during a discussion on a bill that the deceased congressman had been sponsoring, Randolph had his say: "This bill, Mr. Speaker, lost its ablest advocate in the death of my lamented colleague, whose seat," he added caustically, "is still vacant."

Randolph often used his facility with language to withering effect. Andrew Jackson's secretary of state Edward Livingston, he said, "is a man of splendid abilities, but utterly corrupt. He shines and stinks like rotten mackerel by moonlight." Randolph's colleagues Robert Wright and John Rae, he remarked, exhibited two anomalies: "A Wright always wrong; and a Rae without light."

2

Sexcapades

For many congressmen, forbidden sex has been one of the most avidly pursued perks of office, but it's gotten them into heaps of trouble—especially the hypocrites. Representative William Campbell Preston Breckinridge, for one, was as righteous as Moses come down from the mountain (and almost as hammy as Charlton Heston playing him). The congressman from Kentucky liked to play the part of moral crusader, often lecturing on the evils of sex and the virtues of purity. He cautioned one audience of teenage girls to avoid "useless handshaking, promiscuous kissing, needless touching, and all exposures." To another group of girls he declared, "Chastity is the fountain, the cornerstone of human society. . . . Pure home makes pure government." But, alas, Breckinridge's lessons seem to have been lost on his teenage mistress. When young Madeline Pollard slapped the father of five with a $50,000 paternity suit in 1893, one observer noted that "The fall of Breckinridge was like that of an archangel."

Several forces gathered to destroy the congressman, not the least of which was his own stupidity. Breckinridge tried to convince the court that he had no idea Madeline had *three* children by him. Yes, he admitted, they had often had sex, sometimes several times a day. Yes, he had recommended her for a government job and paid her oodles of cash. But kids? Who knew? The jury, not surprisingly, found in Madeline's favor. Breckinridge was wounded, but not yet out of the game. He wanted to be reelected, and in a tearful performance he confessed, "I know the secret sin; I tried to atone for it." But, he said, "I was entangled by weakness, by passion, by sin, in coils which it was almost impossible to break."

Unfortunately for him, Breckinridge's redemption was derailed by the emerging feminist movement. Susan B. Anthony and other activists were first testing their political power, and though they didn't yet have the vote, they rallied hard against the wayward congressman. His "exposed and confessed unchastity," Anthony insisted, rendered Breckinridge unfit for office. He lost by a landslide.

★

William Sharon's fling with Althea Hill was not entirely improper, even if he was twice her age. The senator from Nevada was a wealthy widower and free to pursue whomever he pleased. Nevertheless, the affair did have some unpleasant consequences, including assault and murder charges. It also resulted, directly and indirectly, in *three* U.S. Supreme Court decisions.

Senator Sharon, then sixty, met Althea Hill in California in 1880. She had blown her small inheritance on bad investments, and the senator graciously offered to give her some financial advice. He also offered her $500 a month to let him "love her." The money, he later testified, was the standard fee he offered his mistresses. Althea declined, even after the ante was raised to $1,000. According to her testimony, she immediately rose to depart, saying to Sharon, "You are mistaken in your woman. You can get plenty of women that will let you love them for less than that." Neither Althea nor the senator ever denied that a love affair did eventually commence. It's just that she claimed that it occurred within the confines of a secret marriage. Althea said that Sharon was so smitten that he asked her to marry him after she turned down his lucrative offers to become his mistress. But, she said, he insisted the marriage would have to be secret as he had an ex-mistress in Philadelphia who might make trouble if she heard about it. According to Althea, he told her they could be officially married by simply agreeing in writing to do so. She later produced the signed document in court. He called it a fraud and a forgery.

Althea and the senator set up a household of sorts at two adjoining hotels in San Francisco—she in one; he in the other—connected by a passageway. Back and forth they tiptoed for about a year, apparently in complete harmony. Sharon furnished Althea's room in the style of her choosing and gave her $500 a month spending money (the same amount, incidentally, she would have made as his mistress). For a time they were inseparable. "I used to go everywhere with Mr. Sharon," Althea later testified. "He scarcely went anywhere that I did not go with him—either riding or driving, or attending to business—that he did not take me with him." But then things started to sour. Sharon accused Althea of revealing his business secrets, and even of stealing his private papers. Eventually he demanded that she vacate her room at the hotel, underscoring his seriousness by ordering the door taken off its hinges and all the furniture and carpeting removed. After an abortive reconciliation in 1882, Althea Hill and William Sharon were in court.

In September 1883, Althea made the shocking public announcement that she was Sharon's lawfully wedded wife. Then she had him arrested for adultery with another woman. Sharon vehemently denied there ever was a marriage and vowed to spend as many of his millions as necessary to prove her a liar. His lawyers filed suit in federal court alleging that Althea's marriage document was a fake and asked the court to compel her to surrender it for cancellation. She answered with her own suit in the state court, asking for a divorce and property settlement.

Althea was represented by David Terry, a former chief justice of the California Supreme Court and noted duelist who would soon figure prominently in her personal life. Despite some of Althea's unsavory witnesses, including one who had hidden in Sharon's room to watch him bed another woman, the state judge ruled that a legally binding marriage existed. He granted Althea a divorce and $2,500 a month in alimony. "I am so happy," she cooed after the ruling. "I feel just like a young kitten that has been brought into the house and set before the fire." Sharon promptly appealed, and at the same time pressed his petition in federal court to have the marriage document judged a forgery and nullified.

Althea faced a formidable legal team assembled by Sharon, but she was uncowed. In fact, she was quite feisty—dangerously feisty. During one pretrial examination, while Sharon's lawyers were questioning one witness, Althea sat stewing as she read the unfriendly deposition of another. Suddenly she exploded, demanding that the examination be halted. "When I see this testimony," she screeched, "I feel like taking that man [Sharon's lawyer William M.] Stewart out and cowhiding him. I will shoot him yet, that very man sitting there. To think he would put up a woman to come here and deliberately lie about me like that. I will shoot him as sure as you like." Several attempts by a court officer to stop Althea's tirade were unsuccessful. "They shall not slander me," she shouted. "I can hit a four-bit piece nine times out of ten." With that she withdrew a pistol from her purse, waved it menacingly toward another of Sharon's lawyers, and assured him that she was not going to "shoot you just now, unless you would like to be shot and think you deserve it."

Several weeks after this scene, when all the testimony was completed, circuit judge Lorenzo Sawyer and district court judge Mathew Deadly ruled that the declaration of marriage was a forgery and ordered Althea to surrender it for cancellation. Judge Deadly also gave her a little sermon. Portions of the text bear reprinting here, if only to show that pistol-packin' Althea wasn't the only one a little off the wall:

> [As] the world goes and is, the sin of incontinence in a man is compatible with the virtue of veracity, while in the case of a woman, common opinion is otherwise. . . . And it must also be remembered that the plaintiff is a person of long-standing and commanding position in this community, of large fortune and manifold business and social relations, and is therefore so far, and by all that these imply, specially bound to speak the truth,

> and responsible for the correctness of his statements; and all this, over and beyond the moral obligation arising from the divine injunction not to bear false witness, or the fear of the penalty attached by human law to the crime of perjury. On the other hand, the defendant is a comparative obscure and unimportant person, without property or position in the world. Although of apparently respectable birth and lineage, she has deliberately separated herself from her people, and selected as her intimates and confidants doubtful persons from the lower walks of life. . . . And by this nothing more is meant than that, while a poor and obscure person may be naturally and at heart as truthful as a rich and prominent one, and even more so, nevertheless, other things being equal, property and position are in themselves some certain guaranty of truth in their possessor, for the reason, if no other, that he is thereby rendered more liable and vulnerable to attack on account of any public moral delinquency, and has more to lose if found or thought guilty thereof than one wholly wanting in these particulars.

Althea seems to have taken this judicial homily in stride, perhaps because she viewed it as irrelevant. Senator Sharon had died before the court's decision, and two weeks after it was delivered, she married her attorney, David Terry. As far as the newlyweds were concerned, the judgment had died with Sharon. It was, pronounced Terry, "an ineffective, inoperative, unenforceable pronunciamento," which he didn't bother to appeal. Yet though Sharon was dead, his interests lived on with his children who, through his lawyers, appealed the earlier divorce decree and eventually got the California Supreme Court to reduce Althea's alimony from $2,500 to $500. The court still recognized the marriage as lawful, however, and consequently Sharon's children asked for a new trial. They also filed a petition in federal court to revive the order that Althea surrender her marriage contract, having waited until her time to appeal the order had expired.

The Terrys had been outmaneuvered, but Althea still had some spit in her. One day on a train she encountered Judge Sawyer, who had ruled against her. Marching up to his seat, she started to taunt him. "I will give him a taste of what he will get bye and bye," she said as she leaned over and yanked his hair. David Terry laughed and added, "The best thing to do with him would be to take him into the bay and drown him." Later that summer they met Sawyer again, this time in court, when the petition by Sharon's heirs to revive the federal order to surrender the marriage license was heard. Sitting with Sawyer was Stephen J. Field, associate justice of the U.S. Supreme Court. (In those days, Supreme Court justices were required to hear cases on circuit when the full court was not in session in Washington.) Justice Field, who had already witnessed Althea's exploits on an earlier tour of duty, soon got another taste of her volatile temper when he read the judges' unanimous decision reviving the order against her. Hearing the opinion read, Althea suddenly jumped up and barked at Justice Field: "Judge, are you going to take the responsibility of ordering me to deliver up that marriage contract?"

"Be seated, madam," Field responded coolly.

But Althea wouldn't be silenced: "How much did Newlands [Sharon's son-in-law] pay you for this decision?"

Field had now had about enough. "Remove that woman from the courtroom," he ordered a marshal. "The court will deal with her hereafter."

With that, Althea slumped down in her seat and defiantly said, "I won't go and you can't put me out." Then, as the marshal approached her, she sprung up and slapped him in the face with both hands. "You dirty scrub," she screamed. "You dare not remove me from this courtroom." As the marshal proceeded, Althea's husband moved in and punched him in the mouth. A small riot broke out as a swearing David Terry and a scratching Althea were subdued and removed. During the scuffle, a Bowie knife was taken from Terry's hand and a pistol from Althea's purse. Both were subsequently found guilty of contempt and ordered to prison, Terry for six months and his wife for one. After a petition to revoke the order was denied by Justice Field, the Terrys made two appeals to the U.S. Supreme Court—one on the order imprisoning them for contempt, the other on the order that Althea surrender the marriage contract. They lost both. Then the California Supreme Court decided that the lower court's earlier decision favoring Althea and granting her a divorce from Sharon with alimony was not supported by the evidence.

These reversals set the Terrys off on a furious rampage. David ranted in long letters in the San Francisco *Call,* attempting to smear Justice Field. "He has always been a corporate lawyer, and a corporate judge, and as such no man can be honest," Terry wrote. In conversation, he called the judges "all a lot of cowardly curs," and said he would "see some of them in their graves yet." Terry declared that he would horsewhip Field, "and if [he] resents it, I will kill him." All this from the former chief justice of the California Supreme Court! Althea, too, vowed she would kill both Justice Field and Judge Sawyer. As it turned out, the threats were not idle ones.

In August 1889, Field was traveling by train to San Francisco. Midway through the trip, the Terrys boarded. At a stop in Lathrop, California, Field got off the train to eat breakfast at the station there. He was accompanied by a bodyguard, David Neagle, who had been assigned to protect him after the Terrys' threats reached Washington. Soon after Field sat down to eat, the Terrys walked into the station. Seeing Field, Althea ran back to the train to get her purse. David Terry sat down, whereupon the station manager came up to him and said, "Mrs. Terry has gone out to the car for some purpose. I fear she will create a disturbance." Terry replied, "I think it very likely. You had better watch her and prevent her coming in." When the manager left to do so, Terry rose from his table, strode over behind Field, and viciously slapped him on both sides of his face. With that, Neagle the bodyguard sprang up and ordered him to stop. According to Neagle, Terry shot him "the most malignant expression of hate and passion I have ever seen in my life," while reaching for his Bowie knife. Instantly, Neagle fired his gun twice, and David Terry fell dead. Just then, Althea rushed back into the room, open purse in hand. The manager grabbed her satchel and took a loaded revolver out of it as Althea hysterically screamed for vengeance.

Unfortunately for Neagle, the train station was close to David Terry's home turf of Stockton, California, where the former chief justice had lots of friends. Neagle had none. The local sheriff arrested him for murder and took him into custody. Justice Field was also arrested after Althea swore out a warrant against him, but the governor of California ordered him freed immediately lest the prosecution of a U.S. Supreme Court justice become "a burning disgrace" to the state. Neagle wasn't so lucky, and his case resulted in yet another decision by the Supreme Court arising from Senator William Sharon's broken love affair with Althea Hill Terry.

Neagle's chances of a fair trial in Terry's home county were next to nil. Many believed that he and Field had deliberately provoked Terry's assault so as to have an excuse to kill him. Neagle applied to the federal court for a writ to free him, but there was a serious question as to whether the federal court had the grounds to do that. It depended on whether Neagle had been acting "in pursuance of a law of the United States," yet there was no specific statute calling for him to act as Field's bodyguard. Local authorities in California argued that Neagle should be tried for murder, but the federal court, with Althea's old nemesis Judge Sawyer presiding, overruled all objections and ordered Neagle released. The state's attorney appealed to the U.S. Supreme Court. In 1890, with Justice Field recused, the court ruled that Neagle had indeed been acting "in pursuance of a law of the United States," and that a specific statute was not necessary. Neagle was a free man. The conclusion of this whole sordid episode was not as happy for Althea. Two years after the Supreme Court decision that freed Neagle, she was committed to an insane asylum. And there she lived until her death forty-five years later.

★

Given Althea's penchant for violence, Senator Sharon was lucky to have escaped their affair with his life. Senator Arthur Brown of Utah was not so fortunate. His affair with Anna Addison Bradley began in January 1899. Thirteen months later she gave birth to their son, Arthur Brown Bradley. At the time, Anna was still living on and off with her estranged husband, and Senator Brown with his second wife, Isabel. So desperately did he want to be with his mistress that he separated from his wife and promised to marry Anna. Isabel Brown wasn't about to be shunted aside, however. She had her husband and his lover followed by detectives, then arrested for adultery—twice.

Brown promised his wife that he would stop seeing Anna, and even hired a lawyer, Soren K. Christensen, to stay with him and help keep him faithful. But, alas, Anna's pull was irresistible. Christensen later described the terrible toll the attraction took on the senator. At times, he said, Brown would "call [Anna] vile names, and abuse her, and other times he would tell me he couldn't live without her." Brown resolved his conflicted emotions in favor of Anna, giving Christensen the slip and meeting his lover for a secret tryst in Pocatello, Idaho. Christensen was able to track him down, though, and, accompanied by Mrs. Brown, went to Idaho to fetch him home. The lawyer later described in a deposition the messy confrontation between the senator, his wife, and his lover: "Mrs. Brown said to [Anna], 'How do you do, Mrs. Bradley? I have wanted to talk with you!' Mrs. Bradley sort of cowed over to the wall, and Mrs. Brown walked up towards her and grabbed her by the throat and threw her down, and intended to kill her. . . . I separated them, they got up, and commenced talking in a very low tone of voice, when Mrs. Brown grabbed her again. I separated them, and Mrs. Brown says, 'Let me alone, I will kill her,' and I says, 'Not when I am here.' . . . Finally Mrs. Brown rapped on the door of room 11, and said, 'Arthur, open the door or I will mash it in,' and the door opened and the two women went in. . . . Arthur called me, and said, 'Come in, I don't want to be left alone with them.'"

Having witnessed the force of his wife's fury, Brown provided his mistress with a revolver for her protection. It wouldn't be necessary. Isabel Brown died of cancer in August 1905. The senator was now free to marry Anna. On the very night Isabel died, he called his lover and told her to get a divorce, which she did. But now that the romance was no longer forbidden, Brown seemed to lose interest. He asked Anna to wait until the following June to wed, then left her standing at the altar. Anna was, understandably, a little peeved. Now thirty-three and divorced, with four children, she pleaded with Brown to do right by her, but the good senator said he still needed more time. Instead of a commitment, he gave Anna a ticket to Los

Angeles to rest. She exchanged it for a ticket to Washington. Breaking into his hotel room, she started rifling through his letters and discovered that he was sleeping with someone else. Now Anna had a taste of how poor Isabel must have felt. Her reaction was even more violent. When Senator Brown returned to his room, Anna shot him dead. She used the same gun he had given her for protection from Isabel.

★

Some congressmen of the twentieth century apparently learned little from the travails of their nineteenth-century predecessors. In the case of Representative Wilbur Mills of Arkansas, too much booze and a stripper named Fanne made for some sensational headlines and led to the downfall of the once mighty chairman of the House Ways and Means Committee.

It all started in the early morning hours of October 7, 1974, when Mills and four companions were pulled over near Washington's Tidal Basin by U.S. Park Police for speeding with no lights on. Just as the car was stopped, one of the occupants leapt out and jumped off a bridge into the murky water below. Her name was Anabell Battistella, better known as the stripper Fanne Foxe. Mills, clearly intoxicated, was bleeding from the nose and had scratch marks on his face. He later said the injuries were a result of his trying to restrain Ms. Foxe. The news linking one of the most powerful men in Congress with the bridge-leaping stripper caused an immediate sensation. It was soon revealed that Mills and his wife, Polly, lived in the same apartment building as Foxe, billed as "the Argentine Firecracker," and her husband. Mills and Foxe were reported to have been frequent companions, though he initially denied even being at the scene when she took her famous dive.

Scandalous as the story was, it didn't seem to bother Arkansas voters that much. The following month, Mills was reelected to another term, and the story faded from the front pages. But then in December came another strange twist when Mills appeared on stage with Foxe—now billed as the "Tidal Basin Bombshell"—during one of her appearances in Boston. "I told him not to," the stripper said in an interview with the *Washington Post.* "But I am sure he wanted the audience to see him. . . . He was saying, 'I have nothing to hide.'" To others, however, the message was that Mills had a serious booze problem and exercised very poor judgment. Speaker of the House Carl Albert called him "a sick man," and insisted he step down as chairman of the Ways and Means Committee. The *Arkansas Gazette,* once a supporter of Mills, now editorialized against him: "If Mr. Mills cannot forgo his public indiscretions and if he prefers the life of show business to the life on Capitol Hill, then let him select the former and resign his seat in Congress to devote full time to his new line of work. Whichever course Mills prefers it is past time that he made a choice."

Mills was hospitalized after his bizarre appearance on stage in Boston, and later claimed to have "absolutely no memory" of the spectacle. He returned to Congress and served out his term, although in a much diminished capacity after being stripped of his chairmanship. Fanne Foxe, like so many others propelled to notoriety by scandal, tried to make it in Hollywood. As it turned out, the only splash she ever made was in the Tidal Basin.

★

Less than two years after the Mills debacle, the long career of Representative Wayne Hays of Ohio collapsed when one of his staffers revealed why he had put her on the federal payroll—and it was not because of her secretarial skills. "I can't type. I can't file. I can't even answer the phone," Elizabeth Ray proclaimed to the world in May 1976, explaining her actual job description. Her timing could not have been more inopportune for Hays, seeing as he had just married his legislative assistant, Pat Peak. But it was this marriage, Hays's second, that apparently set Elizabeth Ray off in the first place. When she confronted Hays about her future after his nuptials, he reportedly answered, "Well, I guess that'll make you mistress No. 1." Wrong answer! Ray threw such a tantrum that Hays had to have the police escort her off the Capitol grounds. Immediately afterward she called the *Washington Post* with her scoop.

Hays at first dismissed the report as the rantings of "a very sick young woman," but the FBI nevertheless launched an investigation into the charge that Ray had been given her $14,000-a-year job in exchange for sex. After two days of denials—"Hell's fire! I'm a very happily married man"—Hays finally admitted that there had been a "personal relationship" with Elizabeth Ray, but insisted she could and did type, file, and answer the phone. "I stand by my previous denial of Miss Ray's allegation that she was hired to be my mistress," he said in an address before the House of Representatives. "I further stand by my statement that Miss Ray is a seriously disturbed young lady, and I deeply regret that our relationship, and its termination, has apparently greatly aggravated both her emotional and psychological problems. I am now sixty-five years old, and I have been privileged to serve in this House for twenty-eight years. I know my days on earth are numbered, and my service to this body may well be also . . . but I stand here before you today . . . with my conscience now clear."

Several weeks later, Hays took an overdose of sleeping pills. Although he recovered, his career did not. He resigned that September. Elizabeth Ray went on to write an exposé of her dalliances with Hays and other congressmen, and pursued an acting career (unsuccessfully). The only winners in the whole sordid mess were the street hawkers selling I CAN TYPE T-shirts.

Grover Cleveland's premarital fatherhood becomes a campaign issue.

Part V

Cruel Campaigns

Abraham Lincoln would probably have loved the irony. The president so grandly memorialized in marble today was savagely maligned in his own time. During the 1864 presidential campaign, *Harper's Weekly* compiled a list of slurs used against Honest Abe by supporters of his Democratic opponent (and former subordinate) George B. McClellan: Filthy Story-Teller, Despot, Liar, Thief, Braggart, Buffoon, Usurper, Monster, Ignoramus Abe, Old Scoundrel, Perjurer, Robber, Swindler, Tyrant, Fiend, Butcher. And those were just the insults from the North. The rebellious South, literally at war with Lincoln, had its own arsenal. Brutal as the anti-Lincoln crusade may have been, it was fairly typical of the time. For all the complaints about how negative recent presidential campaigns have been, they are nowhere near as nasty as they were in the good old days.

★

1

"One Continued Tempest of Malignant Passions"

The United States had barely taken its baby steps as a new nation when warring political factions emerged within it. By the end of George Washington's two-term presidency, what he lamentably called the "spirit of party" was in full swing, and not even the revered father of the country was immune to its venomous sting. "If ever a nation has been debauched by a man," wrote Benjamin Franklin Bache, Ben Franklin's grandson, "the American nation has been debauched by Washington." It was the dawn of a virulent American tradition.

George-bashing by Bache and others was an inevitable result of the new factionalism represented by Washington's heir-apparent, Vice President John Adams, and Adams's opponent in the presidential contest, Thomas Jefferson. Jefferson's Republican followers believed that Adams and his Federalist cronies were elitists still attached to Mother England who sought to usurp states' rights and center all power in themselves. Adams's backers saw their ideological enemies as upstart anarchists who reveled in the murderous French Revolution and subsequent Reign of Terror.

"The first real presidential contest in American history turned out to be exuberantly venomous," writes Paul F. Boller Jr. Jefferson's Republicans mocked Adams and labeled him "an avowed friend of monarchy"—a highly toxic charge at a time when the U.S. experiment in democracy was still in its infancy. The Federalists called Jefferson an atheist, demagogue, coward, mountebank, trickster, and Franco-maniac. His followers, they said, were "cut-throats who walk in rags and sleep amidst filth and vermin."

This was a relatively pleasant exchange, given the rematch between President Adams and Vice President Jefferson in 1800. In an era when it was considered unseemly for candidates to campaign actively for office, Adams and Jefferson refrained from slinging mud themselves, at least in public.[1] Their partisans, on the other hand, were happy to get down and dirty. Once again, Adams was caricatured by the Republicans as a licentious fool and criminal tyrant. His presidency, one enemy wrote, was "one continued tempest of *malignant* passions." The Jefferson campaign spread a story that Adams planned to marry one of his sons to a daughter of King George III, start an American dynasty, and reunite with Britain. It was only George Washington's threat to run him through with a sword, the story went, that made Adams abandon the plan. Another tale had President Adams sending Charles Cotesworth Pinckney to England to procure four young mistresses, two for Adams and two for Pinckney. Adams was somewhat amused when he heard the story. "I do declare upon my honor," he chuckled, "if this be true, General Pinckney has kept them all for himself and cheated me out of my two."

For their own part, the Federalists went after Jefferson with unrestrained fury. "Murder, robbery, rape, adultery and incest will be openly taught and proclaimed," warned the Connecticut *Courant,* a pro-Federalist newspaper. "The air will be rent with the cries of the distressed, the soil will be soaked with blood and the nation black with crimes." The invective against the author of the Declaration of Independence in Federalist pamphlets and newspapers included charges that Jefferson was a coward during the Revolutionary War,

1. In private, however, the story was much different. (See Part II, Chapter 1.)

an infidel of dubious parentage, and a thief who once robbed a widow of an estate worth $10,000. One Federalist leaflet posed this question: "Can serious and reflecting men look about them and doubt that if Jefferson is elected, and the Jacobins [a name given French radicals] get into authority, that those morals which protect our lives from the knife of the assassin—which guard the chastity of our wives and daughters from seduction and violence—defend our property from plunder and devastation, and shield our religion from contempt and profanation, will not be trampled upon and exploded?"

Federalist sniping was aimed not only at Jefferson, but at their own man Adams as well. Adams's fellow Federalist and inveterate foe, Alexander Hamilton, concluded that even Jefferson or another Republican would be a better choice for president than Adams. "If we must have an enemy at the head of government," Hamilton exclaimed, "let it be one whom we can oppose, and for whom we are not responsible, who will not involve our party in the disgrace of his foolish and bad measures." Hamilton wrote a blistering attack on President Adams, hoping to turn other Federalist leaders against him. "I should be deficient in candor," he wrote, "were I to conceal the conviction, that he does not possess the talents adapted to the *Administration* of Government, and that there are great and intrinsic defects in his character which unfit him for the office of Chief Magistrate." Among these flaws, Hamilton wrote, were a character "infected with some visionary notions," an "imagination sublimated and eccentric," "a vanity without bounds, and a jealousy capable of discoloring every object."

Hamilton's "Thunderbolt," as James Madison called it, was not meant for public consumption, but it was leaked and gave the Republicans plenty of ammunition. Adams, who most certainly did not appreciate Hamilton's blindside, reacted by calling him "an intriguant, the greatest intriguant in the world—a man devoid of every moral principle—a bastard." Ever the loyal wife, Abigail Adams went even further: "Oh, I have read [Hamilton's] heart in his wicked eyes many a time. The very devil is in them. They are lasciviousness itself, or I have no skill in physiognomy."

The contest of 1800, which Thomas Jefferson ultimately won to become the nation's third president, was so bitterly fought that Abigail Adams remarked sadly that "enough abuse and scandal" was unleashed "to ruin and corrupt the minds and morals of the best people in the world." Yet it was only just beginning.

2

"May God Almighty Forgive Her Murderers"

The presidential campaign of 1828 was a rematch of the contest four years earlier between John Quincy Adams and Andrew Jackson. That election had been settled in the U.S. House of Representatives, with Adams prevailing. According to Jackson's supporters, Speaker of the House Henry Clay had used undue influence to get Adams elected, and their suspicions of a "corrupt bargain" struck between Adams and Clay only intensified when Adams appointed Clay secretary of state. "So you see," Jackson said at the time, "the Judas of the west [Clay] has closed the contract and will receive the thirty pieces of silver. His end will be the same. Was there ever such a bare faced corruption in any country before?"

Jackson's supporters, determined not to have victory snatched away from them again, launched a populist crusade designed to show Adams as an elitist who, like his father, would be delighted to have a monarchy established in the United States. "King John the Second," they called him, a despiser of the people and of the popular will. "His habits and principles are not congenial with the spirit of our institutions and the notions of a democratic people," declared one Jacksonian. Adams, it was said, lived in "kingly pomp and splendor," in his "presidential palace." Old Hickory, on the other hand, was presented as a man of the people, and it was to the ordinary folks that his campaign was directed. Parades, barbecues, and street rallies were organized across the country by Jackson's "Hurra Boys," as his campaign workers were called, while hickory brooms, hickory sticks, and hickory canes became popular gimmicks.

Adams, in the tradition of George Washington, maintained an aloof posture toward campaigning, which he deemed undignified. His followers, however, engaged in an all-out assault on Jackson, helping to make the campaign of 1828 one of the most vicious in U.S. history. "You know that he is no jurist, no statesman, no politician," an Adams pamphlet warned; "that he is unacquainted with orthography, concord, and government of his language; you know that he is a man of no labor, no patience, no investigation; in short his whole recommendation is animal fierceness and organic energy. He is wholly unqualified by education, habit and temper for the station of President." And this was just a tiny BB in the anti-Jackson arsenal.

Old Hickory was lampooned as a homicidal maniac with an insatiable lust for blood. In one memorable broadside, a Philadelphia editor printed a "Coffin Handbill" which excoriated Jackson for the execution of six militiamen charged with desertion during the Creek War in 1813. The widely circulated handbill, with "Some Account of the Bloody Deeds of General Jackson" screaming across the top, was bordered in black and pictured six coffins, one for each of the men executed under Jackson's orders. It went on to detail how the soldiers had served their tour of duty and only wanted to go home. One of them, John Harris, was a "Preacher of the Gospel," the handbill proclaimed, and had patriotically volunteered for service only to be "shot dead" at Jackson's behest. Though the Jackson camp tried to counter the inflammatory circular with their own version of the event—that Harris and the others had tried to incite a mutiny, stole supplies, and burned down a backhouse before deserting, and were fairly tried and convicted—the damage was done. Even if the "Coffin Handbill" exaggerated, Adams partisans argued, there were plenty of other examples of Jackson's blood lust. (In this, they did have a point: See Part II, Chapter 4.)

Far crueler were the attacks on Jackson's family. He was reduced to tears when he saw newspaper accounts branding his mother a "common prostitute," and was enraged when old charges of bigamy were revived against his wife, Rachael.[1] "Ought a convicted adulteress and her paramour husband to be placed in the highest offices of this free and Christian land?" railed one newspaper. Jackson's ultimate victory over Adams was bittersweet. His beloved Rachael died just after his election, and Jackson was convinced the slanders against her were the cause. "May God Almighty forgive her murderers," he exclaimed at her grave site, "as I know she forgave them. I never can." And he never did.

1. See Part II, Chapter 4.

3

"A Horrid Looking Wretch He Is"

Abraham Lincoln had the double misfortune of running for president during two periods of grave national crisis: just as the nation disintegrated in 1860, and then, four years later, in the midst of the bloody Civil War. Needless to say, nerves were raw and political niceties—what few had existed—vanished. Lincoln was abused and reviled as few candidates had been before. Even his looks were the subject of savage commentary.

"A horrid looking wretch he is," opined the Charleston *Mercury,* "sooty and scoundrelly in aspect, a cross between the nutmeg dealer, the horse swapper, and the night man, a creature 'fit evidently for petty treason, small stratagems and all sorts of spoils.' He is a lank-sides Yankee of the uncomeliest visage, and of the dirtiest complexion. Faugh! after him what decent white man would be President?"

The *Southern Confederacy* of Atlanta well reflected the tenor of the times in 1860 when it weighed in on Lincoln's possible presidency. "The South," it proclaimed, "will never permit Abraham Lincoln to be inaugurated President of the United States; this is a settled and sealed fact. It is the determination of all parties in the South. Let the consequences be what they may, whether the Potomac is crimsoned in human gore, and Pennsylvania Avenue is paved ten fathoms deep with mangled bodies, or whether the last vestige of liberty is swept from the face of the American continent, the South, the loyal South, the constitutional South, will never submit to such humiliation and degradation as the inauguration of Abraham." Sure enough, right after Lincoln won the election, the South split from the Union.

Four years later, as the Civil War raged, Lincoln was up for reelection. It didn't look good for the president. As Union setbacks continued and the body count climbed, his party turned on him. "Mr. Lincoln is already beaten," moaned journalist Horace Greeley. "He cannot be elected. And we must have another ticket to save us from utter overthrow." The Republican Party split, and the radical Republicans nominated General John C. Frémont for president. Even this was not enough for some. The Cincinnati *Gazette* suggested that both Lincoln and Frémont withdraw and that the Republicans find someone who "would inspire confidence and infuse a life into our ranks."

The Democrats opted for George B. McClellan, the general Lincoln had fired for his "slows,"[1] as their nominee. "Old Abe removed McClellan," the Democrats crowed. "We'll now remove Old Abe." The vitriol directed at Lincoln during the 1864 campaign was startling. Of the Lincoln–Andrew Johnson ticket, the New York *World* sneered: "The age of statesmen is gone; the age of rail splitters and tailors, of buffoons, boors and fanatics has succeeded. . . . In a crisis of the most appalling magnitude requiring statesmanship of the highest order, the country is asked to consider the claims of two ignorant, boorish, third-rate backwoods lawyers for the highest standings in the Government. Such nominations, in such a conjuncture, are an insult to the common sense of the people. God save the Republic!"

Declared the New York *Herald:*

> President Lincoln is a joke incarnate. His [first] election was a very sorry joke. The idea that such a man as he should be presi-

1. See Part II, Chapter 6.

> dent of such a country as this is a very ridiculous joke. His debut in Washington society was a joke; for he introduced himself and Mrs. Lincoln as 'the long and short of the Presidency.' His inaugural address was a joke. . . . His cabinet is and always has been a standing joke. All his state papers are jokes. His letters to our generals, beginning with those to General McClellan, are very cruel jokes. . . . His emancipation proclamation was a solemn joke. . . . His conversation is full of jokes. . . . His title of 'Honest' is a satirical joke. . . . His intrigues to secure renomination and the hopes he appears to entertain of a re-election are, however, the most laughable jokes of all.

The relentless attacks took their toll on the president, who said sadly, "It is a little singular that I, who am not a vindictive man, should have always been before the people for election in canvasses marked for their bitterness." Lincoln was becoming resigned to the very real possibility of defeat. "It seems exceedingly probable that this administration will not be re-elected," he wrote in a note to his cabinet. "Then it will be my duty to so cooperate with the President-elect as to save the Union between the election and the inauguration, as he will have secured his election on such a ground that he cannot possibly save it afterward."

Yet the president's gloomy forecast was altered by a drastic improvement in Union fortunes. His generals were making great gains. Sherman took Atlanta and began his march across Georgia. Grant was making progress in Petersburg. Sheridan routed Confederate forces in the valleys of Virginia, and Farragut captured Mobile Bay. As a result, the political climate improved as well. Frémont withdrew from the race, and the Republican Party was reunited behind Lincoln. McClellan was defeated. The victorious president marveled at "the extraordinary calmness and good order with which the millions of voters met and mingled at the polls," and he praised the voting public for showing that "a people's government can sustain a national election in the midst of great civil war."

4

"Ma! Ma! Where's My Pa?"

The Republicans' major campaign allegation against Grover Cleveland—that he fathered a child out of wedlock—seems almost quaint in today's tawdry climate. But in 1884 it was a serious smear, and Cleveland's political opponents trumpeted it with glee. "Ma! Ma! Where's my pa?" became the unofficial Republican slogan.

The *Buffalo Evening Telegraph* broke the news of Cleveland's premarital adventures with this blaring headline: "A Terrible Tale: A Dark Shadow in a Public Man's History." The accompanying story revealed that Cleveland, as a young man, had taken up with a widow in Buffalo named Maria Halpin, had a son by her, and was still providing financial support for the two of them. Cleveland, the Democratic governor of New York, opted to come clean and admit the story was true. His supporters argued that their candidate's noted public integrity far outweighed a youthful indiscretion, but backers of Republican candidate James G. Blaine not so respectfully disagreed. "We do not believe that the American people will knowingly elect to the Presidency a coarse debauchee who would bring his harlots with him to Washington, and hire lodgings for them convenient to the White House," opined Charles A. Dana of the New York *Sun*.

The cruel epithets used against Cleveland by the press opposed to him were relentless: "rake," "libertine," "father of a bastard," "a gross and licentious man," "moral leper," "a man stained with disgusting infamy," "worse in moral quality than a pickpocket, a sneak thief or a Cherry Street debauchee, a wretch unworthy of respect or confidence." The religious right was even more indignant. The Reverend Mr. Ball of Buffalo, claiming to speak for a ministerial investigation committee, made Cleveland sound like the mayor of Sodom. "Investigations disclose still more proof of debaucheries too horrible to relate and too vile to be readily believed," Reverend Ball pronounced. "For many years, days devoted to business have been followed by nights of sin. He has lived as a bachelor . . . lodged in rooms on the third floor in a business block, and made those rooms a harem, foraged outside, also, in the city and surrounding villages; champion libertine, an artful seducer, a foe to virtue, an enemy of the family, a snare to youth and hostile to true womanhood. The Halpin case was not solitary. Women now married and anxious to cover the sins of their youth have been his victims, and are now alarmed lest their relations with him shall be exposed. Some disgraced and brokenhearted victims of his lust now slumber in the grave. Since he has become governor of this great state, he has not abated his lecheries."

To some, including Mark Twain, this kind of Puritanical reaction to Cleveland's youthful affair was simply absurd. "To see grown men, apparently in their right mind, seriously arguing against a bachelor's fitness for president because he had private intercourse with a consenting widow!" Twain snorted. "Those grown men know what the bachelor's other alternative was—& tacitly they seem to prefer that to the widow. *Isn't* human nature the most consummate sham & lie that was ever invented?"

Cleveland himself found the smear tactics distasteful, and refused to allow the discovery that his opponent had had—*gasp!*—premarital relations with his wife to become an issue. "The other side can have a monopoly of all the dirt in this campaign," he declared. Nevertheless, the Indianapolis *Sentinel* printed the news of Blaine's wantonness anyway. "There is hardly an intelligent man in the country," the paper noted, "who has not heard that James G. Blaine betrayed the girl who he married, and then only married her at the muzzle of a shotgun . . . if, after despoiling her, he was too craven to refuse her legal redress, giving legitimacy to her child, until a loaded shotgun stimulated his conscience—then there is a blot on his character more foul, if possible, than any of the countless stains on his political record."

Out of this contest of debauchers, Cleveland emerged the victor. His supporters now answered the Republican chant, "Ma! Ma! Where's my pa?" with a celebratory retort: "Gone to the White House. Ha! Ha! Ha!"

Richard Nixon caught on tape.

Part VI

The American Hall of Shame

If an American Hall of Shame were ever to be established, certain standards would have to be met. Spectacular villainy would not be a prerequisite for admission, although it certainly wouldn't hurt. Other qualities would be considered as well—such as stupidity, incompetence, and epic hubris, to name a few. Under these guidelines, nice guys could get in, too. All they would really need is a badly bruised legacy, representing to the world the worst America has to offer. The nine people in the chapters that follow surely would be among the first inductees.

★

1

Benedict Arnold: Hero, Traitor, Whiner

It would have been better for Benedict Arnold had the bullet that tore through his leg at the Battle of Saratoga instead smacked him in the head. He would have died an American hero. But, alas, the Revolutionary War general survived and came to make his name synonymous with traitorous rat.

On the west bank of the Hudson River in upstate New York sits the U.S. Military Academy at West Point. In 1780, it was a key American defensive position that Arnold plotted to surrender to the British—for cash. It was an epic betrayal by an American Judas, a scheme that, had it succeeded, could have so undermined the American quest for independence that today cricket might be the national pastime and "God Save the Queen" the national anthem. What made the man's treachery so astonishing—and what has made the name of Benedict Arnold one of the most puzzling in American history—was that he was not some insignificant mole out to make a few bucks at the expense of his countrymen, but a prominent general in the Continental Army. He was a man esteemed by George Washington himself and the apparent embodiment of American patriotism.

But true patriotism, historians have seen in hindsight, was impossible for Arnold. Despite his military successes and apparent ardor for his country, ultimately he struggled for no greater cause than Benedict Arnold. Nevertheless, his rise to military acclaim was impressive. He had been a New Haven merchant and trader (though not yet traitor) until Britain imposed on her colonies a series of repressive measures such as the Tea and Stamp Acts. Arnold, whose livelihood was at stake, joined the Continental forces immediately after the first skirmish of the Revolutionary War at Lexington. Commissioned a colonel, he proposed an assault on Britain's Fort Ticonderoga on Lake Champlain, in what is now upstate New York. Along with Ethan Allen and the Green Mountain Boys of Vermont, he took the fort and its desperately needed cannons in May 1775.

The following August, he presented himself to the new commander in chief of the Continental Army, George Washington, with a bold proposal to strike Quebec City, a major stronghold of British loyalists. The attack was repelled with staggering losses, but Arnold, wounded in the leg, doggedly maintained the siege with the few men left to him. Now a brigadier general, Arnold was charged with the task of blocking a British invasion of New England by way of Lake Champlain. With minimal resources, he assembled a fleet and successfully thwarted the enemy at the battle of Valcour Island in 1776.

The following year would mark Benedict Arnold's finest hour. The British intended to cut off New England from the rest of the colonies and try to crush the American revolt piecemeal. The plan culminated at the two battles of Saratoga in September and October 1777. Arnold fought fiercely, sustaining a devastating wound to the same leg that had been injured during the siege of Quebec City, and won a decisive victory for the new nation. It proved a turning point in the revolution, allowing Benjamin Franklin to forge a much-needed alliance with France and boosting the morale of the American forces with the very real possibility of ultimate triumph.

Impressive as his résumé may have been, the man himself was fraught with contradictions. Biographer Clare Brandt notes that "Arnold had astonishing physical valor but no moral courage; a rigid code of honor without a shred of inner integrity; superior intelligence with no understanding." The battles he fought for America were a means of gaining the respect he craved, but his personal agenda would constantly interfere with the greater good of the fledgling nation.

Arnold had long had a special knack for making enemies. While planning the attack on Fort Ticonderoga in 1775, he managed to infuriate fellow officers by vehemently insisting that he command the operation even though he was a military neophyte who outranked the other officers only because of the haphazard organization of the military early in the war. Arnold's hunger for personal glory prevented him from taking a back seat, and no amount of cajoling from the other officers would make him waver. "By the time the meeting broke up," Brandt writes, "the others would sooner have murdered Benedict Arnold than take orders from him."

Of all the snits in which Arnold was perpetually engaged, his animosity toward the Continental Congress was the most chronic. During his military ascendancy, his exploits both heroic and petty were not lost on Congress, where he was viewed with both admiration and disdain. His accomplishments could not be ignored. Indeed, he was recognized as a vital part of the war effort, but many people saw him as a self-aggrandizing menace—"our evil genius," as General William Maxwell dubbed him. Consequently, in what Arnold viewed as a deliberate slap in the face, he was passed over for promotion to major general in February 1777, only months after his success at Valcour Island. Doubling the insult, officers more junior were promoted.

"Congress have doubtless a right of promoting those [whom] . . . they esteemed more deserving," he formally wrote General Washington, but "their promoting junior officers . . . I view as a very civil way of requesting my resignation as unqualified for the office I hold." Only Washington's intercession made Congress reconsider, and Arnold got his promotion.

Then there was money—a passionate issue for Arnold with Congress and one that left him bitter. Like most other officers in the war, he often dug into personal assets to help feed and clothe his men and purchase supplies. Rarely could the Continental Congress, perpetually in dire financial straits, reimburse them. Without the authority to tax citizens, it had to rely on the goodwill of the people to pay for the war and, consequently, it was usually broke. Arnold's nagging requests for money were ignored. His resentment festered like the wound on his leg; he was disgusted with the country that so obviously failed to appreciate his service and personal sacrifice.

After Saratoga, Arnold was made military commander of Philadelphia, the nation's new capital after a British evacuation. It was an easy post for the disabled general, and although the revolution continued, he was no longer preoccupied with maintaining the appearance of supreme patriot. His sole concern was to use his position to his best economic advantage. He developed a lavish life style and, having fallen in love with a socially ambitious eighteen-year-old, Peggy Shippen, he needed cash. He found the solution in a series of enterprises that, if not outright illegal, were highly questionable. He made little effort to hide any of them.

Arnold married Shippen, twenty years his junior, in April 1779, but a cloud loomed over the festivities. Earlier the same month, Congress had ordered him court-martialed. His questionable financial schemes, it turned out, had not gone unnoticed. Among the charges was that he had issued an illegal permit to unload a captured enemy ship, *The Charming Nancy,* requisitioned twelve army wagons to transport its cargo to Philadelphia for sale, and received a large cut of the proceeds. When the allegations were aired, he immediately fired off a letter to George Washington: "If your Excellency thinks me criminal, for heaven's sake let me be immediately tried and, if found guilty, executed. I want no favor; I ask only justice."

Within days of writing the letter, however, the audacious Arnold opened correspondence with the British and offered them his services. The court-martial found Arnold guilty on two of eight charges, and Congress demanded that Washington reprimand him. Washington obliged, writing that issuing a permit for *The Charming Nancy* was "peculiarly reprehensible" and using army wagons "imprudent and improper." Meanwhile, Arnold's new relationship with the British was well under way.

Now considering Washington a personal enemy, Arnold was only too happy to get back at him by giving the British what they really wanted—the fort at West Point, Washington's pride and joy. But he needed a plan. Still maintaining the appearance of loyalty, Arnold lobbied Washington relentlessly for command of West Point. The unsuspecting commander in chief gave it to him. Complete ruin of the American cause was now imminent.

By 1780, only an infusion of French money, ships, and men gave the revolution its pulse. King Louis XVI, however, was beginning to fear that the American Revolution was doomed and was looking for any excuse to withdraw. Loss of West Point would have been a lethal blow to the Americans and would have provided Louis with the perfect excuse. A French withdrawal, ironically enough, would have been precipitated by the same man whose victory at Saratoga had convinced France to join the uprising in the first place.

But the plot failed. Arnold and his contact, Major John André, an adjutant to Sir Henry Clinton, the commander in chief of the British forces, met on the banks of the Hudson at midnight, September 22, 1780. Arnold handed over plans for West Point's defenses. But André, carrying the papers to the base of British operations in New York City, was captured by three militiamen. Arnold, who was awaiting a visit from Washington, learned of André's capture the next morning and fled in panic. He raced to the banks of the Hudson and ordered a boat to row him to a waiting British ship, the *Vulture,* which carried him to safety in New York. "One vulture . . . receiving another," as Thomas Paine later described it.

Word of Arnold's treachery spread rapidly through the states, inciting spite and derision. "Whom can we trust now?" Washington asked upon his arrival at West Point. "Judas sold only one man," Benjamin Franklin remarked, "Arnold three million. Judas got for his one man thirty pieces of silver, Arnold not a halfpenny a head. A miserable bargain!"

Arnold served the rest of the war as a brigadier general for the British. General Clinton put him in charge of a marauding expedition in Virginia, where Governor Thomas Jefferson offered a reward of 5,000 pounds for his capture. He forever sealed his infamy when he later led a raid against his former neighbors in Connecticut, burning to the ground the town of New London.

After the war ended in 1783, Benedict Arnold sailed with his family to England and spent the remaining twenty years of his life in bitter exile. A master of self-delusion, Arnold convinced himself—and pronounced publicly—that his switch of allegiance was noble and justified. Offering his services to Britain in the Napoleonic Wars, he was ignored and scorned as a traitor by his adopted country no less than by the country he betrayed. The British even gave him a lower military rank than had the Americans. Destitute, he did what would be expected of him: He whined and badgered King George III and his government for compensation for valiant services rendered. Defeated and ignored, Arnold died in 1801.

2

Aaron Burr: "Embryo-Caesar"

Under the American system of justice, in which a man is deemed innocent until proven guilty, Aaron Burr was no traitor. A jury of his peers acquitted him of that high crime in 1807. But by the same standard, he was no killer either—even if he did shoot Alexander Hamilton clean through the gut.[1] Because he was never tried for the murder, he was legally innocent of it.

Yes, the law was doubly kind to the nation's second vice president, and, except for a brief stint in debtor's prison, he remained a free man. History, on the other hand, has not been quite so benevolent, and today Burr would stand as a pillar of the American Hall of Shame. The slaying of Hamilton alone would probably not be enough to secure his place here—after all, lots of esteemed Americans lived and died by the Code Duello[2]—but his grandiose scheming afterward made him a shoe-in.

Aaron Burr had a crafty brilliance about him that he used to his best advantage. No one was ever quite sure what he was up to—only

1. See Part II, Chapter 2.
2. See Part II, Chapter 3.

that, whatever it was, in all probability it was self-serving. "I found he possessed a talent of making an impression of an opinion upon the subject, on the person with whom he conversed, without explicitly stating or necessarily giving his sentiments thereon," noted Senator William Plumber of New Hampshire. "In everything he said or did, he had a design—and perhaps no man's language was ever so apparently explicit, and at the same time so covert and indefinite."

Because Burr was so adept at masking his intentions and shading the truth, the full extent of his mischief in the years following Hamilton's death—when the former veep was a reviled fugitive seeking his fortune in the American West—remains a mystery to this day. Thomas Jefferson, among others, believed he was engaged in treason, seeking to establish for himself a vast western empire based on the conquest of Mexico and the forced separation of the trans-Appalachian states from the Union. The president called this alleged enterprise, in which Burr reportedly intended to declare himself Emperor Aaron I, "the most extraordinary since the days of Don Quixot[e]." And though Jefferson was sharply criticized for publicly proclaiming Burr's guilt "beyond question" before he was ever tried, the president certainly had plenty of reason to believe his former vice president was up to no good.

Before leaving office, Burr confided his plans to Anthony Merry, Great Britain's minister to the United States, hoping for British financial and naval assistance in his schemes. In a letter dated August 6, 1804, Merry dutifully reported this delicious bit of intelligence to his boss back home: "I have just received an offer from Mr. Burr, the actual Vice President of the United States (which situation he is about to resign), to lend his assistance to his Majesty's Government in any Manner in which they may think fit to employ him, particularly in an endeavoring to effect a Separation of the Western Part of the United States from that which lies between the Atlantick and the [Appalachian] Mountains, in its whole extent. . . ."

Some historians believe that Burr's secret dealings with Britain, and later Spain, were a clever ruse—"a consummate piece of imposture," in the words of one—designed not to aid in the dismemberment of the United States, as he told the ministers of those nations, but to raise funds for an invasion of Mexico. And though such an unauthorized attack on a foreign power certainly would have been illegal, Burr defenders note, it would not be treasonous.

In the spring of 1805, after leaving office, Burr embarked on a tour of the West that took him as far south as New Orleans and as far west as St. Louis. The excursion left some suspicious of his agenda, and led to the publication of a series of anonymous "Queries" that were reprinted in newspapers across the country. "How long will it be before we shall hear of Col. Burr being at the head of a *revolution* party on the western waters?" went one pointed question. Others suggested that the former vice president might be seeking to form his own empire in the West, the reduction and despoiling of Mexico, or both. At the time of their publication, however, the "Queries" were viewed by many as a baseless partisan attack. William Duane, editor of the Philadelphia *Aurora,* wrote that the perfidious designs alleged of Burr were unfairly associated with him because he was "exactly such a character as would be open to the suspicions of all parties," and that his low state might be presumed "to render him fit for any enterprise, however desperate."

Just what Burr was doing on this trip out West remains unclear. He may simply have been speculating on land, or sniffing out the possibility of a political resurrection, or even planning an invasion of Mexico. And though President Jefferson received information that something far more sinister was in the works, he did not appear overly concerned. In fact, he had Burr to dinner soon after his return in the fall of 1805. What is certain, though, is that upon his return Burr was once again entreating with Britain, assuring Anthony Merry that he had found the West ripe for revolution, and that money and ships were still urgently needed to get the enterprise started.

When Burr learned that British assistance would not be forthcoming, he turned to Spain. Through his fellow conspirator, former senator Jonathan Dayton of New Jersey, he informed the Spanish minister, Marqués Casa Yrujo, that his separatist schemes in the West were to be preceded by an attack on the federal government. The plan, as recorded by Yrujo, was "by degrees" to introduce into Washington "a number of men in disguise, well armed." These desperadoes were to seize President Jefferson and other top officials, plunder the local banks, and take possession of the federal arsenal. If there was no resistance to this coup, Burr would "negotiate with the individual states" an arrangement under which he and his confederates would rule the country. If, on the other hand, resistance arose, they would burn the Navy Yard, saving only enough ships to carry them and their plunder to New Orleans. There they would at once "proclaim the emancipation of Louisiana and the Western States."

Though Thomas Jefferson had dismissed a number of earlier warnings he had received concerning Burr's schemes, thinking them politically motivated and unreliable, he later said that he got the "very first intimation of the plot" to divide the Union in a letter from Colonel George Morgan, which he received on September 15, 1806. Burr had visited Morgan's farm outside Pittsburgh on a second and final trip to the West, and tried to enlist his sons in a military expedition he was planning. He also spoke of the future independence of the West, according to Morgan, while disparaging the federal government.

About a month after Morgan's report, Secretary of State James Madison received a letter from General Presley Neville and Judge Samuel Roberts repeating what Morgan had told them about his discussions with Burr. "In short," they wrote, "the whole tenor of [Burr's] conversation was such as to leave a strong impression on the minds of those gentlemen with whom these conversations were held that a plan was arranging or arranged for effecting the separation of the Union, in which Colonel Burr seemed to have no ordinary interest."

Jefferson got additional information about a conspiracy over the next month, the most damaging of which came from General William Eaton, a hero of the Tripolitan War, who claimed that Burr had offered him a top position in the planned quest to attack Mexico and dismember the West. Eaton, who declined the offer, would later be the first witness for the prosecution at Burr's treason trial.

Now thoroughly convinced of Aaron Burr's treachery, the president ordered confidential letters to be written to the governors and district attorneys in the West to have the former vice president "strictly watched, and on his commanding any overt act unequivocally, to have him tried for treason, misdemeanor, or whatever other offence" his actions might amount to. No immediate action was to be taken, though. "We give [Burr] all the attention our situation admits," Jefferson wrote; "as yet we have no legal proof of any overt act which the law can lay hold of."

Burr, meanwhile, was keeping himself quite busy out West, preparing for an expedition that would make him either a criminal (if he merely invaded Mexico), or a traitor (if he invaded Mexico *and* tried to sever the Union). Among his many visits was one to perhaps his most gullible supporter, Harman Blennerhassett, whose private island in the Ohio River Burr intended to use as the launching ground for his assault. In August 1806, he and Blennerhassett contracted for the construction of fifteen bateaux, "ample enough to convey five hundred men," along with "a large keelboat for the transportation of provisions," and other supplies. Blennerhassett happily footed the bill, and as a reward for all his services, Burr offered him the post of ambassador to Britain if his planned empire ever came to be. Blennerhassett hardly needed the inducement. He was already Burr's faithful ally, and worked tirelessly to recruit others to the cause. According to later testimony, he told two possible recruits, brothers John and Alexander Henderson, that "under the auspices of Col. Burr, a separation of the Union was contemplated;" that New Orleans was to be seized, its "bank or banks" emptied, its military stores requisitioned, and the city itself and the country around it "revolutionized in the course of nine months." Blennerhassett also told the brothers, according to their testimony, that "if Mr. Jefferson was in any way impertinent, . . . Burr would tie him neck and heels, and throw him into the Potomac."

The activities of Burr, Blennerhassett, and others associated with them did not escape notice, generating all manner of rumor and speculation, inflammatory press reports, and the unwelcome attention of Kentucky's district attorney Joseph Hamilton Daviess. The federal prosecutor was eager to bring down Burr and thwart whatever enterprise he was planning, but he lacked the evidence to do it. A grand jury was impaneled at his request, but Daviess had to move for its discharge when a key witness failed to show. Undeterred, he renewed his motion for a grand jury inquiry two weeks later. Burr retained Henry Clay, recently elected to the U.S. Senate, to represent him, and wrote to the senator to reassure him of his innocence: "I have no design, nor have I taken any measures to promote a dissolution of the Union." Although Clay agreed to represent Burr, he later became convinced of his client's guilt. The citizens of Kentucky sitting on the grand jury remained unconvinced, however, and on December 5, 1806, found no cause against the former vice president. Burr was to remain a free man for the time being.

It was around this time that one of Burr's chief cohorts, General James Wilkinson— commander in chief of the U.S. Army, governor of the northern part of the Louisiana Territory recently purchased from France, and notorious double-dealer (he was a secret agent for Spain)—decided to betray Burr and cooperate with the government. In a letter to President Jefferson, Wilkinson claimed to be staggered by "the magnitude of [Burr's] enterprise, the desperation of the plan, and the stupendous consequences" it held. Perhaps Wilkinson, described by one historian as "the most skillful and unscrupulous plotter this country has ever produced," turned on Burr because he realized the Western schemes with which he had been so closely involved were doomed to failure, and he wanted to be on the winning side. Though Jefferson had rightly been suspicious of Wilkinson in the past, and believed he exaggerated the size and scope of Burr's plot, the president heeded his warnings.

Several days after receiving Wilkinson's reports, Jefferson issued a proclamation alerting the nation to a conspiracy. Without naming Burr specifically, he lumped together the "sundry persons" whom he had been informed were fitting out and arming vessels, collecting military equipment and provisions, and "deceiving and seducing honest and well-meaning citizens, under various pretences, to engage in their criminal enterprises." The president warned all citizens against participating in such activities, under penalty of prosecution, and enjoined all public officials to help prevent a criminal uprising.

Although Jefferson never mentioned the forced separation of the Western states in his public proclamation, or in his address to Congress a month later—intentionally limiting his comments to any plan to invade Mexico—he later said he interpreted Burr's plot this way: "It appeared that he contemplated two distinct objects. . . . One of these was the severance of the Union of those States by the Allegany [sic] mountains; the other an attack on Mexico." In reference to some 350,000 acres Burr had purchased on the Western frontier, Jefferson said, "This was to serve as the pretext for all his [military] preparations, an allurement for such followers as really wished to acquire settlements in that country, and a cover under which to retreat in the event of a final discomfiture of both branches of his real design."

Jefferson never wavered in his belief that Aaron Burr was a traitor with dangerous designs against the U.S., but it was never borne out under the law. After Burr was arrested and indicted for treason in early 1807, a trial was held in Richmond, Virginia. Burr's defenders claimed he was a victim of Jefferson's personal animosity and of the government's relentless persecution. "Never, I believe, did any government thirst more for the blood of a victim than our enlightened, philosophic, mild, philanthropic government for the blood of my friend," wrote Luther Martin, one of Burr's more flamboyant attorneys.

For his own part, Jefferson believed that the law would benefit Burr because of the strict definition of treason it provided. "Burr's conspiracy has been one of the most flagitious of which history will ever furnish example," he wrote. "Yet altho' there is not a man in the U.S. who is not satisfied of the depth of his guilt, such are the jealous provisions of our laws in favor of the accused, and against the accuser, that I question if he can be convicted." The president was rather astute in this observation, as events would show.

The question before the court was whether or not an *overt* act of treason had occurred. Chief Justice John Marshall, presiding over the trial, determined that the prosecution had not established any overt act, as the law demanded, and thus barred the appearance of most of the prosecution's witnesses because they would be testifying about a conspiracy to commit treason, which would be irrelevant. Marshall's ruling was a devastating blow to the prosecution, and resulted in the jury's verdict of not guilty.

Aaron Burr escaped the noose that would have accompanied conviction, but not the notoriety that clung to him. Harassed by creditors and with no prospect of a return to public life, he slipped away to Europe, where he spent some time in debtor's prison. After an exile of about five years, during which he tried in vain to recoup his fortunes, he returned almost unnoticed to New York in 1812. He spent his remaining years as a moderately successful attorney, though he was never able to erase the stains on his reputation. He died in 1836, at age eighty.

3

Roger Taney: One Mean Supreme

George Washington owned slaves. So did Thomas Jefferson and half the other Founding Fathers. Roger Taney willingly freed his slaves out of personal principle yet it is his reputation that has been forever tarnished by his association with the "peculiar institution." Raw deal? Well, not if you consider that it was Taney, the chief justice of the United States Supreme Court, who tried to cram the legitimization of human bondage into the Constitution. With the *Dred Scott* decision of 1857, Taney affirmed the concept that blacks were an inferior race with no rights of citizenship under the law. Furthermore, he declared that Congress had no right to limit the expansion of slavery into U.S. territories. Taney actually believed the decision would settle the long-festering slavery issue once and for all. Instead, *Dred Scott* inflamed it even further, dragged the nation closer to civil war, and, in the words of Representative Thaddeus Stevens of Pennsylvania, "damned the late chief justice to everlasting fame and I fear everlasting fire."

The Dred Scott case was fairly routine in the beginning, a decade before Roger Taney got his hands on it and made it a landmark decision. Back in 1846, it was simply about a slave named Dred Scott who sought freedom for himself and his family by suing for it in the Missouri circuit court. Scott had good reason to believe then that he would prevail. His owner, an army surgeon, had brought Scott and his family from Missouri to live with him at U.S. Army posts in Illinois and in the Wisconsin Territory, both of which prohibited slavery. Missouri courts in the past had granted freedom to enslaved persons whose owners had taken them for extended periods of residence into free states or territories under the legal principle "Once free, always free." Scott won in the circuit court, but the verdict was appealed, and the politically charged proslavery Missouri Supreme Court reversed it. Dred Scott was still a slave in the eyes of the law. After this setback, Scott sued for freedom in federal court, but there, too, he lost. Finally, after a nearly decade-long legal odyssey, he appealed to the U.S. Supreme Court. He didn't stand a chance.

Dred Scott was facing a nine-member court of which the majority were proslavery Democrats. Chief Justice Taney, having served in that capacity for nearly two decades, enjoyed a decent reputation, but, as historian Kenneth M. Stampp writes, "his judicial robes had only partially concealed his persistent partisanship, especially on matters relating to slavery and the sectional conflict." Furthermore, Scott, though ably represented by his lawyer, Montgomery Blair, had to contend with a formidable team of opposing attorneys who argued that as a black man he was not a U.S. citizen and therefore should never have been permitted to file his suit. They also argued that when Scott was returned to Missouri, his status as a slave was determined by that state's laws, not those of Illinois. The same concept applied to his return from the Wisconsin Territory, although the opposing attorneys broadened the argument considerably when they asserted that the restrictions against slavery imposed by Congress in the various territories under the Missouri Compromise of 1820–21 were unconstitutional in the first place. It was this argument, asserts historian Don Fehrenbacher, that converted "Dred Scott's private case . . . into a public issue," and turned the Supreme Court into a "public arena."

Given the composition of the court and the tenor of the times, Dred Scott's quest for freedom appeared to be doomed. "It seems to be the impression," wrote Montgomery Blair, "that the Court will be adverse to my client and to the power of Congress over the Territories." Blair probably never imagined just how adverse it would be. On the morning of March 6, 1857, a crowd of reporters and spectators crammed into the Supreme Court chamber, then housed in the U.S. Capitol building, to hear the aged and infirm chief justice deliver the court's opinion. With trembling hands and feeble voice, Taney read for more than two hours. His voice may have been weak, but, writes Kenneth Stampp, "his words were not, for they bristled with uncompromising defiance of abolitionists, free soilers, and Republicans." In what Stampp calls "a breathtaking example of judicial activism," Taney had practically rewritten the Constitution to conform to his own proslavery agenda.

The chief justice devoted nearly half of his opinion to the issue of Dred Scott's right "to sue as a citizen in a court of the United States." The question, he said, was whether black people were to be regarded as members of the political community, "and as such become entitled to all the rights and privileges, and immunity guaranteed by [the Constitution] to the citizen." The answer, Taney declared, was *No.* When the Constitution was framed, he reasoned, blacks were regarded "as a subordinate and inferior class of beings, who . . . had no rights or privileges but such as those who held the power and the Government might choose to grant them." In other words, although blacks were not specifically barred from citizenship under the Constitution, that was implicit in the framers' racist attitudes toward them.

To reinforce the argument, Taney dragged in the Declaration of Independence, saying in effect that the assertion "all men are created equal" really meant all *white* men. Blacks, he wrote, were not "acknowledged as a part of the people, nor intended to be included in the general words used in that memorable instrument." In the "civilized and enlightened portions of the world," they were then considered "altogether unfit to associate with the white race . . . and so far inferior, that they had no rights which the white man was bound to respect; and . . . might justly and lawfully be reduced to slavery for his benefit." Therefore, it was "too clear for dispute, that the enslaved African race . . . formed no part of the people who framed and adopted this declaration." The same was true for the Constitution, he said, because racial opinions were no different by the time it was framed.

After this imaginative foray into the minds and intentions of the Founding Fathers, which he conjured to deny citizenship for blacks, Taney moved on to the issue he was certain would silence the antislavery movement forever: Whether or not Congress had the power to legislate slavery in the territories, as it had for seven decades. Were Dred Scott and his family free because of their stay in a territory where slavery was prohibited by the Missouri Compromise? Not in Taney's view, because Congress never had the authority to restrict slavery in a territory to begin with. The provision in the Constitution that allowed Congress to "make all needful rules and regulations" regarding the territories, Taney said, only applied to those belonging to the United States in 1787, not those subsequently acquired. "It was," he wrote, "a special provision for a known and particular territory, and to meet a present emergency, and nothing more." It was certainly not to give "supreme power of legislation." The territories acquired since 1787, Taney asserted, were not intended to be held as colonies "and governed by Congress with absolute authority." Nor could citizens who migrated to a territory "be ruled as mere colonists, dependent upon the will of the General Government, and to be governed by any laws it may think to impose." Also, the people of a territory had the Fifth Amendment on their side, protecting the rights of private property. And that property included slaves! So, because the Taney Court had decided that the prohibition of slavery in the Wisconsin Territory (as well as the others) was unconstitutional, and thus void, it followed, as Taney wrote, "that neither Dred Scott himself, nor any of his family, were made free by being carried into this territory."[1]

As Kenneth Stampp writes, "The Court's opinion meant, of course, that not only the slavery provision of the Missouri Compro-

1. As to Scott's stay in the free state of Illinois, Taney applied an earlier Supreme Court ruling and declared that the laws of Missouri applied, not those of Illinois.

mise but all other acts of Congress excluding slavery from various territories had been equally unconstitutional. A restriction thus imposed on congressional power to govern the territories, unmentioned in the Constitution, unknown to its framers, undisclosed for many years thereafter, but recently devised by . . . pro-slavery partisans, was now, according to the opinion of the court, the law of the land."

Reaction to the *Dred Scott* decision from abolitionists and other slavery opponents was furious. Representative John F. Potter of Wisconsin (by then a state) called it "sheer blasphemy . . . an infamous libel on our government . . . a lasting disgrace to the court from which it was issued and deeply humiliating to every American citizen." The *Chicago Tribune* branded the opinion "shocking to the sensibilities and aspirations of lovers of freedom and humanity," while the *New York Tribune* declared that the decision "is entitled to just so much moral weight as would be the judgment of a majority of those congregated in any Washington bar-room." In the *New York Evening Post,* William Cullen Bryant asked, "Are we to accept, without question, these new readings of the Constitution—to sit down contentedly under this disgrace—to admit that the Constitution was never before rightly understood, even by those who framed it—to consent that hereafter it shall be the slaveholders' instead of the free men's Constitution? Never! Never!"

Proslavery factions, on the other hand, were ecstatic. Abolitionism, proclaimed the Richmond *Enquirer,* had been "staggered and stunned," and the "diabolical doctrines" of Northern fanatics repudiated. Never before, said the Chicago *Times,* had the "creed of an entire political party [the Republicans] been swept away from the consideration of all honest people, by the solemn and profound adjudication of the supreme tribunal."

But the Republican party was hardly swept away by the *Dred Scott* decision; rather, it was given renewed energy and focus that helped elect Abraham Lincoln in 1860. As the abolitionist and former slave Frederick Douglass said in a speech, "All measures devised and executed with a view to . . . diminish the antislavery agitation, have only served to increase, intensify, and embolden that agitation."

Dred Scott did not live to see slavery abolished under the law, but soon after the Supreme Court decision he and his family were purchased and immediately freed. Scott died the following year. Roger Taney served on the Supreme Court until his death in 1864. His last years were not happy ones, plagued by poor health and the ultimate failure of his attempt to bend the Constitution to conform to his own vision. "There was no sadder figure to be seen in Washington during the years of the Civil War than that of the aged Chief Justice," wrote one contemporary. "His form was bent by the weight of years, and his thin, nervous, and deeply-furrowed face was shaded by long, gray locks, and lighted up by large, melancholy eyes that looked wearily out from under shaggy brows, which gave him a weird, wizard-like expression. He had outlived his epoch, and was shunned and hated by the men of the new time of storm and struggle for the principles of freedom and nationality."

In his history of the Supreme Court, Chief Justice William H. Rehnquist acknowledges that the Taney Court "went totally awry" with the Dred Scott case, and that his predecessor's opinion was a "serious mistake." But, he argues, "that opinion should not be allowed to blot out the very constructive work done otherwise in his career." If only history was that accommodating. "Taney," the abolitionist senator Charles Sumner predicted, "will be hooted down the pages of history." And indeed he has been. Who really remembers any other decisions rendered by this chief justice, wise or unwise, anyway? Or that he freed his own slaves long before the law demanded it? *Dred Scott* was a tumor on Taney's reputation that turned out to be malignant.

4

Henry Wirz: Manufactured Monster

Infamy is arbitrary. Usually it's reserved for only the worthiest of villains, but there are occasions when infamy is bestowed a little less selectively. So it was with Henry Wirz, the Swiss immigrant who came to personify all the evils of prisoner abuse during the Civil War. He was hanged for it, too. Wirz, however, was not the source of all the misery, but merely a cog in a terrible machine. Union and Confederate prisoners alike endured unimaginable suffering at places like Point Lookout, Maryland, and Belle Island, Virginia. But while these infernos have faded into history and are largely forgotten, the Confederate prison camp called Andersonville still evokes horror. It was Henry Wirz's misfortune to have been Andersonville's commander, for it was his camp that came under the most intense scrutiny after the war and his life and reputation alone that were sacrificed because of it.

To be sure, the victorious Union could not have targeted a less sympathetic character to atone for the sins of so many. Foul-mouthed and short-tempered, Wirz earned the undying enmity of many prisoners.

Recalled one:

> He would frequently give way to paroxysms of rage so violent as to verge closely on insanity. Brandishing the fearful and wonderful revolver of which I have spoken, in such a manner as to threaten the luckless captives with instant death, he would shriek out imprecations, curses and foul epithets in French, German and English until he fairly frothed at the mouth. One of "Old Switzer's" favorite ways of ending these seances was to inform the boys that he would have them shot in an hour or so and bid them to prepare for death. After keeping them in fearful suspense for hours, he would order them to be punished with the stocks, the ball-and-chain, the chain gang or, if his fierce mood had burned itself out, as was quite likely with a man of his shallow brain and vacillating temper, simply to be returned to the stockade.

Wirz's unpleasant disposition alone would not have been enough to convict him of war crimes, as the North was determined to do, but the prison camp he ran in a remote corner of Georgia provided more than enough ammunition. Dante himself would have been hard-pressed to conjure a place as hellish as Andersonville, where thousands upon thousands of men died of disease and starvation in their own filth. "The smell is fearful!" wrote prisoner Robert Knox Sneden in his diary. "The rains washes the prison filth by the natural declivity of the ground on both sides of the brook [running through the camp] which by constant tramping of the men, kneaded the filth into a muck several inches deep of sand, feces, decomposing vegetable matters, and grease from the cook house outside, in which maggots and flies germinated, and worms, and other species of vermin festered and fattened all about the camp proper. The same filth accumulated while naked skeleton-like corpses lay around in every direction, encroaching on the living, who lay helplessly sick in holes covered partly by ragged blankets, parts of old overcoats, or any other shelter which they had erected from the fierce heat of the sun."

"And now our Sorrow has fairly begun," wrote one Pennsylvanian upon first entering the stockaded camp that held around 41,000 Union prisoners of war between February 1864 and April 1865. Carved out of what was once idyllic farmland, Andersonville at one point became the fifth largest city in the Confederacy, albeit a city of the damned where starving men were reduced to foraging through human feces for the slightest morsel of nutrition and roving bands of "Raiders" preyed upon their fellow prisoners, stealing their meager possessions and clubbing to death anyone who dared resist. "The condition of the prison at Andersonville is a reproach to us as a nation," one Confederate officer wrote, perhaps after sampling some of the food from the camp kitchen. The fare, when it was provided at all, usually consisted of a few ounces of rancid meat, which often had to be eaten raw, accompanied by bug-infested corn mush with the husks ground in. Chronic malnutrition resulted in a number of maladies, including scurvy, while all manner of other diseases swept through the prison camp as well. The few available remedies were primitive and often barbaric, killing far more than they cured. And where disease and starvation failed to take their toll, despair frequently did. Many men simply went mad. "The cases of insanity were numerous," wrote prisoner Charles Hopkins. "Men, strong in mentality, heart and hope were in a few short months, yes, often in a few weeks, reduced to imbeciles and maniacs."

The Civil War ended in April 1865, and Andersonville was liberated. A month later Henry Wirz was arrested. Stories of the brutal conditions at Andersonville, and Wirz's complicity in them, had been spreading for months—each tale more sinister than the last. By the end of the war, the people of the North clamored for revenge against "the demon of Andersonville." Wirz, however, consistently maintained that the prisoners' plight was beyond his control. "My conscience is clear," he wrote in a letter to the New York *News* from his prison cell in Washington, D.C. "I have never dealt cruelly with a person under my charge. If they suffered for want of shelter, food, clothing and necessaries, I could not help it, having no control over these things—things which the Confederate Government could give only in very limited quantity, even to our own men, as everybody knows who will be just and impartial."

Clearly Wirz was attempting a little spin control to save his own skin, but he also happened to have been right. The South in the last years of the Civil War could not adequately supply its own troops—three of whom died of disease for every one killed in combat—let alone all the prisoners of war it held. And as fearsome as the conditions at Andersonville were, they were fairly standard for any prison, Northern or Southern. Even many soldiers in the field endured similar misery. Medical knowledge in the 1860s was almost medieval, sanitation only in its infancy, and any treatment usually meant torture.

The horrors of the Civil War were manifold, and Henry Wirz seemed to have been set up by the victors to pay for them all. His trial before a military tribunal was a joke, the verdict preordained. A long parade of prosecution witnesses presented what William Marvel, author of *Andersonville: The Last Depot,* calls "some of the most absurd hearsay that any American judge ever permitted to stand." Tales of Wirz stomping prisoners to death, torturing them unmercifully, and shooting them for pleasure were laid before the court and accepted without a shred of evidence to back them up. The defense was stymied at every turn. The few witnesses allowed to testify about Wirz's efforts on behalf of the prisoners were dismissed as Southern sympathizers, and those who dared contradict the allegations of the prosecution's witnesses were denounced as traitors. In desperation, Wirz's attorney, Louis Schade, appealed to President Andrew Johnson for justice. "The testimony for the prosecution is loose, indefinite, and in the most part contradictory," Schade wrote. "Before any other court but that military commission it would have been an easy matter to uncover and bring to light a tissue of perjuries [such] as the world has seldom seen. Time will show that this assertion is no empty one."

Schade's efforts on behalf of his client were all for naught. Wirz was sentenced to hang. On November 5, 1865, he was taken to the gallows erected in the shadow of the U.S. Capitol. Amid shouts from the gathered spectators of "Remember Andersonville," Wirz sat on a stool, the instrument of his death dangling above him, as the charges were read. The noose was then fastened around his neck, the trap sprung, and the commandant of Andersonville dropped to his doom. “And thus ended,” wrote one unfriendly correspondent, “the career of a faithful servant of the Devil and Jeff. Davis.”

Now Henry Wirz has his place in the annals of infamy, though obscurity would probably have been a better fit.

5

A. Mitchell Palmer: Seeing Red

A. Mitchell Palmer proved that giving the people what they want is not always such a good idea. In answering the call for drastic action during the Red Scare of 1919–20, Woodrow Wilson's attorney general temporarily soothed a sweeping hysteria by arresting thousands of suspected alien agitators to great acclaim. But with his Gestapo tactics he spit on the Bill of Rights and reduced the U.S. government to the status of a second-rate police state.

After the Great War, the nation was deeply troubled. Fierce political partisanship had been reawakened following a wartime lull, especially over the peace treaty President Wilson had brought back from Versailles and U.S. participation in the League of Nations. Race riots broke out, lynching swept the country, and a crippling recession was exacerbated by explosive labor disputes. By the end of 1919, there were 3,600 different strikes, many violent. For many Americans, the labor unrest had a sinister Red tint about it. "Outside of Russia," the widely respected *Literary Digest* warned, "the storm center of Bolshevism is in the United States." And so it seemed.

The unrest of 1919 was punctuated by a series of bomb attacks on public figures that were popularly attributed to leftist radicals. The first intended victim was Seattle mayor Ole Hanson, an outspoken opponent of such radical groups as the International Workers of the World, whose slogan was, "Every strike is a little revolution and a dress rehearsal for the big one." Fortunately, the bomb mailed to the mayor—big enough he said, "to blow out the side of the County-City Building"—failed to detonate. Another effort, this time directed at Senator Thomas Hardwick of Georgia, was more successful. The senator was uninjured, however, because he was not home when his maid opened the lethal package and had both her hands blown off. A postal worker reading a newspaper description of the package intended for Senator Hardwick recalled seeing sixteen similar packages set aside for insufficient postage. A subsequent examination revealed that each contained a bomb intended for such prominent persons as John D. Rockefeller, J. P. Morgan, Supreme Court Justice Oliver Wendell Holmes Jr., and Attorney General A. Mitchell Palmer. Though the identity of the sender was never discovered, many believed the bomb-laden packages were part of a Red plot.

The parcel meant to kill Attorney General Palmer was not the last attempt on his life. On June 1, 1919, a month after the sixteen packages were discovered (along with sixteen more after further investigation), seven explosions rocked five cities across the eastern United States. That night in Washington, D.C., the attorney general's home was targeted. Palmer, who had been reading in the first-floor library, had retired to bed with his wife around 11 P.M. Soon after, they heard a thump on the front porch, followed by an enormous explosion that shattered windows throughout the quiet neighborhood. Miraculously, the Palmers emerged unharmed, although the front of their home, including the library, was in ruins. The inept assassin had apparently tripped on the front porch, dropped his bomb, and blown himself to bits. Scattered about the wreckage—along with what was described in one report as "great chunks of human being"—were copies of *Plain Words,* an anarchist pamphlet that promised death to government officials. "There will have to be murder," the tract read, proclaiming the triumph of revolution; "we will kill. . . ." Palmer was convinced that an insidious movement was well underway, and that it would be up to him to save the day.

Palmer had only been attorney general for three months when his home was bombed. President Wilson had not really wanted him for the job. He didn't trust Palmer, but he was too busy in Paris trying to negotiate a peace settlement after the Great War to give the appointment much attention. As a result, Palmer's advocates within the administration prevailed. Had the president been more attentive, Wilson's biographer August Heckscher notes, "one of the blackest marks against his administration—the 1920 raids on radicals and aliens—would never have taken place."

After the bombings, Palmer had little difficulty persuading Congress to grant him the necessary funds for his fight against the radical elements. But then nothing happened. The attorney general was becoming increasingly skeptical over how real the Red threat actually was, so he watched and waited. Within the Department of Justice, however, he created the General Intelligence Division, a special arm of the Bureau of Investigation, to monitor subversive threats. He put future FBI director (and fellow Hall of Shame inductee) J. Edgar Hoover, then twenty-four, in charge of the operation. Hoover went right to work, creating an elaborate filing system on individuals, newspapers, and organizations he considered dangerous to the nation. It was the beginning of an autocratic career that would last for another half century. But it wasn't enough for the frightened American public.

The labor strife was unrelenting. Federal troops had to be sent into the nation's steel towns, and when 394,000 coal miners went on strike early in November, the public feared a nationwide strike, or worse—perhaps a revolution. Communist agitators were believed to be lurking in every corner, infiltrating labor unions, churches, and universities—laying siege to the very fabric of America. And what, people wondered, was A. Mitchell Palmer doing about it? "I was shouted at from every editorial sanctum in America from sea to sea," Palmer later said. "I was preached upon from every pulpit; I was urged to do something and do it now, and do it quick and do it in a way that would bring results."

Even the U.S. Senate demanded an explanation for the attorney general's inaction and passed a resolution of censure against him. For a man of Palmer's presidential ambitions, this was a stinging rebuke. It was time to act. The nation, he declared, was besieged by "thousands of aliens, who were the direct allies of Trotsky," and the time had passed when it was possible, or even desirable, to draw "nice distinctions . . . between the theoretical ideals of the radicals and their actual violations of our national law."

To fight the menace, Palmer decided to enforce part of the U.S. immigration code, introduced during the war, that outlawed anarchism in all its forms. That included even reading or receiving anarchist literature. Any violation by an alien meant deportation. It was a good plan, as deportation hearings of the time were a simple matter, handled by immigration officers from the Department of Labor. Although the aliens were supposed to be protected by the procedural safeguards of the Bill of Rights, only minimum proof was needed to show that the immigration code had been violated. There was little oversight of the rulings or opportunity for appeal.

Palmer tested his plan on the night of November 7, 1919, when federal agents and city policemen raided the Russian People's House, a meeting place and recreation center for Russian resident aliens in New York City. Some 200 men and boys were in the building taking night classes. All were put under arrest. When a teacher asked why, since there was no warrant, he was hit in the face and his glasses shattered. The prisoners were herded through a double line of officers armed with clubs. According to one report, thirty-three of them were battered enough to need medical attention. Their injuries, the *New York Times* remarked, were "souvenirs of the new attitude of aggressiveness which had been assumed by the Federal agents against Reds and suspected Reds." That same night other Russian centers in nine cities were also raided and about 450 people arrested. Although half of them were released almost immediately, Palmer's raids were a tremendous success with the public.

The press, which had been pillorying the attorney general for his inaction the week before, now lauded him as a national hero—"a tower of strength to his countrymen," as one paper put it. By December, Palmer had secured deportation orders for 199 Russians found guilty under the immigration laws. The prisoners had been assured that no married man would be expelled, and that plenty of time would be given the others to set their affairs in order. Neither promise was honored. The deportees were taken to Ellis Island on December 21, put on board the *Buford,* an old army transport ship now nicknamed "the Soviet Ark," and shoved out to sea. The action, drastic as it was, was merely a preview of what was to come.

Only a few hundred Russians had been deported; Palmer wanted to snare thousands. To that end, he tried to persuade Secretary of Labor William B. Wilson to amend that part of the deportation law that allowed suspects to secure counsel. He also requested a blanket deportation warrant to cover any aliens discovered once the raids had begun. Wilson balked, but by mid-December he was on sick leave. One of his underlings, John W. Abercrombie, was left in charge of immigration issues and proved much more amiable to Palmer's designs. The right to counsel was suspended, as was the rule that suspects be informed of the charges against them. Also, 3,000 mimeographed warrants were issued, with the aliens' names to be filled in as necessary.

The new series of raids was slated for January 2, 1920. Frank Burke, the assistant director of the Bureau of Investigation, provided some helpful guidelines for the arresting agents to follow: "I leave it entirely to your discretion as to the method by which you gain access to such places [where aliens might be found]. . . . If, due to local conditions in your territory, you find that it is absolutely necessary to obtain a search warrant for the premises, you should communicate with the local authorities a few hours before the time for the arrests is set." Otherwise, Burke ordered, the raids were to be kept top secret and the aliens held incommunicado. The siege began as scheduled in thirty-three cities in twenty-three states. More than 3,000 were arrested, although the actual number remains unclear because of incomplete or nonexistent records. Certainly all 3,000 blank warrants were used, and as many as 2,000 more people were rounded up. All in all, it was an enormous haul.

The popular acclaim was even greater than before, at least initially. Editorials hailed Palmer. Even the *Washington Post,* which had denounced the November raids as "a serious mistake," urged quick deportation for this fresh batch of aliens. "There is no time to waste on hairsplitting over infringement of liberty," the paper declared. But a damper soon came over the excitement as reports of gross abuses began to appear. In Newark, New Jersey, for example, one man had been arrested because, in the words of the arresting officer, "he looked like an alien." Police burst in on a sleeping woman in Boston and arrested her without a warrant, only to discover she was an American citizen with no Communist connections. In Detroit, all the patrons of a foreign restaurant, as well as an entire orchestra, were hauled away. Stories of the mistreatment of suspects were legion. Many were confined under appalling conditions, including 800 suspects in Detroit who were housed in a corridor of the U.S. Post Office building without beds or blankets. No food was distributed for twenty-four hours, and they shared a single toilet. For many of the detainees, a Russian gulag surely would have been more accommodating.

Investigations into Palmer's raids resulted in sharp criticism of his actions. Twelve prominent lawyers, including several from Harvard University's law school, issued "A Report on the Illegal Practices of the United States Department of Justice," in which they sharply noted that the real danger to the nation was not a Red revolution, but the blatant abuse of federal power. Examples of egregious violations of the Fourth, Fifth, Sixth, and Eighth Amendments were cited. Palmer, the authors said, had ignored due process of law in favor of "illegal acts," "whole sale arrests," and "wanton violence." The attorney general, however, was unrepentant. As he saw it, drastic times called for drastic measures.

"Like a prairie-fire," he wrote in *Forum,* "the blaze of Revolution was sweeping over every institution of law and order. . . . It was eating its way into the homes of the American workman, its sharp tongues of revolutionary heat were licking the altars of the Church, leaping into the belfry of the school bell, crawling into the sacred corners of American homes, seeking to replace marriage vows with libertine law, burning up the foundations of society."

Yet despite Palmer's dire warnings, America was still standing. The January raids had yielded almost nothing in the way of arms or revolutionaries, just a sickening sense that things had gone too far. "Palmer," President Wilson said at his first cabinet meeting since a debilitating stroke the previous fall, "do not let this country see red." The admonition was a little late, but the president had been shielded from news of his attorney general's unlawful excesses because of concern for his health. Others, however, were painfully aware of the mess Palmer was making. Labor Secretary William Wilson and his assistant Louis Post took the bite out of Palmer's program by restoring the rule of law. Many of those arrested in January were released, and ultimately fewer than 600 aliens were deported. Indignant, Palmer demanded that Post be called to account for his "tender solicitude for social revolution," but a congressional committee cleared him.

Palmer was getting desperate. He issued a series of warnings of a revolutionary plot to overthrow the U.S. government that was to be launched on May 1, 1920. The National Guard was called out and the nation was in a state of nervous agitation. Yet when the date of doom came and went without incident, Palmer was derided as the Fed who cried wolf one too many times. That July his presidential dreams were grounded for good when he failed to get the Democratic nomination. In January 1921, he was called before the Senate Judiciary Committee to answer charges that he had misused his office during the great Red Scare. Palmer defended himself vigorously. "I apologize for nothing," he told the committee. "I glory in it. I point with pride and enthusiasm for the results of that work. . . . [If my agents] were a little rough and unkind, or short and curt, with these alien agitators . . . I think it might well be overlooked in the general good to the country which has come from it."

6

Warren G. Harding: Nice Guy Finishes Last

My God, this is a hell of a job! I can take care of my enemies all right. But my friends, my God-damn friends, they're the ones that keep me walking the floor nights!

—WARREN G. HARDING

At least Julius Caesar's friends had the decency to kill him. Harding's poker-playing pals, who also served as members of his cabinet, did far worse: They disgraced him. The Teapot Dome scandal and other instances of corruption by his high-ranking circle helped destroy the twenty-ninth president, a basically good man, and secured his position in history as one of the nation's worst chief executives.

No one ever expected anything great from Warren Harding, and he did not disappoint. "We must go back to Franklin Pierce,"[1] wrote the *New York Times* in 1919, "if we would seek a president who measures down to his political stature." Indeed, even Harding's main benefactor, Ohio political boss Harry Daugherty, thought him a

1. See Part III, Chapter 2.

dimwit, once confessing that he had pushed Harding for the presidency only because "he looked like a president." Daugherty was not unaware of the fact that Harding was a handsome devil, and that the election of 1920 was the first in which women could vote.

Harding brought to the presidency something no man has before or since—an overwhelming awareness of his own incompetence. "I am not fit for this office and never should have been here," he once said in despair. He was bewildered by the job from the beginning. His inability to grasp its complexities only fed his enormous self-doubt. "I don't think I'm big enough for the presidency," he once confided to Judge John Barton Payne.

Taxes, foreign affairs, the economy—all overwhelmed him. "I don't know what to do or where to turn on this taxation matter," Harding once blurted out in desperation. "Somewhere there must be a book that tells all about it, where I could go to straighten it out in my mind. But I don't know where the book is, and maybe I couldn't read it if I found it! My God, this is a hell of a place for a man like me to be!"

The president found reassurance in the letters he received from the public and spent an inordinate amount of time answering mail that should have been handled by his staff. He promised to buy tickets from an eleven-year-old boy raising funds for a swimming pool and reminisced about the creek where he used to swim as a lad. In a reply to the maker of Dodson's Bird Houses and Famous Sparrow Traps, who had suggested that the White House grounds be turned into a bird sanctuary, he asked that the crackpot inventor postpone his request "for the present."

Harding delighted in greeting visitors to the White House, shaking hands and making small talk. "I love to meet people," he explained to an adviser who questioned the amount of time he spent at the activity. "It's the most pleasant thing I do; it is really the only fun I have. It does not tax me, and it seems to be a very great pleasure to them."

Harding's fatal flaw was obviously not as classically epic as pride or ambition. It was something more innocuous, but for him equally lethal—the chronic need to be liked. It defined his presidency. Such vulnerability gave those who would take advantage of it license to use their appointed posts to whatever benefit they could. Their president would be loath to offend his friends by interfering. Friends were important to Harding. His nagging self-doubt required them, and high government posts were filled with them. They played poker together in the White House, with the Prohibition-era booze provided courtesy of good old Warren. Alice Roosevelt Longworth described it as "a general atmosphere of waist-coat unbuttoned, feet on the desk, and the spittoon alongside."

Among the players was kingmaker Harry Daugherty, the skilled, if somewhat unscrupulous, political Svengali who guided Harding from Ohio politics to Pennsylvania Avenue. Harding rebuffed warnings not to appoint Daugherty attorney general: "Harry Daugherty has been my best friend from the beginning of this whole thing . . . He tells me that he wants to be attorney general and by God he will be attorney general!"

Daugherty set up an influence-peddling office at the Department of Justice and became the subject of two congressional investigations. After resigning he was twice indicted for malfeasance during his tenure (only because the statute of limitations had expired for the real charge of accepting bribes).

There also was Harding's affable friend Colonel Charlie Forbes, who was appointed director of the Veterans' Bureau. Forbes convinced Harding to transfer the planning and construction of all future hospitals from the army to his department, along with the authority for purchase and disposal of veterans' supplies. Forbes supplemented his government salary quite lavishly with hospital construction kickbacks and the sale of the veterans' supplies for a fraction of what the government had paid for them. "I am heartsick about it," Harding said when told of his friend's treachery. The colonel had been a treasured favorite.

There was no warmly welcomed guest in the White House who did more to devastate the reputation of the president than his good friend Secretary of the Interior Albert Fall, a passionate poker player and architect of the great Teapot Dome swindle. Harding befriended the fiery, anticonservationist senator from New Mexico when he himself was the new senator from Ohio. After he was elected president, Harding appointed Fall, "that star of a fellow," to his cabinet. Fall's fellow senators voted with jovial unanimity to confirm him without reference to committee. The Department of the Interior was his, and he didn't ignore the advantage.

Although he was born in Kentucky, Albert Fall epitomized the spirit of the West. One of Theodore Roosevelt's "Rough Riders," he owned a sprawling ranch in New Mexico and was a fierce and vocal opponent of the government setting aside land for conservation—including a series of oil reserves controlled by the U.S. Navy. It was one of those reserves, Teapot Dome in Wyoming (so named for its vague resemblance to a giant sandstone teapot), that gave its name to one of the greatest scandals in the nation's history.

Fall succeeded in transferring control of several of the oil reserves, including Teapot Dome, from the Navy to the Department of the Interior. He then leased them out to the private interests of Harry Sinclair and E. L. Doheny, multimillionaire oil producers doing business as Mammoth Oil Company and Pan-American Petroleum and Transport Company respectively. The leases were granted without competitive bidding, which was not illegal, but Fall received "loans" from Sinclair and Doheny amounting to $400,000 in exchange for their licenses to secretly plunder the reserves. The loans were never documented or acknowledged, which made them bribes, and Fall, the man Teddy Roosevelt once called "the kind of public servant of whom all Americans should feel proud," came to be the first cabinet member in history to serve time in prison.

Fortunately, Harding would never know the extent of Fall's activities. He died in 1923, before completing his first term as president. Nor would he feel the full brunt of a stunned public's reaction to their gradual discovery of an administration teeming with dirty dealers. "No one can hurt you now, Warren," his wife said at his casket. No one but History.

7

Joe McCarthy: Wisconsin Sleaze

Calling Joe McCarthy a common bully is a little like calling Hitler a run-of-the-mill racist. It just doesn't do him justice. McCarthy, perhaps the most notorious demagogue of the twentieth century, exceeded the boundaries of ordinary bullies, aiming his devastating lies and distortions not just at weaker government workers, but also at some of the nation's most powerful people—including the president of the United States. He might, then, be called an *über*-bully, one who smeared reputations without regard to the strength or status of his victims.

Before launching his now infamous crusade against Communists and other subversives he claimed were lurking in all levels of government, McCarthy was just a poorly regarded junior senator from Wisconsin—part of the famed congressional class of 1946 that included John F. Kennedy and Richard M. Nixon.[1] Aside from a few questionable financial dealings that brought him unwelcome atten-

1. McCarthy was elected after campaigning on a much-embellished record of military service during World War II, dubbing himself "Tail-Gunner Joe," for example, despite having never actually served as a tail-gunner.

tion, McCarthy's greatest claim to fame during his early years in the Senate was perhaps the complete ass he made out of himself during what was known as the Malmédy affair. It was a disturbing preview of the senator's later career, although instead of chasing enemies of the United States—in this case, a group of Nazi murderers—McCarthy was actually coddling them.

The Germans in question had been tried and convicted in 1949 for the massacre of American prisoners of war five years earlier near the French village of Malmédy. The defendants claimed to have been framed by the U.S. Army and alleged their confessions had been beaten out of them. McCarthy, aghast, demanded a Senate hearing on the matter. It was quite a spectacle, with the senator from Wisconsin ranting about an elaborate conspiracy against the Nazis and the special committee's utter indifference to it. At one point, McCarthy stormed out of the hearings, declaring dramatically that he would no longer be party to such "a shameful farce . . . a deliberate and clever attempt to whitewash the American military." The incident failed to enhance the senator's reputation. Clearly he needed something other than mistreated Nazis to make a national name for himself. It didn't take him long to latch onto the threat of domestic communism as a career-making cause.

On February 9, 1950, in a speech before a Republican ladies group in Wheeling, West Virginia, McCarthy made his debut as a Red hunter, alleging that the U.S. Department of State was crawling with Communists. "While I cannot take the time to name all of the men in the State Department who have been named as members of the Communist Party and members of a spy ring," McCarthy gravely told the gathered women, according to a report in the Wheeling *Intelligencer,* "I have here in my hand a list of two hundred and five that were known to the Secretary of State as being members of the Communist Party and who nevertheless are still working and shaping the policy of the State Department." It was a preposterous lie, but McCarthy clung to it with the ferocity of a rottweiler. He had finally hit upon a theme that resonated quite nicely with an American public thoroughly paranoid over mounting Soviet aggression, the emergence of Red China, and the ever present threat of nuclear annihilation. Joe McCarthy, once voted the worst U.S. senator in a press corps poll, was finally getting a little respect, and he was not about to let the truth interfere with that.

"McCarthy was surely the champion liar," Richard Rovere writes in his biography of the senator. "He lied with wild abandon; he lied without evident fear; he lied in his teeth and in the teeth of the truth; he lied vividly and with bold imagination; he lied, often, with very little pretense to telling the truth." And while his widely scattered accusations occasionally bore fruit, far more often they were total nonsense—like his charge against the Truman administration for conniving with Communists several weeks after his speech at Wheeling. "The Democratic label is now the property of men and women who have . . . bent to the whispered pleas from the lips of traitors," he said, "men and women who wear the political label stitched with the idiocy of a Truman, rotted by the deceit of a [Secretary of State Dean] Acheson. . . ."

Indeed, McCarthy had a special loathing for Acheson, "that striped-pants asshole," as he privately called the dapper secretary of state who he felt personified the very worst of two decades' worth of Democratic administrations. It didn't help that Acheson had spoken in support of Alger Hiss, who had been convicted of perjury for lying about passing secret documents to the Soviets—just the kind of ammunition McCarthy craved. Acheson and his ilk exerted "a tremendous, almost hypnotic influence" on President Truman, McCarthy charged, warning that the American people would have to suffer the consequences, including the continued growth of the "sinister, many-headed and many-tentacled monster" that was the Communist conspiracy within the government—"one which was conceived in Moscow and given birth to by Dean Gooderham Acheson."

Whenever McCarthy uttered Acheson's name, William White of the *New York Times* noted, he made it sound like an expletive. And in attacking him, he went right for the throat: "When this pompous diplomat in striped pants, with the phony British accent, proclaimed to the American people that Christ on the Mount endorsed Communism, high treason, and betrayal of a sacred trust, the blasphemy was so great that it awakened the dormant indignation of the American people." Acheson received so much threatening mail after McCarthy's assaults that guards had to be posted at his home around the clock. The senator, always a gutter brawler, was unrepentant. Nevertheless, he was actually surprised, and even a little hurt, when he encountered Acheson one day in an elevator and the much maligned secretary of state pointedly refused to acknowledge his presence.

For his own part, President Truman believed McCarthy was all bluster, "a ballyhoo artist who has to cover up his shortcomings by wild charges." But the once insignificant senator began to get plenty of attention after Senate Democrats called for a complete investigation of his charges concerning hidden Communists within the State Department. The Democrats had hoped the special hearings would expose McCarthy as a fraud, but instead the press was dutifully reporting almost everything he said, and the public was lapping it up. McCarthy's popularity was beginning to soar as Truman's plummeted.

"You are not fooling me," McCarthy at one point challenged the committee chaired by Senator Millard Tydings, a Democrat from Maryland. "This committee [is] not seeking to get the names of bad security risks, but . . . to find out the names of my informants so they can be kicked out of the State Department tomorrow." The senator was setting himself up as a national savior, fighting a growing evil all alone. "In his own mind, it was Joe McCarthy against the world," writes historian Arthur Herman in his reexamination of the senator's legacy, "playing a sudden-death, high-stakes game against a Communist conspiracy that, in more expansive moments, seemed to include the entire Democratic administration and Washington establishment." And he seemed to be winning—despite the fact that he had yet to prove a single instance of subversion within the government. When President Truman was asked at a press conference in March 1950 whether he expected McCarthy to find any Communists in the State Department, he replied, "I think the greatest asset that the Kremlin has is Senator McCarthy."

In July 1950, the Tydings Committee issued an interim report that stated McCarthy had imposed a "fraud and a hoax" on the Senate with his unfounded allegations. "Starting with nothing," the report said, "Senator McCarthy plunged headlong forward, desperately seeking to develop some information which, colored with distortion and fanned by a flame of bias, would forestall the day of reckoning." Uncowed as usual, McCarthy called the report "a green light for the Reds." Stepping up his fight, he went after a genuine American hero.

General George C. Marshall had served as chief of staff of the U.S. Army during World War II, building perhaps the greatest fighting force in history. Under his command, Generals Eisenhower and MacArthur led American forces to victory in Europe and the Pacific. After the war, while serving as Truman's third secretary of state (before Acheson), he pushed for the European Recovery Program, or Marshall Plan, that helped check the spread of Communism in Western Europe and later earned him the Nobel Peace Prize. At the outbreak of the Korean War in 1950, he became secretary of defense. Historian David McCullough writes that Marshall was often compared to George Washington, "a figure of such flawless rectitude and self-command he both inspired awe and made description difficult." Churchill called him "the noblest Roman." Joe McCarthy called him a traitor: "A man steeped in falsehood . . . who has recourse to the lie whenever it suits his convenience . . . [part of] a conspiracy so immense and an infamy so black as to dwarf any previous venture in the history of man . . . [one in whose activities can be seen] a pattern which finds his decision maintained with great stubbornness and skill, always and invariably serving the world policy of the Kremlin."

McCarthy's attack on Marshall showed that no one was safe from his assaults. By late 1952, however, the Truman administration was coming to a close, and someone else was going to have to suffer the senator's outrageous slings and arrows. Adlai Stevenson, the Democratic candidate for president, was a natural target. McCarthy at one point called him "Alger . . . I mean Adlai," and declared that he would "continue the suicidal Kremlin-shaped policies of this nation." But the Republican candidate, Dwight D. Eisenhower, once the supreme Allied commander in World War II, also seemed intimidated by McCarthy's power.

This was made sadly apparent when Eisenhower was preparing to campaign in McCarthy's home state of Wisconsin. There had been much speculation that Ike was going to repudiate McCarthy's attacks on his old boss, George Marshall. "Just you wait till we get to Milwaukee, and you will find out what the general thinks of Marshall," Eisenhower's campaign manager told reporters, hinting that McCarthy was in for a stinging rebuke. Indeed a paragraph praising Marshall "as a man and as a soldier, . . . dedicated with singular selflessness and the profoundest patriotism to the service of America" had been drafted as part of Eisenhower's planned speech. It was never delivered. Instead, Ike sounded a lot like Joe McCarthy in the speech he did give, declaring that the Communist penetration of the government "meant—in its most ugly triumph—treason itself." McCarthy was of course delighted with the speech, and vigorously shook Eisenhower's hand at its conclusion. Others were appalled. "Yesterday could not have been a happy day for General Eisenhower," the *New York Times* editorialized, "nor was it a happy day for many supporters."

Though Eisenhower came to loathe McCarthy and his methods, even if he did agree with him in principle, he was reluctant to tangle with him after he became president—at least not directly. The senator had become far too powerful, and was shielded by the support of millions of Americans. "I just won't get into a pissing contest with that skunk," the president told friends. Eisenhower believed the best way to fight this enemy was to ignore him. "This he cannot stand," Ike wrote in his diary. Given enough time, he believed, McCarthy would destroy himself. The president would not have to wait much longer to prove this point.

On the surface, in 1953, McCarthy seemed invincible. He chaired the Permanent Subcommittee on Investigations, and made it his personal fiefdom. With a staff that included chief counsel Roy Cohn, soon to be an instrument of his downfall, and assistant counsel Robert Kennedy, whose father was an avid supporter of the senator and got his son the job, McCarthy went on a Red-hunting rampage. There were investigations of the State Department (an old favorite), the Voice of America, the Government Printing Office, and the United Nations, among others. He even planned to target the CIA, "a breathtaking choice," writes Arthur Herman. "The notion of Joe McCarthy pawing through the intelligence agency's files and personnel records made not just administration officials but many senators blanch."

The White House ordered McCarthy to back off, which McCarthy reluctantly did. But he still stood in the way of the Eisenhower administration on several key issues, including the nomination of Charles Bohlen as ambassador to Moscow. The president was furious. "McCarthy has the bug to run for the presidency in 1956," he fumed to his staff, adding with an angry slap to his knee, "The only reason I would consider running again would be to run against him." But any hopes Joe McCarthy may have harbored for the White House, or even another term in the Senate, were severely diminished when he and his staff took on the U.S. Army. It was this confrontation that ultimately destroyed him.

The assault on the army was classic McCarthy. At one point, for instance, he lashed out at General Ralph Zwickler, a war hero and field commander during the Battle of the Bulge. McCarthy called him a protector of Communists "unfit to wear [his] uniform." What the senator failed to realize, though, was that the army was preparing a counterattack of its own, focusing on the activities of chief counsel Roy Cohn. It seems Cohn had a crush of sorts on another McCarthy staff member, David Schine, and was upset when Schine got drafted into the army. Cohn was determined to get his pal special treatment and went all the way to the secretary of the Army to see that he did. Not one to have his will thwarted, Cohn became enraged when he found out Schine's weekend passes were to start on Saturday rather than Friday night as he had requested. In a snit, he called the army's chief lawyer, John Adams.

"The army has double-crossed me for the last time," Cohn screamed. "The army is going to find out what it means to go over my head."

"Is this a threat?" Adams asked.

"It's a promise," Cohn replied. "I always deliver on my promises. . . . We are not going to stop at this. Joe [McCarthy] will deliver, and I can make Joe do whatever I want."

It was true. Cohn did have a strange hold on the senator and was now making it clear that McCarthy's investigation of the army was directly related to the army's willingness to bend to Cohn's will. It was just one instance of many the army assembled into a dossier and made public, showing the world how McCarthy and his staff sought to hound the army to further their own ends. Ironically, McCarthy agreed to have his own subcommittee investigate the army's charges, with him and Cohn, as implicated parties, recusing themselves. So sure was the senator of a positive outcome that he agreed to have the hearings televised. It was perhaps the greatest mistake of his life.

Millions tuned in to watch the spectacle. For many, it was the first time they were able to see Joe McCarthy in action. It was not a pretty sight. Day after day viewers watched the senator and his staff bully and harass witnesses while failing to produce any hard evidence to back up increasingly outrageous accusations. McCarthy's credibility crumbled before the eyes of the nation. In one dramatic moment, after McCarthy attacked a young associate of Joseph N. Welch, chief attorney for the army, Welch stood up, faced the senator, and said: "Until this moment, Senator, I think I never really gauged your cruelty or your recklessness. Let us not assassinate this lad further, Senator. You have done enough. Have you no sense of decency, sir, at long last? Have you no sense of decency?"

The cloak of righteousness that had long shielded McCarthy in the eyes of the American public was now shredded. The end was near. "In this long, degrading travesty of the democratic process," the *Louisville Courier-Journal* noted, "McCarthy has shown himself to be evil and unmatched in malice." On December 2, 1954, the Senate voted 67–22 to condemn McCarthy for "conduct contrary to Senatorial traditions." Less than three years later, he was dead of alcohol-induced cirrhosis.

8

J. Edgar Hoover: What a Drag

The sight of J. Edgar Hoover in an evening gown would be enough in itself to propel the notorious FBI director straight into the American Hall of Shame. But since that horrifying spectacle has yet to be proven, the fact that Hoover sashayed his way over the civil liberties of thousands—for nearly a quarter of the nation's history—will have to suffice.

Red-baiter and blackmailer extraordinaire, the director-for-life made the bureau a model secret police force that infiltrated the lives of suspected enemies ranging from Eleanor Roosevelt to Albert Einstein. For J. Edgar Hoover, information meant power—the more lurid, the better—and he wielded what he knew like a spiked club. The abuses of office are legion, but the FBI's relentless campaign against Martin Luther King Jr.—or "that burrhead," as Hoover preferred to call the civil rights leader—show the director at his most vicious.

The FBI's interest in King started out as routine. Red-hunting had long been the bureau's stock in trade—even before Hoover became its director in 1924—and the civil rights movement was thought to be prime for Communist infiltration. As one of the movement's most prominent leaders, King naturally merited watching. The attention was passive, however, until 1961, when Hoover himself became directly involved. King, heading the Southern Christian Leadership Conference (SCLC), had taken a leading role in the "Freedom Rides" that year, hoping to desegregate interstate bus transportation facilities across the Deep South. Alerted to this, the director wanted more information on this uppity Negro who was making such a fuss. He was disappointed to find that there wasn't much in the FBI files. On a memo sent to him noting that King had never been formally investigated, Hoover wrote, "Why not?" The basilisk's glare had now been focused and would not be diverted until well after King was dead.

Increased FBI surveillance soon revealed that one of King's closest associates, Stanley Levison, had been involved with the Communist Party in the early 1950s. And though it became apparent from further investigations—including wiretaps on Levison—that he had had nothing to do with the party since becoming associated with King, Hoover reacted as if a Soviet invasion was being plotted. King was added to the FBI's enemies list, and government officials were put on Red alert. "This Bureau has recently received additional information showing the influence of Stanley David Levison, a secret member of the Communist Party, upon Martin Luther King Jr.," Hoover wrote in a memo to Attorney General Robert Kennedy.

When it came to stirring J. Edgar Hoover's eternal animosity, King's alleged Communist connections were nothing compared to his public criticism of the FBI in late 1962. A *New York Times* reporter had asked King if he agreed with a report on the civil rights protests that had taken place the previous summer in Albany, Georgia, in which the FBI was criticized for ignoring patent abuses of blacks by local law enforcement. King said he did agree with the report, particularly as it concerned the FBI. "One of the great problems we face with the FBI in the South is that the agents are white Southerners who have been influenced by the mores of the community," he told the reporter. "To maintain their status, they have to be friendly with the local police and people who are promoting segregation. Every time I saw FBI men in Albany, they were with the local police force." The *Times* story, in which King went on to suggest that non-Southerners be assigned to FBI offices in the Deep South, appeared in many other newspapers across the country. Allergic to criticism of any sort, Hoover was wild.

"In a very real sense there was no greater crime in Mr. Hoover's eyes than public criticism of the Bureau," recalled former Attorney General Nicholas deB. Katzenbach. "All public critics of the Bureau, if they persisted," were treated as enemies. "The only thing unique about Dr. King was the intensity of the feeling and the apparent extremes to which the Bureau went in seeking to destroy the critic."

Hoover's wrath was evident just before the famous 1963 March on Washington at which King delivered his stirring "I Have a Dream" speech. The FBI's domestic intelligence division had prepared a lengthy and detailed report on the Communist Party's efforts to infiltrate the civil rights movement, concluding that such efforts had been a failure. But with a vendetta against Martin Luther King to pursue, Hoover was not satisfied with the benign contents of the report.

"This memo reminds me vividly of those I received when Castro took over Cuba," the director wrote on the report's cover letter. "You contended then that Castro & his cohorts were not Communists & not influenced by Communists. Time alone has proved you wrong. I for one can't ignore the memos re King . . . et al. as having only an infinitesimal effect on the efforts to exploit the American Negro by the Communists."

Hoover's underlings were smart enough to know that their jobs depended upon their interpretation of the facts meshing harmoniously with the autocratic director's. Accordingly, two days after the March on Washington, Assistant Director William C. Sullivan—no doubt fearing Hoover's wrath—prepared a new memo that completely reversed the position taken in the one sent a week earlier. "The Director is correct," Sullivan wrote in humble response to Hoover's critique. "We were completely wrong about believing the evidence was not sufficient to determine some years ago that Fidel Castro was not a communist or under communist influence. On investigating and writing about communism and the American Negro, we had better remember this and profit by the lesson it should teach us." Sullivan went on to characterize King's "I Have a Dream" oration as a "powerful demagogic speech," and warned that "We must mark [King] now, if we have not done so before, as the most dangerous Negro of the future in this Nation from the standpoint of communism, the Negro and national security."

With the menace of Martin Luther King now fabricated to Hoover's specifications, Attorney General Robert Kennedy was confronted with the "evidence" of King's continuing Communist connections. Fearing the effect a public disclosure of this might have on the pending civil rights legislation backed by his brother's administration, Kennedy authorized wiretaps on King's home, as well as the SCLC's offices in Atlanta and New York. On its own initiative, the FBI planted bugs in his hotel rooms. A new phase of official harassment was beginning. It would drive King to the edge of despair.

Much of what the bugs picked up was useless noise, but the juice that did seep through was enough to send J. Edgar Hoover pirouetting across his office with glee. There was King laughing at the Kennedys. King telling raunchy stories. King cheating on his wife. It was a bonanza—dirt both to destroy the sinful minister and to satisfy the voyeuristic pleasure the director derived from hearing about the sex lives of others. Of course, Hoover's public reaction was moral outrage, a posture dutifully emulated by the FBI rank and file. "King must, at some propitious point in the future, be revealed to the people of this country and to his Negro followers as being what he actually is—a fraud, demagogue and moral scoundrel," Assistant Director Sullivan wrote in a memo. "When the true facts concerning his activities are presented, such should be enough, if handled properly, to take him off his pedestal and to reduce him completely in influence so that he will no longer be a security problem and no longer will be deceiving and misleading the Negro people." Hoover put it more succinctly: "[This] will destroy the burrhead."

The director was stunned and angered, therefore, when it became obvious that the derogatory information the FBI had so painstakingly gathered was having little effect. When King went to

Europe in 1964, for example, the bureau learned that he wanted to meet Pope Paul VI. Anxious to prevent such a credibility-building encounter, an agent alerted Francis Cardinal Spellman of New York, shared the dirt on King, and encouraged him to pass it on to the Vatican. The meeting took place anyway, and Hoover was shocked. "I am amazed that the Pope gave an audience to such a degenerate," he scrawled on a news clipping of the event.

A month later, something even worse happened. King won the Nobel Peace Prize. This was just too much for the director. "King could well qualify for the 'top alley cat' prize," he wrote on a news clipping of the announcement. In light of this latest outrage, fresh accounts of King's behavior behind closed doors were sent to the White House, the attorney general's office, and all the government offices, including the State Department, which would play a part in King's trip to Oslo to accept the prize. Hoover's fury was unsated, however, and in a rare meeting with a group of female reporters, he went on a rampage. Martin Luther King was "the most notorious liar in the country," he informed the reporters—a response to King's criticism of the FBI two years earlier. Ignoring the frantic notes of an aide imploring him to keep his comments off the record, Hoover continued to rant, calling King "one of the lowest characters in the country." The blistering attack became front page news.

King's public response was restrained. "I cannot conceive of Mr. Hoover making a statement like this without being under extreme pressure," he said in a statement. "He has apparently faltered under the awesome burden, complexities and responsibilities of his office. Therefore, I cannot engage in a public debate with him. I have nothing but sympathy for this man who has served his country so well." Behind the scenes, though, King was preparing for battle. He instructed his aides to ask other public figures and organizations to speak out against Hoover's outburst. In a phone conversation with one SCLC staffer—taped by the FBI, of course—King said that the director "is old and getting senile" and should be "hit from all sides" in order to force President Johnson to censure Hoover publicly.

The war was escalating, but King's arsenal was sorely limited next to Hoover's. This was a man who demanded results and had all the resources to get them. When Hoover complained in one memo that "we are never taking the aggressive," he had an army below him that got the message. Assistant Director William Sullivan was no doubt inspired by the boss when he ordered the "highlights" of King's taped misdeeds assembled into a sort of "greatest hits" recording and sent to King himself. To accompany this damning package, Sullivan, posing as a black person, wrote the following anonymous letter:

> KING,
> In view of your low grade . . . I will not dignify your name with either a Mr. or a Reverend or a Dr. And, your last name calls to mind only the type of King such as King Henry VIII. . . .
>
> King, look into your heart. You know you are a complete fraud and a great liability to all of us Negroes. White people in this country have enough frauds of their own but I am sure they don't have one at this time that is anywhere near your equal. You are no clergyman and you know it. I repeat you are a colossal fraud and an evil, vicious one at that. You could not believe in God. . . . Clearly you don't believe in any personal moral principles.
>
> King, like all frauds your end is approaching. You could have been our greatest leader. You, even at an early age, have turned out to be not a leader but a dissolute, abnormal moral imbecile. . . . Your "honorary" degrees, your Nobel Prize (what a grim farce) and other awards will not save you. King, I repeat you are done.
>
> No person can overcome facts, not even a fraud like yourself. . . . You are finished. . . . And some of them to be ministers of the Gospel. Satan could not do more. What incredible evilness. . . . King, you are done.
>
> The American public, the church organizations that have been helping—Protestant, Catholic and Jews will know you for what you are—an evil, abnormal beast. So will others who have backed you. You are done.
>
> King, there is only one thing left for you to do. You know what it is. . . . You are done. There is but one way out for you.

> You better take it before your filthy, abnormal, fraudulent self is bared to the nation.

"They are out to break me," King said in despair after receiving the package—a reaction that must have delighted Hoover when it was caught on a wiretap. Though King was able to rally and continue his mission, the FBI's harassment campaign continued until his assassination in 1968, and even beyond. Hoover approved the following proposal by his aide Cartha DeLoach after Martin Luther King's murder: "I would like to suggest that consideration be given to advising a friendly newspaper contact on a strictly confidential basis, that Coretta King and Reverend Abernathy [King's widow and his close associate, respectively] are deliberately plotting to keep King's assassination in the news by pulling the ruse of maintaining that King's murder was definitely a conspiracy and not committed by one man. This, of course, is obviously a rank trick in order to keep the money coming in to Mrs. King and Abernathy. We can do this without any attribution to the FBI and without anyone knowing that the information came from a wiretap."

Although many of the FBI's shameful secrets were exposed after Hoover's death in 1972, including the ones involving Martin Luther King, the bureau's headquarters in Washington still bears the director's name. Until the American Hall of Shame is erected, that building remains his monument.

9

Richard Nixon: Say *What!?*

Ah, Tricky Dick. So much has already been said and written about the disgraced thirty-seventh president. There's almost nothing left of Nixon to kick around anymore. Perhaps, then, it's time to let the man speak for himself. All the president's rants were captured on recording equipment installed at the White House, reminding us, as Gene Weingarten of the *Washington Post* notes, "that the leader of the free world was buggier than a flophouse blanket."

On the Decline and Fall of the Roman Empire:

"Do you know what happened to the Romans? The last six Roman emperors were fags!"

On Jews (Part I):

"The Jews are [an] irreligious, atheistic, immoral bunch of bastards."

On Civilian Casualties in Vietnam:

To National Security Advisor Henry Kissinger: "You're so goddamned concerned about the civilians, and I don't give a damn. I don't care."

On Jews (Part II):

"What about the rich Jews? The IRS is full of Jews. . . . Go after them like a son of a bitch. The Jews, you know, are stealing in every direction."

On House Majority Whip Thomas P. "Tip" O'Neill Jr.:

"An all-out dove and a vicious bastard."

On Senator Edward M. Kennedy:

"I'd really like to get Teddy taped."

On Panda Mating:

"The only way they learn how is to watch other pandas mate, you see."

On Jews (Part III):

"Most Jews are disloyal, you can't trust the bastards. They turn on you."

On the Media:

"*Newsweek* is totally—it's all run by Jews and dominated by them in their editorial pages. The *New York Times,* the *Washington Post,* totally Jewish, too."

On Rival Democrats:

To White House Chief of Staff H. R. Haldeman: "Keep after 'em. . . . Maybe we can get a scandal on any, any of the leading Democrats."

On Bugging the Watergate Offices of the Democratic National Committee:

"The reaction is going to be primarily in Washington and not the country because I think the country doesn't give much of a shit about bugging. . . . Most people around the country think it's probably routine, [that] everybody's trying to bug everybody else — it's politics."

On the Chicago Seven:

"Aren't the Chicago Seven all Jews?"

On the Federal Bureaucracy:

"We have no discipline in this bureaucracy. . . . We never fire anybody. We never reprimand anybody. We never demote anybody. We always promote the sons of bitches that kick us in the ass. That's true in the State Department. It's true in HEW. It's true in OMB, and true for ourselves, and it's just got to stop."

On Obtaining Tax Records of Prominent Democrats:

"We have to do it artfully so that we don't create an issue by abusing the IRS politically. And, there are ways to do it. Goddamn it, sneak in in the middle of the night."

On the Supreme Court:

"You've got a senile old bastard in [Justice Hugo] Black. You've got an old fool and black fool in that [Justice] Thurgood Marshall. Then you've got [Justice William] Brennan, I mean, a jackass Catholic."

On the District of Columbia:

"There's a hell of a lot of Jews in the District, see . . . the Gentiles have moved out."

On *Washington Post* publisher Katharine Graham:

"An old bitch" and "a terrible old bag."

On the Art of Political Warfare (Part I):

To H. R. Haldeman: "You're to break into the place [the Brookings Institution, a liberal-leaning Washington think tank], rifle the files and bring them out. . . . Just go in and take them [the president demands, almost shouting]. Go in around 8 or 9 o'clock . . . and clean them out."

On the Art of Political Warfare (Part II):

The next morning: "We're up against an enemy, a conspiracy that are using any means [the president says, pounding his desk repeatedly]. We are going to use any means. Is that clear? Did they get the Brookings Institute [sic] raided last night? Get it done! I want it done! I want the Brookings safe cleared out." (The president's order, coming a year before the Watergate break-in, apparently was never carried out.)

On the Ideal IRS Director:

"I want to be sure he is a ruthless son of a bitch, that he'll do what he's told, that every income tax return I want to see, I see. That he'll go after our enemies, not our friends. . . . Now, it's as simple as that. If he isn't, he doesn't get the job."

On Homosexuals (Part I):

"You know what happened to the popes? It's all right that popes were laying the nuns. That's been going on for years, centuries, but when the popes, when the Catholic Church went to hell in—I don't know, three or four centuries ago—it was homosexual. . . . Now, that's what happened to Britain, it happened earlier to France. And let's look at the strong societies. The Russians. Goddamn it, they root them out, they don't let 'em hang around at all. You know what I mean? I don't know what they do with them."

On Drugs:

"Dope? Do you think the Russians allow dope? Hell, no. Not if they can catch it, they send them up. You see, homosexuality, dope, uh, immorality in general: These are the enemies of strong societies. That's why the communists and the left-wingers are pushing it. They're trying to destroy us."

On Jews (Part IV):

"You know, it's a funny thing. Every one of the bastards that are out for legalizing marijuana is Jewish. What the Christ is the matter with the Jews. . . . What is the matter with them? I suppose because most of them are psychiatrists."

On Homosexuals (Part II):

"I won't shake hands with anybody from San Francisco."

On the Television Sitcom *All in the Family*:

"Archie's sitting here in his sloppy clothes and here's his hippie son-in-law who's married to his screwball-looking daughter. The son-in-law obviously is—apparently goes both ways."

On Homosexuals (Part III):

Referring again to Meathead's imagined bisexuality on *All in the Family*: "The point that I make is that, goddamn it, I do not think that you glorify on public television homosexuality. And the reason you don't glorify it . . . any more than you glorify whores. It outrages me because I don't want to see this country go that way. Well, in other countries, you know what happened to the Greeks. Homosexuality destroyed them. Aristotle was a homo, we all know that. So was Socrates."

On Ambassador (to France) Arthur K. Watson's Drunken Behavior Aboard an Airplane:

"Look, people get drunk. People chase girls. And the point is, it's a hell of a lot better for them to get drunk than to take drugs. It's better to chase girls than boys."

On the U.S. Justice Department:

"Listen, the lawyers in government are damn Jews."

On the United Nations:

"The problem is the U.N. The United States is getting kicked around by a bunch of goddamned Africans and cannibals and horrible people and the rest."

On Women in Government:

". . . a pain in the neck, very difficult to handle."

On Blacks in Government:

"With blacks you can usually settle for an incompetent, because there are just not enough competent ones, and so you put incompetents in and get along with them, because the symbolism is vitally important. You have to show you care."

On Mexicans in Government:

"That's the problem, finding a Mexican that is honest. And Italians have somewhat the same problem."

On the U.S. Military:

"Goddamn it, the military, they're a bunch of greedy bastards. They want more officers' clubs and more men to shine their shoes. The sons of bitches are not interested in this country."

On His Cabinet and Staff:

"I'm sick of the whole bunch. The others are a bunch of goddamned cowards. The staff, except for Haldeman and Ehrlichman, screw them. The cabinet, except for [Treasury Secretary John B.] Connolly, the hell with them."

On His Vietnam Policy:

"I'd rather use the nuclear bomb."

On His 1973 Address to the Nation Regarding Watergate:

"Goddammit, I'm never going to discuss this son of a bitching Watergate thing again. Never, never, never, never." (Nixon resigned the following year.)

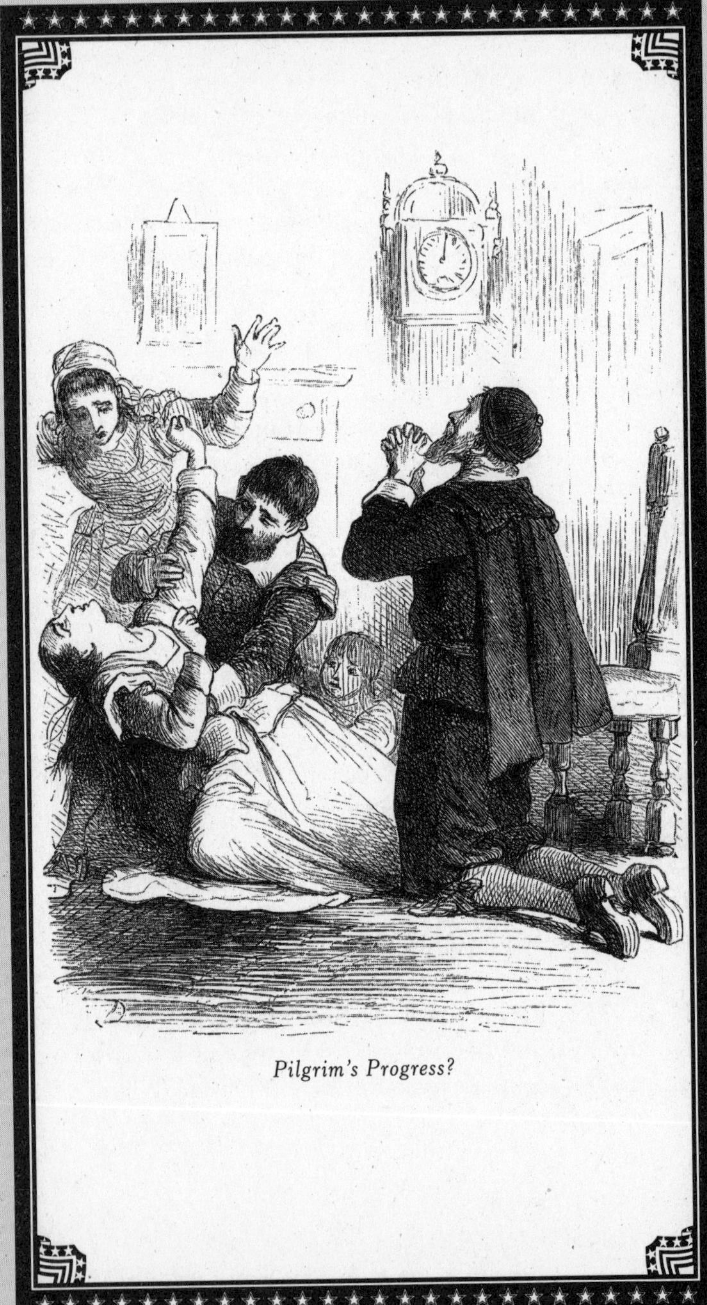

Pilgrim's Progress?

Part VII

Murder, Madness, and Just Plain Strange Episodes

In the great melting pot that is America, a few oddballs are bound to bubble up—some deranged, others just a bit weird. A number have had quite an impact on the nation. Following is a survey of some of the most unsettling personalities and episodes in American history.

★

1

Bewitched

The English Puritans brought a little of the Old World with them when they settled in America during the seventeenth century, including that quaint old custom of killing accused witches. Though the slaughter never reached the epic scale it did in Europe, many innocent women and men lost their lives across New England, perhaps most infamously in a small Massachusetts hamlet called Salem Village. It was here that a band of attention-starved girls, all claiming to be tormented by witches, actually gained enough power through their hysterical performances to send twenty of their neighbors to the gallows. Adolescent angst was never so lethal.

The girls who launched the witch hunt in 1692 were, in all probability, just plain bored. Salem Village was not the most exciting place to grow up, and the strict Puritan ethic that suffused the town only made things more unbearable. Any respite from such an oppressive environment surely would be embraced by the children living in it. For some young women, this came at the feet of a strange woman named Tituba, a slave in the household of Reverend Samuel Parris, the town's minister. Tituba's superstitious tales entranced the girls, and the more they gathered around to hear her speak of the occult, the closer Salem came to madness.

Samuel Parris's daughter Betty, nine, and her cousin Abigail Williams, eleven, were the first to exhibit signs that all was not well in Salem, barking like dogs, for instance, and screaming in agony during prayer services. Others were quick to copy them, and soon the girls became known to the town as "the afflicted ones." The devil was clearly at work, and all of Salem's collective energy was directed at rooting out his minions. The girls would have to lead the way. And with everyone's attention focused on them—a welcome change from their normal invisibility—"the afflicted ones" had to start producing. The strange storyteller was an obvious target. "Tituba . . . she . . . oh Tituba!" wailed Betty Parris in apparent delirium. The other girls immediately echoed her, and came up with a few more witches as well: Sarah Good, a tough, pipe-smoking woman who had fallen on hard times, and Sarah Osburne, a moderately well-to-do widow who had earned the scorn of the town for having lived with her second husband before marrying him. The three accused witches were arrested and imprisoned to await an official inquiry into their evil activities.

The two magistrates assigned to conduct the pretrial examinations were diligent in their preparations, learning all they could about the ways of witchcraft. The one unquestioned legal precept was the Biblical injunction, "Thou shalt not permit a witch to live," but the good book was short on specifics. For the details, the magistrates turned to the available literature of the day, including works by Cotton Mather, the contemporary Puritan expert on the devil. All the research resulted in a number of rational, well-conceived principles of evidence. Proof of guilt would include the "devil's mark," which meant any "unnatural" blight upon the body. People with psoriasis or eczema, therefore, might have found themselves in big trouble. Also, if an accused witch had been in a dispute with a neighbor and anything untoward happened to that neighbor, like a wheel breaking off his cart or his livestock falling ill, witchcraft was surely at work. The most important principle was that of "spectral evidence," in which a person could be condemned if their spirit, or "shape," visited an accuser with the intention of causing mischief—never mind that providing an alibi for the activities of one's "shape" would be impossible.

The magistrates were most judicious in determining what would be allowed as evidence, disregarding, for example, the medieval water test—in which an accused witch was tossed into a body of water and if she sank and drowned, she was proved innocent, but if she floated, she was condemned and executed. Either way, the defendant ended up dead. This test, the judges wisely concluded, was superstitious and unchristian.

The initial inquiry of the accused women began on March 1, 1692. Most of Salem Village, and many from surrounding towns, took the day off to witness such a momentous event in their midst. Sarah Good was brought into the crowded meetinghouse first, and as she arrived, her accusers, sitting in a place of honor in the front row, trembled and went into fits and convulsions. Few doubted this unsavory crone, feisty as ever in the face of the magistrates, was the devil's own. Why, the judges asked, did she not attend church? "For want of clothes," she snapped. Sarah Good had a contemptuous answer to every question aimed at her and was eventually escorted out of the room. Sarah Osburne, ailing and in need of assistance, was next. Her best defense was that she was as tormented and afflicted as the girls writhing and shrieking in her presence. It was a desperate gambit that did no good. But Sarah Osburne successfully avoided a public execution: She died in prison two months later.

The much anticipated appearance of Tituba, the last of the three accused, was greeted with even louder howls of frenzy from the girls in the front row. Here, it seemed, was the wickedest witch of them all. Tituba didn't deny it, and this, perversely enough, was her salvation. A sound thrashing by her master, Reverend Parris, had helped elicit the "truth" from her before the inquest, and Tituba, having discovered that an admission of guilt was the only way to stop the torture, carried this lesson into the courtroom. For three days she told the people of Salem exactly what they wanted to hear. Conjuring for them episodes of unspeakable evil, she stunned even her histrionic accusers into silence. There was, she said, a thing she could describe only as "something like a cat," with wings and a woman's face, that ordered her to serve it. It was Sarah Osburne's creature, she said. Other denizens of Hell came to her, too—red cats and red rats, all with one order: "Serve me." The devil's creatures demanded that she send her shape to torment the girls. Sometimes she resisted, like when she was told to harm young Betty Parris. "I could not hurt Betty," she insisted. "I loved Betty." But Sarah Good and Sarah Osburne always forced her to comply.

Tituba told tales of witches' sabbaths, and of a "tall man"—presumably the devil himself—who came to her often and offered her "pretty things." The tall man, "he tell me he God and I must believe and serve him six years," Tituba testified. "The first time I believe him God and he was glad." The most startling of Tituba's revelations was that the tall man had a book signed by nine other witches whose names she could not read. The audience gasped at this development. It meant there were others out there, and Salem was facing an epidemic of evil.

Tituba had by her "apparently witless wanderings . . . laid down a pattern which would wreck the peace of mind of Massachusetts for months and even years to come," writes historian Marion L. Starkey. But she had saved herself by illuminating the evil in Salem and turning her back on it with her confession. When the girls, quiet during most of Tituba's testimony, started acting up again, she was asked, "Who hurts the children now?" In responding, Tituba wisely stepped into her new role as an ex-witch who had renounced her calling. "I am blind now," she said. "I cannot see."

Tituba's revelation that there were more witches to be identified gave the girls a renewed sense of purpose, and they quickly settled on their next victim. Martha Cory, a respectable matron and prominent member of the congregation, was an unlikely witch, but any presumption of innocence was erased after her haughty dismissal of the accusation. "I don't believe that there are witches," she told two members of the community who had come to her home to warn her that she had been named. This was blatant heresy. In the Puritan universe, the devil was every bit as real as God himself. To deny his existence, or that of his earthly servants, would be to deny God. When her visitors demanded to know how she she could deny the existence of witches when three had already been identified (though not yet formally tried), Martha Cory remained obstinate. "Well, if they are," she snorted, "I could not blame the devil for making witches of them, for they are idle slothful persons and minded nothing that was good." Besides, she demanded, what did they have to do with her, a pillar of faith, a woman of the gospel? "Woman," one of the visitors pronounced before leaving, "outward profession of faith cannot save you."

A warrant was sworn out for Martha Cory's arrest on Saturday, March 19, but she wasn't taken until the following Monday. That left Sunday for her to disrupt religious services by her very presence. The community was shocked that such a depraved servant of Satan would dare sit among them. But there she was, staring straight ahead, ignoring the sidelong glances of her neighbors and the tormented shrieks of her accusers. "Look!" Abigail Williams suddenly screamed. "There sits Goody Cory on the beam suckling a yellow bird betwixt her fingers." Of course it was not the physical body of Martha Cory Abigail saw perched above the congregation, but her "shape." And only the girls could see it. The next day Martha—the physical Martha, that is—was hauled before the magistrates. Her request to pray was abruptly denied, and the examination began. Why, she was asked, did she torment the girls?

"I don't torment them," she replied.

"Who doth?"

"I do not know. How should I know?"

Indignant, Martha argued that it would be impossible for her to do the devil's work. "I am a gospel woman," she proclaimed.

"She's a gospel witch!" shouted one of the girls in response. As if on cue, the rest of the pack cried out too: "Gospel witch! Gospel witch!"

One of the girls, little Ann Putnam, spoke of having seen Martha Cory praying to the devil. "Nay," the accused answered. "We must not believe these distracted children." It was the most reasonable statement of the entire hearing, but few cared to listen. Instead, the girls started imitating every move Martha made, as if she was compelling them to do it. If she shifted her feet, so did they. If she bit her lip, they drew blood doing the same. Then, looking out the window of the meetinghouse, the children announced that an assembly of witches had gathered just outside. "Don't you hear the drumbeat?" said one. "Why don't you go, gospel witch? Why don't you go too?"

While Martha Cory's spectral shape might have gone out to join the gang, the rest of her was sent away to await trial. She was joined in jail by Sarah Good's five-year-old daughter, Dorcas, whose shape had apparently been running around like a vicious little dog and biting the ankles of the girls who had dared to expose her mother. Others were rounded up as well, including seventy-one-year-old Rebecca Nurse and her sisters Sarah Cloyce and Mary Esty. When Rebecca Nurse, housebound and bedridden, heard she had been named, she maintained her Puritan stoicism. "Well, if it be so," she said, "the will of the Lord be done." Then, after sitting silently for a moment, as if in a trance, she said, "As to this thing I am innocent as a child unborn, but surely, what sin hath God found in me unrepented of that He could lay such an affliction on me in my old age?"

At her examination, Rebecca Nurse made a pitiful sight. "I can say before my eternal father that I am innocent," she pleaded before the judges, "and God will clear my innocence." Even the normally stern and unforgiving magistrates seemed moved by the aged and infirm woman before them. "Here is never a one in the assembly but deserves it," said Magistrate John Hawthorne gently. "But if you be guilty, I pray God discover you." The testimony then began, and no longer was it just young hysterical girls pointing fingers and swooning. Henry Kenny reported that when Rebecca came to his house he was "seized with an amazed condition." Edward Putnam said that she had tormented his niece in his presence. To this Rebecca responded: "I am innocent and clear and have not been able to get out of doors these eight–nine days. I never afflicted no child, no, never in my life." Hawthorne seemed moved by this, and wondered aloud if the accusers might be mistaken. Perhaps he forgot that, bedridden as she may have been, Rebecca Nurse still had her "shape" to do her bidding. In any event, the girls' frenzied response to his wavering quickly settled any doubts.

Out of the crowd, Ann Putnam's mother yelled, "Did you not bring the Black Man with you? Did you not bid me tempt God and die? How often have you eat and drunk to your own damnation?" Hawthorne turned to Rebecca for a response. "What do you say to them?" he demanded. She probably never heard him in the din of the room. "Oh, Lord help me!" she cried, spreading her hands helplessly. The girls did the same. If this wasn't proof enough of witchcraft, her failure to weep cinched it. Everyone knew witches could not cry. "It is awful for all to see these agonies," said the magistrate, pointing to the girls, "and you an old professor thus charged with the devil by the effects of it, and yet to see you stand with dry eyes when there are so many wet."

"You do not know my heart," Rebecca answered quietly.

"You would do well if you were guilty to confess," said the judge. "Give glory to God."

This was asking too much. Rebecca Nurse was no Tituba. "Would you have me belie myself?" she asked. With that, Hawthorne read the most serious charge against her. Ann Putnam had sworn that a succession of dead children had come to her in their burial sheets and told her that it was Witch Nurse who had killed them.

"What think you of this?" Hawthorne asked.

"I cannot tell what to think," she responded, still steadfast. "The devil may appear in my shape." After several more questions, Rebecca was led away to make room for the Lecture Day sermon to be held that afternoon in the meetinghouse.

It was an edifying sermon. Satan had come to Salem because he worked most effectively through the righteous, pronounced Reverend Deodat Lawson. In carrying out his purposes, he needed human mediums; these he sought among "the adopted children of God . . . for it is certain that he never works more like the Prince of Darkness than when he looks most like an angel of light." This answered that nagging question as to why seemingly good people like

Martha Cory and Rebecca Nurse could embrace such evil. Satan wanted to undermine the entire community through its most devout and pious members. "You are therefore to be deeply humbled and set down in the dust," cried Lawson, "considering the signal hand of God in singling out this place, this poor village, for the first scene of Satan's tyranny, and to make it . . . the rendezvous of devils. . . . I thus am commanded to call and cry . . . to you. Arm! Arm! Arm! Let us admit no parley, give no quarter. Prayer is the most proper and potent antidote against the old Serpent's venomous operations. . . . What therefore I say unto one, I say unto all—Pray! Pray! Pray!"

Reverend Lawson may have been preaching to the converted, but there were still a few in Salem who believed the wrong people were being targeted. If anyone was doing the devil's work, it was those godforsaken girls making all the accusations. "They should be at the whipping-post!" exclaimed John Proctor. "If they are let alone we should all be devils and witches." There was a simple solution, he said: "Hang them! Hang them!" But what would be considered good common sense today was blasphemy in the Salem Village of 1692, and John Proctor would pay dearly for making such a suggestion. He and his wife Elizabeth were both called out, with John Proctor named "a most dreadful wizard" by the girls he sought to expose.

The arrest of John and Elizabeth Proctor was followed by a brief lapse into sanity, however. The Proctors' servant, Mary Warren, had been among the girls pointing their fingers at the witches all around them. But when the Proctors, the people closest to her, were swept up in the frenzy, Mary had a conversion of sorts. She distanced herself from the howling pack of girls who were causing such misery. Her betrayal was costly, as Mary went from accuser to accused.

"You were a little while ago an affected person; now you are an afflicter," said John Hawthorne when Mary was brought before him after her arrest. "How comes this to pass?" The girl was almost speechless with fear, but believed she was on the path of righteousness in renouncing her false ways. "I look to God," she quavered, "and I take it to be a mercy of God."

"What!" Hawthorne shouted. "Do you take it as a mercy to afflict others?"

Mary Warren saw her former companions' contrived agony for what it was—she had been part of the troupe, after all—but the situation in which she found herself now was becoming untenable. A stint in jail with the other witches she had helped identify only made it more so. It didn't take long for Mary Warren to recognize where safety lay. She was no martyr. In front of the judges, Mary pretended to fight off the shape of Elizabeth Proctor. "I will tell! I will tell!" she howled. "Thou wicked creature, it is you that stopped my mouth. . . . It shall be known, thou witch. Hast thou undone me body and soul?" Soon after this catharsis, the judges declared Mary Warren free from sin and allowed her to rejoin the girls in their place of honor. And though she never again took a leading role in their hysterical demonstrations, neither did she ever again lapse into what Marion Starkey calls "the dangerous, unbelievable world of reality."

With Mary Warren now restored to the ranks of the accusers, the business of identifying witches could resume once again. And indeed it did—with a vengeance. Three had been indicted with Mary Warren: Martha Cory's slow-witted husband, Giles, Bridget Bishop, a tavern keeper who offended Puritan sensibilities with her flashy way of dressing, and Abigail Hobbs, a wild child from the adjacent town of Topsfield. Abigail had always unsettled people with her peculiar behavior, like walking alone through the woods at night. One of her accusers claimed she was unafraid because "she had sold herself body and soul to ye old boy [the devil]." Perhaps unbalanced to begin with, Abigail pulled a Tituba and eagerly admitted to everything, including the names of nine other witches who had attended unholy sabbaths with her in Reverend Parris's own pasture. She also confessed to murder in a private session with the judges.

"Were they men or women you killed?"

"They were both boys and girls," came the answer.

"Was you angry with them yourself?"

"Yes, though I don't know why now."

The judges seem to have forgotten to ask whom specifically Abigail Hobbs had murdered, but the day after her alarming testimony an unprecedented nine arrest warrants were sworn out—two of them for her parents.

It was beginning to seem that almost the entire village of Salem was part of a wicked coven, yet there were still many more arrests to come. And the contagion was spreading. In Maine, the grand wizard of all the witches was identified: George Burroughs, who happened to have been Salem Village's minister a decade before, was dragged away from his dinner table, leaving behind his third wife and a large brood of children. Mrs. Burroughs was familiar enough with the law to know that all the property and goods of a convicted witch would be forfeit, and wasted no time in selling them off herself. Loyal to the end, she took the one daughter she had with Burroughs and moved away, leaving all her stepchildren to fend for themselves.

Given his status as a minister, Burroughs was well provided for in Salem, though he was still stripped naked before a panel of jurors looking for the telltale "devil's mark" on his body. A special session of the magistrates that included Massachusetts deputy governor William Stoughton, a Harvard graduate, was called to conduct a hearing. During the examination Burroughs was instructed to face the gang of girls, most of whom had been babies or young children when he had served as Salem's minister. They immediately launched into their now familiar (except to Burroughs) routine. The minister showed no evidence of the "devil's mark," but the girls' reaction to him was damning evidence indeed, as was the subsequent testimony that he—or rather his shape—was a murderer.

The judges were informed that whenever a soldier died during the Indian trouble in "the eastward country," where Burroughs lived, it wasn't the Indians who did the killing. It was the minister standing before them. Not surprisingly, Burroughs had no answer for this or any of the other accusations. "It is amazing and humbling evidence," he stammered at one point. "But I understand nothing of it." The judges did understand, though. The man was clearly a wizard and was sent to prison to await trial with all the rest. There would be no more cushy accommodations for this spawn of Satan. And just to be sure that neither he nor his fellow prisoners practiced their black arts from their cells, Massachusetts Governor William

Phips ordered them all chained, with the added cost of such confinement billed to the witches.

George Burroughs, supreme wizard though he may have been, was still relatively inconsequential next to John Alden. This son of John and Priscilla Alden, whose romance in the early days of the Plymouth Colony was later immortalized by Longfellow, was identified as Tituba's elusive "tall man." Curiously, he had never met the girls who accused him—"the Salem wenches," as he came to call them. But they had certainly heard of him, for Alden had earned an impressive reputation as a sea captain and soldier fighting in the wars against the Indians. Because the girls had never seen Alden before, only his shape, they had a little trouble identifying him when he came into the courtroom from Boston. They pointed to the wrong man, in fact, but the judges helped clarify the situation and the accusers redirected their fingers. "There stands Alden," shouted one of them. "A bold fellow with his hat on before the judges. He sells powder shot to the Indians and French and lies with Indian squaws and has Indian papooses." All this on top of being the devilish "tall man" of Boston.

The girls gave extra-strong performances befitting such a dangerous man. When he was ordered to look at them, they screamed that he was hurting them. Alden was indignant. "Just why do your honors suppose I have no better things to do than come to Salem to afflict these persons that I never knew or saw before?" he asked the judges. It was a good question, and Alden followed it with an even better one: "What's the reason *you* don't fall down when I look at you? Can you give me one?" Later, before being led away to jail, he gave vent to his frustration. "I wonder at God in suffering these creatures to accuse innocent people." Other than those charged, few shared the sentiment.

Most citizens were grateful to the girls for helping deliver them from the evil infestation and eagerly anticipated the upcoming trials that would rid Salem of such wickedness once and for all. Any hope the accused may have had that justice would prevail when their cases came before a new panel of trial judges—most of whom were not from Salem—was quickly dashed. As far as the court was concerned, the facts were already established during the pretrial examinations. "There was little occasion to prove witchcraft," noted Cotton Mather, "this being evident and notorious to all beholders."

Bridget Bishop, the flashy tavern keeper, was among the first to stand trial. She didn't stand a chance. For starters, a panel of female examiners had discovered a "witch's tet" between "ye pudendum and anus." She also visited witnesses in various shapes, like a black pig, and once with the body of a monkey, the feet of a cock, and the face of a man. There was other horrifying evidence as well, and Bridget Bishop was duly condemned and hanged from the branches of a great oak tree.

Rebecca Nurse was next. The jury seemed to have the same reservations about her guilt as Magistrate John Hawthorne initially had several months before at the preliminary examination. She just didn't seem like witch material. The jury's doubts were fueled by the recommendations of a group of ministers who had been consulted after Bridget Bishop's trial. They established some new, more enlightened standards of judgment, recommending, for instance, that "exquisite caution" be taken in considering spectral evidence, and that conviction should be based on something "more considerable than the accused persons being represented by a spectre unto the afflicted." They also urged "an exceeding tenderness" toward "persons formerly of an unblemished reputation."

Rebecca Nurse certainly met the new guidelines; her piety and goodness were attested to by more than a score of respectable citizens. The jury was convinced and voted for acquittal. The girls, however, were not pleased with the verdict. It meant their witch radars were being called into question. Their displeasure was made known by furious roars and convulsions, and the spectacle was enough to give the judges pause. Perhaps the jury had made a mistake. "I will not impose on the jury," announced Chief Justice William Stoughton, "but I must ask you if you considered one statement made by the prisoner. When Deliverance Hobbs was brought into court to testify, the prisoner, turning her head to her, said, 'What, do you bring her? She is one of us.' Has the jury weighed the implications of this statement?" As a matter of fact, they had not, mainly because none of them remembered hearing it. The only thing to do now was to ask the defendant to explain herself. Only problem was, with the continuing uproar of the girls, the buzz in the courtroom, and the fact that Rebecca Nurse was practically deaf, she failed to hear the question directed at her. Oblivious, she stared straight ahead. This was eerie-enough behavior in the minds of the jury, already becoming more and more convinced by the agonized reaction of the girls that they had made a terrible misjudgment in acquitting this strange woman. It was now apparent to the panel that the defendant's "one of us" reference had been an involuntary admission of guilt. Accordingly, they revised their verdict.

Now that she had been condemned under the law, the leaders of her church made sure she was condemned by God as well. In a formal ceremony, into which the old lady had to be carried, they excommunicated her, thereby insuring her soul's eternal damnation. Yet while the rest of the community abandoned her to her fate, her children did not. They appealed to the governor, laying before him all the evidence of their mother's innocence. Phips took pity on them and signed a reprieve. Rebecca Nurse had been saved from a hideous fate, or so it seemed. After signing the reprieve, Phips received some distressing news from Salem. Rebecca Nurse had sent her shape to kill her accusers, and some were already on the verge of death. Did the governor really want to spare the source of such wickedness? the people wanted to know. Could he live with the deaths of these innocent children while this guilty witch went free? The answer was no, and the reprieve was canceled. Rebecca Nurse would hang after all.

The execution took place on Saturday, July 19, 1692. Five women were hanged that day, including Sarah Good, the feisty pipe smoker who had been among the first accused. She did not go quietly. The attending minister appealed to her to save her soul and confess, reminding her that she knew very well that she was a witch. "You're a liar!" Sarah shouted back. "I am no more a witch than you are a wizard! If you take my life away, God will give you blood to drink."

After the corpses were taken down from the gallows, they were buried in a shallow grave nearby. But the children of Rebecca Nurse dug up her body later that night and took it home for a dignified, though secret, burial. It was their final act of kindness to the mother they loved and fought in vain to save.

Seeing the fate of their fellow defendants convinced some of the accused that there would be no mercy when their time came. They had to act immediately to save themselves. Some, like John Alden, managed to escape from prison and flee Massachusetts. Mostly poor and without resources, many were quickly recaptured. John Proctor tried to save his life by addressing a petition to five ministers in Boston on behalf of himself and the others. In it he appealed to them to use their influence and have the trials moved to Boston, or, if that were not possible, at least to substitute other judges, the present incumbents "having condemned us already before our trials." Proctor also advised the ministers that "full and free confessions" were being wrung out of the male suspects by torture. "These actions," he wrote, "are very like the Papish cruelties." This odious comparison to the Church of Rome would be enough to rile any good Puritan, and resulted in several of Proctor's relatives being hauled in as witches.

The petition did get the interest of some powerful people in Boston, though. Increase Mather, the president of Harvard (and Cotton's father), called a conference of several ministers in Cambridge to discuss the pesky question of spectral evidence. His proposition was, "Whether the devil may not sometimes have permission to represent an innocent person as tormenting such as are under diabolic manifestation." The ministers, pondering the question with all their collective wisdom, agreed that the shapes of innocent people might be manipulated by Satan, but "that such things are rare and extraordinary." Increase Mather traveled to Salem to check out the witch trials for himself, though the fate of his petitioner John Proctor was not his primary interest. George Burroughs was. "Had I been one of his judges," Mather later noted of the Burroughs trial, "I could not have acquitted him." And neither could the jury. Burroughs and Proctor, along with three others, were sentenced to hang.

The condemned were placed in a cart and driven through the streets of Salem Village to the place of execution. All eyes were on

Burroughs as he stood on the scaffold and spoke his final words. They were so simple and moving that some in the gathered crowd wept. Burroughs concluded by reciting the Lord's Prayer, which caused a loud murmuring among the assembled. Everyone knew a witch wasn't supposed to be able to say this prayer. Was an innocent man about to hang? Responding to the crowd's mounting agitation, one of the accusers yelled out that she had seen the devil at the condemned man's shoulder whispering the prayer into his ear. This would have explained it, except the girl apparently forgot that the devil couldn't say the prayer either. The crowd surged forward as Burroughs mounted the ladder, almost as if they were preparing to seize him away.

Fortunately, Cotton Mather, the authority on the ways of the devil, was there to save the day. He reminded the people that Satan is never so subtle than when he appears like an angel of light. Besides, Burroughs was not even an ordained minister. Though the point was irrelevant, and Reverend Mather failed to explain why the condemned wizard was able to recite the Lord's Prayer, his words quieted the crowd and the execution proceeded. Still, George Burroughs haunted the people for years to come, and Cotton Mather later wrote that he wished he had never heard "the first letters of his name."

The executions of Burroughs and the rest were followed a month later by eight more, including those of Martha Cory, whose husband Giles had been pressed to death three days earlier for having "stood mute" in the face of the charges against him, and Rebecca Nurse's younger sister, Mary Esty. After her condemnation, Mary Esty made a final appeal to the judges: "I petition to your Honours, not for my own life, for I know I must die, and my appointed time is set, but . . . that no more Innocent Blood be shed, which undoubtedly cannot be avoided in the way and course you go in. I question not by your Honours do to the utmost of your pains in the discovery and detection of witchcraft and witches; but by my own Innocency I know you are in the wrong way."

Mary Esty and the others executed with her on September 22 were the last to die in the insanity that swept over Massachusetts in

1692. Others would be tried, but reason was slowly returning. Spectral evidence was abolished as a basis for accusation, resulting in mass acquittals, and Governor Phips freed the remaining suspects, numbering more than a hundred, the following spring. "Such a jail delivery," wrote Thomas Hutchison, "has never been known in New England." Freedom came at a price, though. The released prisoners were expected to pay all the expenses of their incarceration, and those who couldn't remained behind bars.

Gradually, life in Salem returned to some semblance of normalcy. "The afflicted ones" quietly withdrew from the deadly spectacle they had created. Some repented; others reportedly went on to lead lives of ill repute. Farms neglected for much of that unquiet year were sown again, while severed relationships and damaged reputations were slowly restored. Yet few could ever forget what had happened. "We walked in clouds and could not see our way," wrote Reverend John Hale. "And we have most cause to be humbled for error . . . which cannot be retrieved."

2

The Man Who Would Be Queen

Prior to the Revolution, most Americans were still loyal to the British crown. But Edward Hyde, Lord Cornbury, the royal governor of New York, seems to have taken his allegiance to the queen a bit to the extreme. By some accounts, Lord Cornbury, who governed from 1702 to 1708, believed that since he was the colonial representative of Queen Anne (Britain's monarch of the time), he bloody well ought to look like her. The result wasn't pretty. A portrait on display at the New-York Historical Society identified as Lord Cornbury shows him dressed in all his female finery. The image of majesty is marred somewhat by the five o'clock shadow, but otherwise the governor looks every bit the queen.[1]

In 1786, Sylvester Douglas, Lord Glenbervie, recorded in his diary a conversation he had with Horace Walpole, son of the great English statesman Robert Walpole, a contemporary of Cornbury's.

1. It should be noted that in her book *The Lord Cornbury Scandal: The Politics of Reputation in British America,* Patricia U. Bonomi offers convincing though not conclusive evidence that the portrait is actually of a woman, and that Lord Cornbury was the victim of a political smear campaign.

"[Lord Cornbury] was a clever man," Glenbervie was told. "His great insanity was dressing himself as a woman. [Walpole] says that when Governor in America he opened the Assembly dressed in that fashion. When some of those about him remonstrated, his reply was, 'You are very stupid not to see the propriety of it. In this place and particularly on this occasion I represent a woman and ought in all respects to represent her as faithfully as I can.'"

Some of Lord Cornbury's contemporaries failed to appreciate his extravagant displays of loyalty. "Tis said he is wholly addicted to his pleasure . . . ," Robert Livingston wrote to London in 1707. "His dressing in womens Cloths Commonly [every?] morning is so unaccountable that if hundred[s] of spectators did not daily see him it would be incredible." New York catechist Elias Neau had something similar to say: "My Lord Cornbury has and does still make use of an unfortunate Custom of dressing himself in Womens Cloaths and of exposing himself in the Garb upon the Ramparts to the view of the public; in that dress he draws a World of Spectators about him and consequently as many Censures, especially for exposing himself in such a manner all the great Holy days and even in an hour or two after going to the Communion."

There are no surviving accounts of what Queen Anne thought of Lord Cornbury's homage to her, but given that they were both rather homely, as well as first cousins, she may have been struck by the resemblance—and not especially flattered.

3

Cellar Dweller

"Give me liberty or give me death," Patrick Henry famously demanded on the eve of the American Revolution. His wife, Sarah, might have said the same thing, since she was confined in the basement of the couple's Virginia estate for almost four years. Not that the accommodations were all that bad. "It was an English-style basement," insists Edith Poindexter, an historian with the Patrick Henry Memorial Foundation. That means it was partially aboveground, letting in plenty of light and fresh air. "Warm in the winter and cool in the summer," says Poindexter. Yet it wasn't quite the Ritz, especially when Sarah found herself in a straitjacket. What had driven the poor woman to such an unfortunate state?

It seems her children were part of the problem. She had five of them, starting when she was seventeen, but after the birth of the sixth in 1771, Sarah lost it. She exhibited what Patrick Henry biographer Robert Meade calls "a strange antipathy" toward her children. It might be called postpartum psychosis today. Sarah's "antipathy" became so dangerous that she had to be kept away from the kids. But Patrick Henry was a loyal husband and knew how horrific insane asylums of the day could be. So, the family lived upstairs while Sarah ranted and raved below. It was in this sad state that she died in 1775 at age thirty-seven.

4

Explorer Off Course

Things were not going very well for Meriwether Lewis after he returned from his epic trek across the American continent with William Clark in 1806. Sure, he was hailed as a hero by President Jefferson and the rest of the nation, but he was drinking too much, suffering from malaria and bouts of mental illness, and, despite his superstar status, unable to find himself a wife.

"I am now *a perfect widower with rispect [sic] to love,*" he wrote his friend Mahlon Dickerson after one failed courtship. "I feel all that restlessness, that inquietude, that certain indiscribable [*sic*] something common to old bachelors [he was thirty-four at the time], I cannot avoid thinking, my dear fellow, proceeds from that *void in our hearts,* which might, or ought to be better filled. Whence it comes I know not, but certain it is, that I never felt less like a heroe [*sic*] than at the present moment. What may be my next adventure God knows, but on this I am determined, *to get a wife.*" Alas, he never did.

Meanwhile, Jefferson, to reward Lewis for his great service to the country, appointed him governor of the Territory of Louisiana. But the president was also getting a little annoyed with his old friend, waiting impatiently for the publication of the journals Lewis meticulously kept during his adventure. With the wealth of information they contained about the previously unexplored West—scientific, geographic, and commercial—the published work would help Jefferson justify his faith in Lewis and the enormous sums of government money spent on the expedition. "We have no tidings yet on the forwardness of your printer," the president wrote. "I hope the first part [of the proposed three-volume set] will not be delayed much longer." Lewis didn't bother to answer, perhaps because he had done nothing to prepare his journals for printing. "It is astonishing we get not one word from him," Jefferson said to Secretary of War Henry Dearborn.

Dearborn's successor at the War Department, William Eustus, was less concerned about the journals than he was about the bills Lewis was sending. Under the auspices of the St. Louis Missouri River Fur Company, which Governor Lewis had organized in 1808 (and perhaps joined as a silent partner), a large military expedition was gathered, at government expense. The plan was to travel up the Missouri River and return an Indian chief named Big White—whom Lewis had taken with him to Washington after his travels—back to his people. After dropping off Big White, the expedition would set up a fur trading post at the mouth of the Yellowstone River and there enjoy a monopoly granted by Lewis.

The only snag was, Secretary of War Eustus wasn't buying it. He rejected a number of Lewis's claims for reimbursement for the project, writing, "As the object and destination of the Force [beyond getting Big White home] is unknown, and more especially as it combines commercial purposes, so it cannot be considered as having the sanction of the Government of the United States, or that they are responsible for the consequences." In other words, Lewis was stuck with the bill. This was not good news for the governor, who was already in debt and now adding opium and morphine to his malaria medicine. Furthermore, his champion and protector, Thomas Jefferson, was no longer in office and could not help him. Besides, Jefferson was still nagging him about the journals, which Lewis had *still* not prepared for publication.

"I am very often applied to know when your work will begin to appear," the former president wrote in 1809 from his retirement at Monticello, "and I have so long promised copies to my literary correspondents in France, that I am almost bankrupt in their eyes. I shall be very happy to receive from yourself information of your expectations on this subject. Every body is impatient for it." Lewis, once again, failed to reply. Instead, he decided to go to Washington and justify the St. Louis Missouri River Fur Company to President Madison.

Lewis had been stung by Secretary Eustus's letter rejecting his claims, believing it implicated him in some dirty dealing. "The feelings it excites are truly painful . . . ," he wrote Eustus. "I have been informed Representations have been made against me." What these representations might have been is unclear, though it appears a story was circulating that the St. Louis Missouri River Fur Company intended to go outside of U.S. territory, and that Lewis was seeking to establish a new country for himself, not unlike Aaron Burr.[1] "Be assured, Sir, that my Country can never make 'A Burr' of me—She may reduce me to Poverty; but she can never sever my Attachment from her." Sadly, Lewis never got to prove his patriotism, or at least justify his expenses, for the journey to Washington was his last voyage.

Twice he tried to kill himself on the boat carrying him down the Mississippi River. When the boat reached Chickasaw Bluffs (now Memphis, Tennessee), the commander of Fort Pickering, Captain Gilbert Russell, was informed of Lewis's suicide attempts and, as he later wrote, "resolved at once to take possession of him and his papers, and detain them there until he recovered, or some friend might arrive in whose hands he could depart in safety." For days Lewis ranted disjointedly, drank heavily, and indulged in his narcotic "medicines," but after about a week Captain Russell reported "all symptoms of derangement disappeared and he was completely in his senses," though "considerably reduced and debilitated." He was also ashamed,

1. See Part VI, Chapter 2.

telling Russell that he was resolved "never to drink any more spirits or use snuff again." Several weeks later, Lewis seemed fit enough to resume travel. But it was an illusion. Before long he was boozing again and "appeared at times deranged in mind," as Major James Neelly, who accompanied Lewis, later reported to Jefferson.

While traveling through Tennessee, Lewis came to Grinder's Inn, about seventy miles from Nashville, and took a room. Mrs. Grinder, the proprietress, served him a meal during which, she said, he started "speaking to himself in a violent manner," his face flushed, "as if it had come on him in a fit." Later that night he started pacing in his room, back and forth for hours, talking to himself, Mrs. Grinder said, "like a lawyer." Then he took a pistol and shot himself in the head. The bullet only grazed him, though, so Lewis took another pistol and shot himself in the chest. This time the bullet traveled down through his torso, emerging low on his back. Surviving this shot as well, Lewis staggered to the door of his room and called out for Mrs. Grinder. "Oh Madam!" he cried. "Give me some water, and heal my wounds." He then went outside briefly before making his way back to his room.

Terrified, Mrs. Grinder sent her children to find the servants accompanying Lewis on the trip. When they got to his room they found him cutting himself from head to foot with a razor. "I have done the business, my good servant, give me some water," he said before showing them the second wound. "I am no coward," he continued, "but I am so strong, [it is] so hard to die." He then begged the servants to shoot him in the head and put him out of his pain. They refused, but just after sunrise that morning the great explorer finally expired from the wounds he had inflicted upon himself.

5

The Case of the Cuckolded Congressman

"Of course I intended to kill him. . . . He deserved it."

—Representative Daniel Sickles

Murder has always been a frequent-enough occurrence in the nation's capital that a single killing does not ordinarily attract much attention—unless, of course, it involves a cuckolded congressman, a famous composer's son, and an attempted cover-up by the president of the United States. Then, almost everyone will sit up and take notice, just as they did in February 1859, when Representative Daniel Sickles of New York killed his friend Philip Barton Key, son of "Star-Spangled Banner" composer Francis Scott Key, right in front of the White House. Sickles did the deed in broad daylight, with a number of witnesses present, after learning that Key had been sleeping with his wife. But with a little help from President James Buchanan, and the then-novel defense of temporary insanity, he got away with it.

By most accounts, Key and Sickles's wife, Teresa, conducted their affair with all the discretion of mating elephants. Everyone in Washington seemed to know about it, except Daniel Sickles. Key rented a house near Lafayette Square, where the Sickleses lived, so they could get together whenever they felt like it, which might be as often as three times a day. From the park in front of Teresa's home, Key would wave his handkerchief when he wanted her to come out and play. "Here comes Disgrace to see Disgust," servants in the Sickles household would mutter whenever they saw the familiar sight.

The adulterous couple had been sniffing each other out for some time before their affair actually began. Key, Washington's district attorney (a post Sickles helped him retain after the Buchanan administration came to power in 1857), often escorted Teresa to social events when her husband was too busy with congressional duties—or other women—to accompany her. A widower with four children, Key was pushing forty, almost twice Teresa's age. He claimed to be like a father to his friend's wife, regarding her, as he told Representative John Haskin of New York, "as a young person who stood towards him in the relation of a child." He spoke of how "childlike she was," Haskin later testified, "and how innocent." Many people who saw them out on the town got an entirely different impression, though. Key's attentions seemed far more amorous than paternal, and Teresa's response to them was hardly one of sweet innocence.

Gossip about an improper relationship between his wife and his friend filtered back to Sickles, but Key vigorously denied what he called "the vile calumnies" against him. "It is the highest affront which can be offered to me," Key declared, "and whoever asserts it must meet me on the field of honor, at the very point of the pistol." Though Sickles accepted Key's denials, he was still suspicious—just not suspicious enough, as it turned out.

Sickles seemed to miss all the signs of the affair that commenced on a sofa in his own parlor, while Key grew ever bolder, ignoring warnings that violence could result if the affair was ever discovered. "I am prepared for any emergency," he said defiantly, patting the left breast pocket of his coat where, it was implied, he kept a weapon. Teresa herself maintained a façade of respectability, despite all the chatter swirling around her increasingly brazen trysts with Key. Virginia Clay, one of Washington's leading hostesses, recalled seeing

Teresa at a reception during this time and never forgot the "innocent" impression she made: "She was so young and fair, at most not more than twenty-two years of age, and so naive, that none of the party of which I was one was willing to harbour a belief in the rumours which were then in circulation." But all the gossip was true, and Sickles couldn't stay oblivious forever.

The congressman's cocoon of ignorance finally came apart when he received an anonymous letter advising him of his wife's infidelity. "I do assure you, [Key] has as much the use of your wife as you have," the letter stated. And on the night he received it, family friend Octavia Ridgely recalled, "Mr. Sickles had a very wild, distracted look." He wasn't fully convinced, however, until further investigation proved the anonymous letter writer's allegations all true. This "unmanned him completely," said House clerk George Wooldridge, who had verified the facts himself. The congressman's "exhibitions of grief" were so violent, Wooldridge said, that the two men had to retreat to a private room near the House chamber to avoid a public spectacle.

An ugly scene ensued when Sickles went home and confronted Teresa with what he knew. That same evening she wrote a long, detailed confession. Whether it was dictated by Sickles or written in her own words is unknown, but the document was quite explicit for the prudish era in which it was written—a time when sex and nudity were rarely mentioned, even in private. "I did what is usual for a wicked woman to do," Teresa wrote. That night she slept on the floor of her friend Octavia's room, while Sickles stayed in the bedroom. Servants later reported loud sobs coming from both bedrooms well into the night.

Key, unaware that the jig was up, showed up at Lafayette Park the next morning looking for a little action. When Teresa failed to respond to his signals, he went away, but he came back a little while later, again waving his hankie in vain. On his third trip to the park that day, Key was greeted by the Sickleses' dog, Dandy, who bounded out of the house upon seeing him. Key made a show of playing with the dog, waving his handkerchief all the while. Still no Teresa. Sickles, though, had seen the less than subtle display out front. "That villain has just passed my house," he stormed, telling Wooldridge and another visitor, Samuel Butterworth, that he had "seen the scoundrel making signals." Butterworth tried to placate him, arguing that a public scene with Key would only alert people to the affair. But Sickles brushed him off, snorting that the whole town knew of it anyway. He was right about that. Butterworth persisted, however, telling him to keep calm "and look this matter square in the face. If there be a possibility of keeping the certain knowledge of this crime from the public, you must do nothing to destroy that possibility. You may be mistaken in your belief that it is known to the whole city." By now, though, Sickles was well past reason and hardly concerned about appearances.

Arming himself with two derringers, he rushed out of the house and into the park. "Key, you scoundrel," Sickles shouted, "you have dishonored my house—you must die!" As Key thrust his hand inside his coat, Sickles fired. But the shot only grazed him. "Murder!" Key cried. Sickles raised his arm to fire again, but Key seized him by the collar of his coat. The gun fell during the struggle, but Sickles was able to break away and draw his other gun. "Don't murder me," Key pleaded as he backed away, tossing a pair of opera glasses at his assailant in a desperate bid to ward him off. Sickles fired again. This time the bullet penetrated, striking Key near the groin. "I'm shot," he gasped, pleading again for his life while falling against a tree. Sickles approached him and pulled the trigger again. It misfired. "Murder! Murder!" Key screamed in desperation as Sickles reloaded his weapon, put it close to his ex-friend's chest, and fired again. This proved to be the fatal one, but Sickles wasn't through yet. He put the gun to Key's head, but it misfired again. "Is the scoundrel dead?" he asked Thomas Martin, a Treasury Department clerk who witnessed the crime. "He violated my bed," Sickles said over and over while Key was taken to a nearby building, where he died shortly after.

Sickles turned himself in immediately after the murder. At about the same time, President Buchanan was receiving the news from a young page, J. H. W. Bonitz, who had witnessed the killing. After hearing the report, Buchanan told a bold lie intended to help his old pal Sickles. He warned Bonitz to get out of town quickly. Otherwise, he would be jailed and held without bond as a witness to the crime. Perhaps the president was unaware that plenty of other people had seen Sickles kill Key, but his tactic worked on Bonitz at least. The page took some money offered by Buchanan, packed his bags, and left Washington immediately.

Before being taken away to jail, Sickles was permitted a brief return home. A large crowd was gathered outside. Inside, Teresa was lying on a bedroom floor stricken with despair. Coming upon her, Sickles uttered one terse sentence: "I've killed him." Then he left. News of the murder, meanwhile, was spreading all over the city. Ridiculous rumors abounded. Some said Teresa was pregnant with Key's child, others that the congressman had tried to kill himself after killing Key. The truth was juicy enough, though, and the story soon dominated the front pages of the nation's newspapers. Editorials on the greater significance of the murder flourished. It reflected the moral decay of society in general, it was said, as well as an ever-increasing lawlessness, especially in Washington. "Can any of us be surprised?" asked *Harper's Weekly*. "When the newspapers declare, and private testimony asserts, that no capital in the world is more rotten than ours, is it remarkable that a wife should be faithless and her husband shoot her seducer?"

Sickles, indicted for murder, assembled a nineteenth-century version of "The Dream Team"—eight of some of the nation's best lawyers—to defend him. The prosecution, on the other hand, was hamstrung from the beginning. Robert Ould, who was appointed by President Buchanan to replace Key as Washington's district attorney, was an inexperienced trial lawyer and a poor choice to handle such an explosive case, especially by himself. Yet despite pleas from the Key family, the president—still doing his darnedest to help Sickles—refused to assign Ould an experienced assistant. So Key's family and friends decided to hire an assistant themselves. It was a futile gesture.

The trial, which began on April 4, 1859, and ended three weeks later, was a spectacle. The courtroom was crammed with curious spectators—all men, as the case was considered too scandalous for the tender sensibilities of women—while those left outside resorted to climbing windows to get a peek at the proceedings. The case itself should have been simple. Sickles, whom the prosecutor described as "a walking magazine" who stalked and killed Key in an act of "remorseless revenge," had done the deed in the wide open, with plenty of people watching. But the defense complicated the issue by arguing that Congressman Daniel Sickles had been temporarily insane at the time, and that Key's defilement of his wife had made him so. While the insanity defense had been well established in American jurisprudence, there was no precedent at all for what the defense called an "irresistible impulse." Sickles, the defense declared, had acted "in a transport of frenzy" that was ultimately fleeting in nature. "Was Mr. Sickles, at the time of the homicide, such a creature of instinct, of impulse, that he could not resist, but was carried forward, like a mere machine, to the consummation of that so-called tragedy?" asked defense attorney John Graham. The jury thought the answer was yes and acquitted Sickles after deliberating for little more than an hour.

Jury foreman Reason Arnold later expressed gratitude that he had "lived to render such a verdict," adding that he "hoped and believed the great God would acquit as the jury has done." Another juror, William Hopkins, also felt the homicide was justified, punctuating his opinion by saying he "would not for himself have been satisfied with a derringer or revolver, but would have brought a howitzer to bear on the seducer." The *New York Times* summarized the temper of the jurors, which mirrored that of the public at large, reporting that "they gave their verdict on the principle that, in the absence of any adequate punishment by law for adultery, the man who violates the honor and desolates the home of his neighbor, does so at the peril of his life, and if he falls by the outraged husband's hands he deserves his doom."

The verdict was followed by spontaneous celebrations in the streets of Washington, including an impromptu parade down Pennsylvania Avenue led by the U.S. Marine Band. And if Daniel Sickles wasn't quite acclaimed as a hero, he was certainly absolved of the crime in the minds of most. The congressman had taken appropriate action after being grievously wronged, and the public was prepared to welcome him back to his proper place in society.

But then Sickles did the unthinkable. He reconciled with Teresa.

All the goodwill that had been generated suddenly evaporated, and a furious uproar ensued. "If Mrs. Sickles was herself guilty before the death of Key she is guilty still, and if one can be forgiven now, Key ought to have been forgiven in February," wrote the Washington correspondent of the Philadelphia *Press,* again reflecting the general public sentiment. "All the feeling for poor Key has been revived," the writer continued, "all the grief suppressed by the verdict in favor of Mr. Sickles has been called forth anew by the forgiveness extended by Mr. Sickles to his wife, and Heaven knows where it will end." The congressman's friends "have been completely disgusted by the announcement of the fact that he has taken the polluted female again to his bosom as a wife," reported the Sunday *Atlas,* while the Washington *Evening Star* noted that Sickles had now shown "his true colors" and "opened the eyes of the dupes of his late melodramatic programme, so as to enable them to realize the facts that the aspersions showered upon Key, for [Sickles's] benefit, were . . . baseless." The *Star* concluded by stating that "this *denouement* . . . will do some good, we trust, in teaching District of Columbia juries their duty between law and justice on one side, and vulgar bastard public opinion manufactured for the moment by theatrical appliances to cheat law and justice, on the other."

Daniel Sickles was ruined not for murder, but for reconciliation. The public reaction was so virulent that the congressman was compelled to justify himself in a lengthy statement published in the New York *Herald* and reprinted in newspapers across the country. In it, he made no apologies for murdering Key or for taking back Teresa. Instead, he appealed for the right to conduct his personal family life in private. "I am not aware of any statute, or code of morals, which makes it infamous to forgive a woman," he wrote defiantly, "nor is it usual to make our domestic life a subject of consultation with friends, no matter how near and dear to us. And I cannot allow even all the world combined to dictate to me the repudiation of my wife, when I think it right to forgive her, and restore her to my confidence and protection."

The open letter did little good. Sickles remained a pariah, ostracized by his colleagues in Congress and rendered virtually impotent there. "He was left to himself as if he had smallpox," observed Mary Chestnut, wife of Senator James Chestnut of South Carolina. Despised and rejected, he decided not to run for reelection. But the colorful career of Daniel Sickles was far from finished.

His reputation was gloriously revived during the Civil War, in which he served as a major general and lost his leg after being hit by an artillery shell at the battle of Gettysburg. (The amputated limb is still on display at the National Museum of Health and Medicine in Washington, D.C., where for years Sickles used to visit it on the anniversary of its removal.) After the war, Sickles was appointed by President Andrew Johnson to be the military governor of the Carolinas during Reconstruction. The position made him, as he wrote, "a sort of Sultan, a sort of Roman Consul. I was not only the military commander, I was the Governor of those two states; I was the legislature of those two states; I was the Court of Chancery of those two states. I was a sort of Poobah." He was also way too full of himself, from the president's point of view, and was relieved of his duties in 1867.

Earlier that year, Teresa died at age thirty-one. Sickles was remarried four years later to Carolina Creash, whom he met while serving as the American minister to Spain. He was apparently a bit big for his britches in this position too, earning the sobriquet "the Yankee King of Spain." He was forced to resign in 1873, but not before reportedly carrying on a torrid affair with the deposed Queen Isabella II. His second marriage was a failure, as he and his wife were estranged for nearly three decades because she refused to return with him to the United States. Sickles kept busy though, serving another term in Congress and taking his maid on as a mistress. Even into his nineties he was still chasing the ladies. In 1914, more than half a century after killing Philip Barton Key in cold blood, Sickles died a natural death at age ninety-four.

6

The *Other* Assassinations

Is it possible for an American president to be murdered in office and have the world forget about it? The millions who remember precisely where they were that November day in 1963 when John F. Kennedy was shot would say no. They would insist that the terrible event would be forever seared into the nation's conscience. Maybe so. After all, the assassination of Abraham Lincoln still remains vivid more than a century later, even with no one alive who would remember it. On the other hand, the national memory is selective. Few Americans can name the other two presidents slain in office. Time has obscured the names of James Abram Garfield and William McKinley, yet their violent deaths once traumatized the nation.

James Garfield never actively sought the presidency. The former Civil War general and college president was content to represent Ohio in Congress. After sixteen years in the House, he was elected to the Senate in 1880. Before he could take his seat, though, events at the Republican National Convention—where Garfield was heading the Ohio delegation—inexorably altered the course of his life. The party was hopelessly divided between the "Stalwart" faction supporting former president Ulysses S. Grant, who was seeking a third term, and the more progressive "Half-Breeds," who wanted to make Senator James G. Blaine of Maine the nominee. Out of this disunity, the forty-nine-year-old Garfield's name emerged and gathered momentum, much to his surprise and chagrin.

"General, they are talking about nominating you," a political associate warned.

"My God," Garfield replied in agitation. "I know it. I know it! And they will ruin me. I am here as a friend of [John] Sherman [another hopeful Republican nominee] and what will he and the world think of me if I am put in nomination? I won't permit it." Garfield nevertheless received the nomination and proceeded to defeat his Democratic opponent, General Winfield Scott Hancock, in the election of 1880. The prospect of being president troubled him. "I am bidding goodbye to private life," he wrote, "and to a long period of happy years which I fear terminate in 1880."

Presidents at the time faced the awesome task upon entering office of filling thousands of government jobs left open when workers from the previous administration were automatically fired in a well-established spoils system. Most of Garfield's brief time as president was taken up with this task, which he found odious. "My services ought to be worth more to the government than to be thus spent," he lamented.

Everywhere he went, hordes of eager office seekers harassed the new president. Thousands streamed through the White House, trolling for lucrative jobs. In those days, White House security was almost nonexistent, even though Lincoln had been killed only sixteen years earlier. Almost anyone could walk in and ask to see the president. Job seekers marauded through the mansion and onto Pennsylvania Avenue, making "the sounds of beasts at feeding time," as the statesman John Hay put it. "These people would take my very brain, flesh and blood if they could," Garfield groaned.

One of the most persistent hopefuls was Charles Julius Guiteau, a mentally unbalanced drifter. Consumed with a grand vision of himself and his place in the world, this slight, unimposing thirty-seven-year-old was a failure at everything he tried—except, as it would turn out, at killing the president of the United States. He had been frozen out of a semireligious cult he joined as a young man for what was labeled "excessive egoism." Undeterred and fully intending to run the sect that had rejected him, Guiteau tried to start a newspaper based on the cult's teachings. When that plan quickly fizzled, the tenacious loser tried blackmail, threatening to expose "how nightly innocent girls and innocent young women [in the sect] are sacrificed to an experience easier imagined than described." Next, Guiteau decided to become a lawyer after passing a less than rigorous bar exam. It appears that he argued only one case, during which he ranted incoherently while invoking God and the rights of man. His client was convicted, and Guiteau settled on a new profession as a debt collector. But he pocketed almost everything he recovered, and business soon evaporated.

After another try at religious revivalism, a failed marriage, and a stint in prison, Guiteau turned to politics. Though he quickly proved himself a nuisance while hanging around Republican Party headquarters, Guiteau became convinced that he was responsible for Garfield's election. The office of consul general in Paris, he decided, was a fitting reward for his services. He sent the president-elect a copy of an unsolicited, disjointed speech that he had written for Garfield during the campaign. "I presume my appointment will be promptly confirmed," Guiteau wrote in a note. "There is nothing against me. I claim to be a gentleman and a Christian."

Intending to press the point in person, Guiteau traveled to Washington and joined the long line of office seekers winding through the White House office of the newly inaugurated president. When Guiteau finally reached Garfield, he handed the bewildered president yet another copy of the campaign speech with the words "Paris Consulship" scrawled on the cover. Frustrated by the lack of response to his request and growing increasingly belligerent, Guiteau appeared repeatedly at the White House demanding to see the president. His erratic behavior soon got him banned from the premises.

Guiteau became convinced that Garfield was deliberately foiling his rightful destiny and that, as he later stated, "if he [Garfield] was out of the way, everything would go better." Garfield had been in office only three months when Guiteau began stalking him around

Washington, awaiting the perfect opportunity. That came a month later, on July 2, 1881, when the president arrived at the Baltimore & Potomac railway station, then on Washington's Mall, to embark on a summer-long vacation. Guiteau had been lurking there all morning, anticipating Garfield's well-publicized arrival. "I had no ill will toward the president," Guiteau had written in a note to the press earlier on the morning of the murder. "His death was a political necessity."

Deep in conversation with Secretary of State James Blaine, the president was oblivious to his killer's presence. Guiteau rushed up behind him and, from just a yard away, raised a pistol and fired at Garfield's back. "My God! What is this?" the stunned president exclaimed, staggering from the shot. As Garfield crumpled to the ground, the assassin took two steps forward and shot him again. "I am a Stalwart," he screamed, "and [Vice President Chester] Arthur is president now." A police officer on the scene pounced on Guiteau, who was struggling to escape, while agitated onlookers demanded that he be lynched on the spot.

Garfield, meanwhile, lay on the station floor. One bullet had grazed his arm, but the other had penetrated deeply. At the time, rigorous sterilization was not yet commonplace, and a physician, seeking the bullet, probed the wound with his fingers. Believing that the president was hemorrhaging internally, the doctor nevertheless reassured him, saying, "I don't believe the wound is serious." But Garfield, pale and quickly losing strength, knew otherwise. "Thank you, doctor," he said with a weak smile, "but I am a dead man."

The president was taken to the White House, where he lingered near death as a shocked nation kept vigil. Medical advice poured in from all over the country. Alexander Graham Bell, inventor of the telephone, made several appearances at Garfield's bedside with a primitive metal detector he had rigged to locate the bullet in the absence of X-rays, which would not be discovered until the 1890s. Though the bullet was never found, the president rallied enough to be taken to a seaside cottage in Elberon, New Jersey. Infection overtook him, however, and he died on September 19, 1881, two and a half months after being shot.

As Americans mourned the fallen president they never really

knew, Garfield's murderer was put on trial in Washington. It was a spectacle from the beginning. Guiteau, who had pleaded not guilty by reason of temporary insanity brought about by "divine power," constantly disrupted the proceedings with his ranting. He called the prosecutor a "low-livered whelp" and prosecution witnesses "dirty liars." At one point he jumped up and told the judge, "I had a very happy holiday," and at the conclusion of the lengthy trial, he insisted on making his own summation before the jury. "God told me to kill," he shrieked. "Let your verdict be that it was the Deity's act, not mine."

Guiteau was convicted and sentenced to death by hanging at the Washington Asylum and Jail. He went to the gallows, thrilled to be the center of attention, reciting an epic poem he had written for the occasion. It was called, "I Am Going to the Lordy."

★

Twenty years after Garfield's assassination, William McKinley met the same fate. Like Garfield, McKinley was from Ohio, served in the Civil War, and represented Ohio in Congress. Unlike his predecessor, however, McKinley served a full term and more in the White House before being murdered. During that time, the United States was emerging as a world leader, winning the Spanish-American War in 1898 and taking possession of Guam, Hawaii, the Philippines, Puerto Rico, and part of Samoa. American confidence was growing, big business was booming, and new technology was changing the nation. "We have prosperity at home and prestige abroad," McKinley said as he was elected to a second term in 1900.

Although he had once favored growth of big business, McKinley modified that position at the beginning of his new term, fearing monopolies and the resulting high prices. He also changed his views on protective tariffs designed to help U.S. businesses against foreign competition. McKinley now favored reciprocal trade agreements with other countries and introduced the new policy in a speech at the Pan American Exposition in Buffalo, New York, on September 5, 1901. "By sensible trade relations which will not interrupt our home production, we shall extend the outlets for our increasing surplus," he said. "The period of exclusiveness is past," he concluded. It would be his last speech.

The next day, the president appeared at the exposition's Temple of Music for a mass reception. Always affable and outgoing, McKinley was eager to shake as many hands as possible. A dense crowd had assembled, erupting into great applause when the president arrived. Among the thousands was a twenty-nine-year-old anarchist by the name of Leon Czolgosz. He had come to kill.

A disaffected youth who had grown up in poverty in Michigan, Czolgosz became obsessed with anarchist literature of the day. He hated the American system of government and believed that killing anyone branded an "enemy of the people" by anarchist leaders was just. He was thrilled to learn that King Humbert I of Italy had been assassinated by an anarchist in 1900, and he soon set out to make his own mark. Reading that McKinley would be in Buffalo for the trade exposition, Czolgosz staked out the grounds there, including the Temple of Music, where he knew the president would be appearing. He purchased a small revolver and bided his time.

On the morning of September 6, Czolgosz arrived at the temple and joined the milling thousands waiting for the president. He had wrapped the revolver in a handkerchief, knowing he would have to pull it out unseen when the president greeted him. "Let them come," McKinley said with a smile as he arrived at the temple amid a fanfare of music. Crowds immediately poured in, and the president began shaking hands in earnest. In the line moving forward, his face expressionless, was the assassin.

Agents guarding the president didn't notice anything unusual as Czolgosz repeatedly took out the handkerchief wrapped around the gun and pretended to wipe his forehead. When the killer reached the president, McKinley graciously extended his hand to greet him. In a flash, Czolgosz slapped it away and fired two shots into McKinley's midsection from inches away. As the president clutched his abdomen in shock, six agents rushed the the assassin and knocked him to the floor. Seeing this, McKinley weakly told an aide: "Don't let them hurt him. Be easy with him, boys." Looking up at his secretary, George Cortelyou, McKinley whispered, "My wife, be careful, Cortelyou, how you tell her—oh, be careful!"

The president was taken to a small hospital on the exposition grounds, where it was decided that an immediate operation was necessary. With no electricity in the makeshift hospital, physicians used a mirror to reflect the sun's dying rays as they worked. One bullet had grazed the president, possibly deflected by a button, but the other had pierced his stomach front and back. The doctors cleaned the peritoneal cavity and sutured the stomach. The wound was closed and covered with an antiseptic bandage, and McKinley was taken to a friend's home to recuperate.

Initially, it seemed that the fifty-seven-year-old president might recover. But gangrene set in, and doctors argued among themselves about whether McKinley was strong enough to withstand another operation. He grew progressively weaker and lapsed into a coma a week after being shot. McKinley revived briefly to say to those around him: "It is useless, gentlemen. I think we ought to have a prayer." The Lord's Prayer was recited, with the dying president silently moving his lips to the words. He then said, "Goodbye, goodbye, all," adding, "It is God's way. His will, not ours, be done." With death very near, the president drew his wife closer and whispered the words of his favorite hymn, "Nearer, My God, to Thee, Nearer to Thee." After Ida McKinley was led away weeping, the president groped for a hand to hold. A doctor took it as McKinley drew his last breath on September 14, 1901.

"I killed President McKinley because I believed it was my duty," Czolgosz told reporters from his jail cell. He was tried for the crime and never denied his guilt, maintaining that he followed the teachings of American anarchist leader Emma Goldman. Czolgosz was sentenced to death. Asked if he had any last words as he was being strapped in the electric chair, he responded, "I am not sorry for my crime."

Although Americans grieved for the murdered president, crowding the funeral route and erecting memorials across the country,

McKinley's death soon was overshadowed by the dynamic vice president who succeeded him, Theodore Roosevelt. It would be another six decades before a presidential assassin would successfully strike again. When he did, Americans thought back almost a century and remembered Lincoln.

Abraham Lincoln is laid to rest . . . the first time.

Part VIII

Remains to Be Seen

For deceased Americans of renown, R.I.P. has always been more of a plea than a promise. Take Zachary Taylor, who lay peacefully buried for nearly a century and a half before someone got the idea that maybe it wasn't a surfeit of cherries on a hot day that killed the twelfth president, as has been commonly accepted, but a nefarious plot to assassinate him with arsenic. Armed with this theory, and little to back it up, an amateur historian succeeded in having President Taylor's corpse dug up and tested for poison. Although no arsenic was found, putting the kibosh on the conspiracy theory, it was noted that Old Rough 'n' Ready was still recognizable by his "protruding eyebrows." The indignity of this exhumation was just one instance in a long, grisly tradition of discommoding the dead. Indeed, old Zach fared better than most, at least being treated to the formality of a flag-draped coffin. Disinterment has not always been so decorous.

★

1

Boiling "Mad"

"Mad" Anthony Wayne was not your run-of-the-mill Revolutionary War hero. He had an extra streak of boldness—sometimes bordering on recklessness—that earned him his "Mad" appellation, as well as the almost universal affection of his troops. Wayne's willingness to defy the odds helped him achieve one of the greatest American victories in the War of Independence when he attacked the nearly impregnable fort at Stony Point on the Hudson River and subdued the entire 700-man enemy garrison there. It was a devastating blow to British operations in the North, and gave sagging American morale a much needed boost. That Mad Anthony succeeded in this enterprise despite being wounded in the head by a musket ball only added to his luster. Because he was such a great man, his brethren in the Society of the Cincinnati naturally wanted to honor him with a memorial after his death in 1796. Yet if the general had had any notion of what this would entail, he no doubt would have preferred to be forgotten.

It was decided that the churchyard at St. David's parish in Radnor, Pennsylvania, would be the most appropriate place for the memorial, as generations of Waynes were buried there. The only problem was, Mad Anthony himself was buried all the way across the state in Presque Isle (now Erie), where he had died. So, in 1809, his son Isaac set out in a small carriage to bring his father's remains back to Radnor. When he arrived in Presque Isle, though, Isaac discovered that taking his dad's body away with him would not be so easy. Accounts differ as to what the problem was. Some say the locals, proud to have such a great American hero buried in their midst, were loath to have him removed; others maintain that Isaac Wayne discovered that his father's well-preserved corpse would not fit into the small, one-horse carriage he had driven across the state. Whatever the problem may have been, the solution was ghastly. Mad Anthony Wayne was removed from his burial place and his remains were boiled. After his flesh and bones were separated, the spoils were divvied up. Presque Isle kept the corpse soup, while Isaac Wayne took the lighter load of bones away with him for reburial in the family plot.

2

Tom Paine's Farewell Tour

"These are the times that try men's souls," Thomas Paine wrote during what he later called "a passion of patriotism" at the onset of the American Revolution in 1776. Sadly for the British-bred Founding Father who wrote so eloquently against tyranny and for basic human dignity, the years after his death in 1809 were the times that tried his body.

Despite having been one of the leading voices of both the American and French Revolutions, author of such works as *Common Sense* and *The Rights of Man,* Paine died reviled and nearly friendless. The radical views on religion he expressed later in his life certainly contributed to his unpopularity, and an attack on his former friend George Washington didn't exactly enhance his standing with the public either. Only six people came to his funeral.

One of Paine's harshest critics was the English pamphleteer William Cobbett, a staunch conservative who despised Paine's revolutionary ideas and repeatedly savaged him in print. Cobbett, alas, did not remain an enemy for long. Exposed to the ravages of the Industrial Revolution on Britain's rural poor, he was stunned by what he witnessed and as a result transformed himself into a radical reformer. Paine's worst critic was now his greatest disciple, preaching the new gospel against monied interests and monarchical privileges. Of course, this did not go over very well with Britain's ruling elite, and Cobbett, after serving two years in prison for sedition, was forced to flee to the United States in 1817. It was here that Paine's most loyal adherent started acting a little loony.

Cobbett was outraged at how poorly his hero's grave in New Rochelle, New York, was being maintained. "Paine lies in a little hole under the grass and weeds of an obscure farm in America," he wrote. "There, however, he should not lie, unnoticed, much longer. He belongs to England. His fame is the property of England; and if no other people will show that they value that fame, the people of England will." Cobbett could not have been more mistaken about his countrymen, as he would soon discover.

His plan to glorify Thomas Paine in perpetuity was twofold: He would remove his corpse from the ungrateful United States and take it to Britain, where he would build a magnificent monument for it, a rallying place for the poor and downtrodden. Obtaining the body was no problem. Cobbett simply stole Paine's remains under cover of night. "I have done myself the honor to disinter his bones," he reported. "I have removed them from New Rochelle . . . they are now on their way to England. When I myself return, I shall cause them to speak to the common sense of the great man; I shall gather together the people of Liverpool and Manchester in one assembly with those of London, and those bones will effect the reformation of England in Church and State."

Cobbett was bubbling with enthusiasm, but money was another matter. He didn't have any. This cast a bit of a pall on his plans to honor Paine with a lavish funeral featuring "twenty wagon loads of flowers . . . to strew before the hearse," not to mention the monument he wanted to build. To raise funds, he decided to take his revered relic, Paine's body, on a tour of Britain. It was a flop. No one came to his "bone rallies"; instead, he was laughed at. Lord Byron even penned a mocking poem for the occasion:

In digging up your bones, Tom Paine,
Will Cobbett has done well;
You visit him on earth again,
He'll visit you in hell.

Eventually Cobbett was reduced to selling locks of Paine's hair, but the demand was minimal. He was soon forced to realize that nobody cared, and he reluctantly shelved his plans. The bones he had removed from New Rochelle were shoved under his bed, where they stayed until his death in 1835. After that, Cobbett's son inherited them. But the younger Cobbett was arrested for debt and the remains were seized for auction, along with his other possessions. There was a reprieve, however, when a court ruled that Thomas Paine's skeleton was not a marketable asset, and it was returned to Cobbett's son. After that, the bone trail grows cold. And though history has rehabilitated Thomas Paine's reputation, his final resting place remains a mystery.

3

Abe Lincoln's Indecent Exposure

Most accounts of the life of Lincoln end with the solemn funeral procession that carried the martyred president by train from Washington back home to Springfield, Illinois. There is an epilogue, but it is not often included—perhaps because it is so unseemly. The Great Emancipator died in 1865, but he wasn't left alone until almost a half century later. In the intervening years, his corpse was subjected to a succession of abuses, including an abortive body-snatching scheme that came off more like a Keystone Kops caper.

Lincoln was laid to rest, the first time, in a temporary vault at Oak Ridge Cemetery in Springfield. And though his body would never leave the precincts of the graveyard, it would be disinterred no fewer than a dozen times. The first exhumation came just six months after Lincoln arrived at Oak Ridge, when his corpse was moved to another temporary vault pending completion of a permanent monument. His coffin was opened, ostensibly to identify the six-month-old corpse for the record. Then, in 1871, he was moved again—after being reidentified and reboxed in an iron coffin—to another temporary resting spot inside the partially completed monument. When a stone sarcophagus intended to be the president's permanent grave was completed three years later, officials were stunned to discover that Lincoln's iron coffin would not fit into it. They had to remove the body from the casket and place it in a smaller one made of wood. Of course, a formal identification of the remains was included in the process. Finally, on October 15, 1874, President Ulysses Grant dedicated the now completed National Lincoln Monument at Oak Ridge. Abraham Lincoln, safely ensconced in stone, was now at peace—or so it seemed.

A year after the monument's completion, Benjamin Boyd, a master engraver in the employ of counterfeiter "Big Jim" Kinelly, entered the state prison at Joliet, Illinois. This was a blow to Kinelly's criminal operations, depending as they did on Boyd's skill in making quality engravings of U.S. currency. Kinelly wanted his man back and settled upon a plan to make it happen. He would steal Lincoln's body and hold it for ransom in exchange for Boyd's release, plus $200,000 in cash. It seemed simple enough, but word of the plot leaked out to the U.S. Secret Service. Patrick Tyrell, the agent in charge of the service's Chicago branch, ordered one of his paid informers, a petty crook named Lewis Swegles, to infiltrate Kinelly's gang and find out how and when they planned to make their move against Lincoln's remains. Tyrell wanted to catch them in the act.

On the night of November 7, 1876, a group of Secret Service agents and detectives borrowed from Pinkerton's and other detective agencies waited in the darkness of the National Lincoln Monument for the invasion of the body snatchers. Swegles, who was accompanying the robbers, was supposed to give the waiting lawmen a signal as soon as the crypt was entered, but he couldn't slip away in time. It was only after the thieves had entered the tomb, pried open the sarcophagus, and began dragging away the coffin that Swegles was able to get outside, under the pretext of fetching the wagon, and give the signal that the crime was in progress. All at once, the agents charged the tomb, but to their dismay they found no thieves. Rushing back outside, they started shooting at each other in the darkness and confusion. Miraculously, no one was killed, but the grave robbers, who had decided to wait for Swegles and the wagon outside, escaped into the night when they heard the gunshots.

The would-be thieves were eventually captured and imprisoned, but there would be no happy endings for Lincoln. His coffin was removed from the crypt and hidden within the walls of the monument to discourage any further attempts to steal his body. For years, people paid their respects to an empty sarcophagus. By 1900, the Lincoln monument had become so dilapidated that it had to be almost entirely torn down and rebuilt. While this project was being completed, the late president and his family were buried in a temporary hole in the yard for about a year. Then, in 1901, the remains were returned to the reconstructed monument. Lincoln's son Robert, determined to foil any future robbery attempts, ordered that his father's body be buried deep inside the tomb and covered with twenty inches of concrete to seal it forever. He also ordered that the coffin not be opened again before reburial. But local officials ignored that command. They had to be sure the president was still there.

A pungent odor reportedly filled the room as workers pried off the coffin lid. The gathered moved in closer to see the great man who had been dead for almost forty years. His skin had turned black, and the chalk applied to his face by the undertaker made it appear a "grayish chestnut" color, according to one witness. His hair, beard, and the distinctive mole on his face were all well preserved, while the gloves he was wearing had rotted away. "Yes, his face was chalky white," recalled Fleetwood Lindly, another witness. "His clothes [were] mildewed, and I was allowed to hold one of the leather straps as we lowered the casket for the concrete to be poured. I was not scared at the time, but I slept with Lincoln for the next six months."

4

The "Resurrection" of John Scott Harrison

Despite all the disruptions to his perpetual rest, Abraham Lincoln was lucky that the thieves aiming to steal his body were thwarted in their ghoulish enterprise. John Scott Harrison was not so fortunate. This congressman from Ohio has the distinction of being the son of one U.S. president (William Henry Harrison), the father of another (Benjamin Harrison), and the victim of a horrible postmortem ordeal.

When John Scott Harrison died in 1878, body snatching was still a fairly common occurrence. There was money to be made selling corpses to medical schools, which used them to teach anatomy, and "resurrectionists," as the thieves were called, did brisk business. During Harrison's funeral, it was noticed that the grave of a recently buried friend, William Devin, had been disturbed. Further investigation revealed that the body had been stolen. To avoid such a fate for their deceased dad, the Harrisons bricked up his grave, cemented it, and laid a ton of marble slabs upon it. They also hired two watchmen. The body of John Scott Harrison, they believed, was safe and sound.

After the burial, Harrison's son John Jr. and his nephew George Eaton went to Cincinnati to look for their friend William Devin's missing corpse. A search of the Ohio Medical College proved fruitless, until the two men were about to leave. One of them noticed a rope hanging in the chute through which cadavers were hoisted up to the school's dissecting room. The rope was taut, as though something heavy was hanging from it inside the chute. Pulling it up, they found a naked body with its head and shoulders covered by a cloth. When the cloth was removed, the men got quite a shock. "My God," gasped John Jr. in horror, "that's my father!" Indeed, it was Harrison instead of Devin who had been buried at the disturbed grave the day before.

The gruesome discovery caused an immediate uproar, led by Benjamin Harrison, who arrived the following day. Although it was never discovered who took the corpse to the Ohio Medical College, the school was blasted in the press and subjected to an investigation. Dr. William Seely tried to defend the institution, saying that the entire affair "matters little, since it would all be the same on the day of resurrection." This was not something the Harrisons wanted to hear, especially future president Benjamin, who never got over "the taste of hell which comes from the discovery of a father's body hanging by the neck, like that of a dog, in the pit of a medical college."

5

John Paul Jones: Pickled in Paris

John Paul Jones commands a place of honor at the U.S. Naval Academy in Annapolis, Maryland, where he is buried in a magnificent sarcophagus at the center of a marble crypt beneath the academy's chapel. It is a fitting monument to the Revolutionary War hero and father of the U.S. Navy, who is famous for his wartime declaration, "I have not yet begun to fight." But the dignity accorded him in this serene setting was about a century overdue. Before Jones was finally laid to rest at the academy in 1913, the hero and his remains were treated with appalling disregard by the nation he had served so well.

After his illustrious career during the American Revolution, and later in the service of Russia's Catherine the Great, Jones retired to Paris in 1790. He was hoping for a commission from the French government, but his glory days had passed and his health was failing. The great historian Thomas Carlyle described the deflated hero's final years: "In faded naval uniform, Paul Jones lingers visible here; like a wine-skin from which the wine is drawn. Like the ghost of himself!" Suffering from kidney disease and bronchial pneumonia, John Paul Jones died quietly and nearly alone on July 18, 1792.

Gouverneur Morris, the American minister to France, ordered the body to be buried privately and as cheaply as possible. With an additional touch of sensitivity, he had most of the dead man's uniforms, medals, and other personal treasures auctioned off to satisfy demands on Jones's estate. Morris later tried to explain his desire to dispose of the body with minimal cost or fanfare: "Some people here who like rare shows wished him to have a pompous funeral, and I was applied to on the subject; but . . . I had no right to spend on such follies either the money of his heirs or that of the United States."

Morris's cold frugality was ultimately circumvented by the French, who apparently thought more of the great American than did the Americans. Pierre-François Simmoneau, a royal commissary of King Louis XVI, not only paid for a decent funeral, but had the corpse preserved in alcohol and placed in a lead coffin so that "in case the United States should claim his remains, they might be more easily removed." A dignified funeral procession wound its way through the streets of Paris to the Protestant cemetery outside the city walls. There the gathered mourners, mostly French, were exhorted by the presiding minister to imitate this "illustrious foreigner" and his contempt for danger, his devotion to his country, and "his noble heroism, which after having astonished the present age, will continue to be the object of the veneration of future generations." While the French paid their respects to "le célèbre capitaine Paul-Jones," Gouverneur Morris didn't bother to attend the funeral. The American minister was too busy flitting around Paris on social calls.

A little more than three weeks after John Paul Jones was buried, a Paris mob stormed the royal palace of the Tuileries, and the bodies of the Swiss Guards killed while trying to protect the king and queen were tossed into a common grave adjoining that of Jones. With France in the midst of revolution and a crushing foreign war with Austria and Prussia, any hope of recovering Jones's body and bringing it back home would have to be postponed indefinitely—not that there was any great clamor in the United States to do so. John Paul Jones was quietly fading into obscurity as the years passed, and, except for his heirs pestering Congress for his unpaid salary and other monies, no one gave the great man much thought. The cemetery where he was buried closed in 1804 and was soon covered over by the expanding city.

There were several attempts to find the burial site as the nineteenth century progressed, but all were futile. It seemed that Jones would be lost forever. But then, in 1899, General Horace Porter, the American ambassador to France, initiated his own search and eventually found the site of the old graveyard. As word of the discovery leaked out, though, the owners of the buildings on the site saw an opportunity for profit and demanded exorbitant sums for the right to excavate beneath their property. Ambassador Porter had no choice but to postpone his project until 1905, when the initial excitement had died down and he was able to secure permission to dig on more favorable terms.

An army of workers immediately set about sinking shafts and digging tunnels. Around the clock they toiled, at one point encountering the badly deteriorated remains of those unfortunate Swiss Guards who had been, according to one report, "stacked like cordwood" in their graves. Eventually, a series of lead coffins were found. One of them surely contained the remains of John Paul Jones. But which one? A group of anthropologists and pathologists were called in to help sort through the corpses. When the coffin thought to be Jones's was opened, it proved to be a bonanza. "To our intense surprise," wrote Ambassador Porter, "the body was marvelously preserved, all the flesh remaining intact, very slightly shrunken, and of grayish brown or tan color." Simmoneau's decision to cure the corpse in alcohol had paid off. The gathered experts were able to match the well-preserved face with a bust of Jones known to be an accurate likeness, and an autopsy confirmed the cause of death. The search for John Paul Jones was over. Now it was time to finally give him his propers.

President Theodore Roosevelt, sensing the propaganda value for the U.S. Navy, which he was looking to strengthen, sent a fleet of ships over to France to escort Jones back home. First, though, an elaborate service was held over the body, which now reposed in a sleek new mahogany coffin. This was followed by a big parade and a special trip to Cherbourg, where, after another ceremony, the casket was transferred to the U.S.S. *Brooklyn* for the trip back to the United States.

Still more obsequies awaited the arrival home, yet despite all the tributes and long-delayed expressions of gratitude, John Paul Jones was still getting dissed in some quarters. Midshipmen at the U.S. Naval Academy, Jones's final resting place, sang a parody of a popular song called "Everybody Works but Father":

Everybody works but John Paul Jones!
He lies around all day,
Body pickled in alcohol
On a permanent jag they say.
Middies stand around him
Doing honor to his bones;
Everybody works in Crabtown [Annapolis]
But John Paul Jones.

And though Congress had settled on the academy over many other places vying for the remains, it was too cheap to fund a proper shrine. As a result, Jones's body was stashed behind a set of stairs until Congress finally came through with the cash. That only took seven years.

Appendix I

Presidents of the United States

1) **GEORGE WASHINGTON**
Born: February 22, 1732, Westmoreland County, Virginia
Political Party: Federalist
State Represented: Virginia
Vice President: John Adams
First Lady: Martha Dandridge Custis Washington
Term of Office: 1789–1797 (two terms)
Died: December 14, 1799, aged 67, Mount Vernon, Virginia
Distinctions: Only president inaugurated in two cities (New York, 1789, and Philadelphia, 1793). Only president to not live in Washington, D.C. Only president unanimously elected, receiving 69 of the 69 electoral votes cast in 1788.
Pages: 4, 7–8, 37–39, 172–73

2) **JOHN ADAMS**
Born: October 30, 1735, Braintree (now Quincy), Massachusetts
Political Party: Federalist
State Represented: Massachusetts
Vice President: Thomas Jefferson
First Lady: Abigail Smith Adams

Term of Office: 1797–1801 (one term)
Died: July 4, 1826, aged 90, Quincy, Massachusetts
Distinctions: First president to live in the White House. First to have his son elected president.
Pages: 37–46, 155–57

3) **THOMAS JEFFERSON**
Born: April 13, 1743, Albermarle County, Virginia
Political Party: Democratic-Republican
State Represented: Virginia
Vice President: Aaron Burr (first term); George Clinton (second term)
First Lady: None (Jefferson was a widower.)
Term of Office: 1801–1809 (two terms)
Died: July 4, 1826, aged 83, Charlottesville, Virginia
Distinctions: First president inaugurated in Washington, D.C. First elected by the U.S. House of Representatives.
Pages: 32, 41–46, 155–58, 178, 180–83, 250–52

4) **JAMES MADISON**
Born: March 16, 1751, Port Conway, Virginia
Political Party: Democratic-Republican
State Represented: Virginia
Vice President: George Clinton (first term); Elbridge Gerry (second term)
First Lady: Dolley Dandridge Payne Todd Madison
Term of Office: 1809–1817 (two terms)
Died: June 28, 1836, aged 85, Montpelier, Virginia
Distinctions: Shortest president (5 feet 4 inches). First to have been a congressman. Last surviving signer of the Declaration of Independence.
Pages: 42, 157, 180, 252

5) **JAMES MONROE**
Born: April 29, 1758, Westmoreland County, Virginia
Political Party: Democratic-Republican
State Represented: Virginia
Vice President: Daniel D. Tompkins
First Lady: Elizabeth Kortright Monroe
Term of Office: 1817–1825 (two terms)
Died: July 4, 1831, aged 73, New York, New York

Distinctions: First president to have been a U.S. Senator. First to ride on a steamboat.
Page: 75

6) **JOHN QUINCY ADAMS**
Born: July 11, 1767, Braintree (now Quincy), Massachusetts
Political Party: Democratic-Republican
State Represented: Massachusetts
Vice President: John C. Calhoun
First Lady: Louisa Catherine Johnson Adams
Term of Office: 1825–1829 (one term)
Died: February 23, 1848, aged 80, Washington, D.C.
Distinctions: Only ex-president to serve in the U.S. House of Representatives.
Pages: 9–11, 159–61

7) **ANDREW JACKSON**
Born: March 15, 1767, Waxhaw, South Carolina
Political Party: Democratic
State Represented: Tennessee
Vice President: John C. Calhoun (first term); Martin Van Buren (second term)
First Lady: None (Jackson was a widower)
Term of Office: 1829–1837 (two terms)
Died: June 8, 1845, aged 78, Nashville, Tennessee
Distinctions: First president to be born in a log cabin. First target of assassination attempt.
Pages: 12, 56, 58–63, 64–71, 136–37, 159–61

8) **MARTIN VAN BUREN**
Born: December 5, 1782, Kinderhook, New York
Political Party: Democratic
State Represented: New York
Vice President: Richard M. Johnson
First Lady: None (Van Buren was a widower.)
Term of Office: 1837–1841 (one term)
Died: July 24, 1862, aged 79, Kinderhook, New York
Distinctions: First president not born a British subject.
Pages: 64, 67, 69, 120

9) **WILLIAM HENRY HARRISON**
Born: February 9, 1773, Charles City County, Virginia
Political Party: Whig
State Represented: Ohio
Vice President: John Tyler
First Lady: Anna Tuthill Symmes Harrison (never went to Washington)
Term of Office: 1841 (32 days)
Died: April 4, 1841, aged 68, Washington, D.C.
Distinctions: Shortest term in office.
Pages: 131, 281–82

10) **JOHN TYLER**
Born: March 29, 1790, Charles City County, Virginia
Political Party: Whig
State Represented: Virginia
Vice President: None
First Lady: (1) Letitia Christian Tyler, (2) Julia Gardiner Tyler
Term of Office: 1841–1845 (one partial term)
Died: January 18, 1862, aged 71, Richmond, Virginia
Distinctions: First accidental president. First to marry while in office.
Page: 131

11) **JAMES K. POLK**
Born: November 2, 1795, Mecklenburg County, North Carolina
Political Party: Democratic
State Represented: Tennessee
Vice President: George M. Dallas
First Lady: Sarah Childress Polk
Term of Office: 1845–1849 (one term)
Died: June 5, 1849, aged 53, Nashville, Tennessee
Distinctions: First presidential inauguration reported by telegraph.

12) **ZACHARY TAYLOR**
Born: November 24, 1784, Orange County, Virginia
Political Party: Whig
State Represented: Louisiana
Vice President: Millard Fillmore
First Lady: Margaret Smith Taylor
Term of Office: 1849–1850 (one partial term)

Died: July 9, 1850, aged 65, Washington, D.C.
Distinctions: First president to represent a state west of the Mississippi River.
Pages: 115, 271

13) MILLARD FILLMORE
Born: January 7, 1800, Summerhill, New York
Political Party: Whig
State Represented: New York
Vice President: None
First Lady: Abigail Powers Fillmore
Term of Office: 1850–1853 (one partial term)
Died: March 8, 1874, aged 74, Buffalo, New York
Distinctions: Only president to run for a term on the American ("Know-Nothing") Party ticket.
Page: 113

14) FRANKLIN PIERCE
Born: November 23, 1804, Hillsborough (now Hillsboro), New Hampshire
Political Party: Democratic
State Represented: New Hampshire
Vice President: William Rufus King (died before serving any functions of V.P.)
First Lady: Jane Appleton Pierce
Term of Office: 1853–1857 (one term)
Died: October 8, 1869, aged 64, Concord, New Hampshire
Distinctions: First president born in the nineteenth century. Only one to affirm rather than swear the oath of office.
Pages: 116–17

15) JAMES BUCHANAN
Born: April 23, 1791, Cove Gap, Pennsylvania
Political Party: Democratic
State Represented: Pennsylvania
Vice President: John C. Breckinridge
First Lady: None (Buchanan was a bachelor.)
Term of Office: 1857–1861 (one term)
Died: June 1, 1868, aged 77, Lancaster, Pennsylvania

Distinctions: Only bachelor president.
Pages: 118–19, 254, 255, 257–58

16) **ABRAHAM LINCOLN**
Born: February 12, 1809, Hardin (now Larue) County, Kentucky
Political Party: Republican
State Represented: Illinois
Vice President: Hannibal Hamlin (first term); Andrew Johnson (second term)
First Lady: Mary Todd Lincoln
Term of Office: 1861–1865 (one full term; one partial term)
Died: April 15, 1865, aged 56, Washington, D.C. (assassinated)
Distinctions: Tallest president (6 feet 4 inches). First to be assassinated. First to wear a beard. First depicted on a noncommemorative coin.
Pages: 15–16, 72–78, 162–64, 278–80

17) **ANDREW JOHNSON**
Born: December 29, 1808, Raleigh, North Carolina
Political Party: Democratic (elected vice president on Republican ticket)
State Represented: Tennessee
Vice President: None
First Lady: Eliza McCardle Johnson
Term of Office: 1865–1869 (one partial term)
Died: July 31, 1875, aged 66, Carter's Station, Tennessee
Distinctions: First president to be impeached. Only one to have been a tailor.
Pages: 120–21, 261

18) **ULYSSES S. GRANT**
Born: April 27, 1822, Point Pleasant, Ohio
Political Party: Republican
State Represented: Illinois
Vice President: Schuyler Colfax (first term); Henry Wilson (second term)
First Lady: Julia Dent Grant
Term of Office: 1869–1877 (two terms)
Died: July 23, 1885, aged 63, Mount McGregor, New York
Distinctions: First president to run (unsuccessfully) for a third term.

First to have both parents alive at inauguration.
Pages: 32, 122, 262–63

19) RUTHERFORD B. HAYES
Born: October 4, 1822, Delaware, Ohio
Political Party: Republican
State Represented: Ohio
Vice President: William A. Wheeler
First Lady: Lucy Webb Ware Hayes
Term of Office: 1877–1881 (one term)
Died: January 17, 1893, aged 70, Freemont, Ohio
Distinctions: First president to visit West Coast while in office.

20) JAMES A. GARFIELD
Born: November 19, 1831, Orange, Ohio
Political Party: Republican
State Represented: Ohio
Vice President: Chester A. Arthur
First Lady: Lucretia "Crete" Rudolph Garfield
Term of Office: 1881 (199 days)
Died: September 19, 1881, aged 49, Elberon, New Jersey (assassinated)
Distinctions: First left-handed president. First to review inaugural parade in front of White House.
Pages: 262–66

21) CHESTER A. ARTHUR
Born: October 5, 1829, Fairfield, Vermont
Political Party: Republican
State Represented: New York
Vice President: None
First Lady: None (Arthur was a widower.)
Term of Office: 1881–1885 (one partial term)
Died: November 18, 1886, aged 57, New York, New York
Distinctions: Amazing whiskers.
Page: 265

22 AND 24) GROVER CLEVELAND
Born: March 18, 1837, Caldwell, New Jersey
Political Party: Democratic

State Represented: New York
Vice President: Thomas A. Hendricks (first term); Adlai E. Stevenson (second term)
First Lady: Frances Folsom Cleveland
Term of Office: 1885–1889; 1893–1897 (two nonconsecutive terms)
Died: June 24, 1908, aged 71, Princeton, New Jersey
Distinctions: Only president married in the White House. Only one to serve two nonconsecutive terms.
Pages: 123–24, 165–67

23) **BENJAMIN HARRISON**
Born: August 20, 1833, North Bend, Ohio
Political Party: Republican
State Represented: Indiana
Vice President: Levi P. Morton
First Lady: Caroline Scott Harrison
Term of Office: 1889–1893 (one term)
Died: March 13, 1901, aged 67 years, Indianapolis, Indiana
Distinctions: More states admitted to the Union during his administration (six) than any other president.
Pages: 281–82

25) **WILLIAM MCKINLEY**
Born: January 29, 1843, Niles, Ohio
Political Party: Republican
State Represented: Ohio
Vice President: Garret A. Hobart (first term); Theodore Roosevelt (second term)
First Lady: Ida Saxton McKinley
Term of Office: 1897–1901 (one full term and one partial term)
Died: September 14, 1901, aged 58, Buffalo, New York (assassinated)
Distinctions: First president to use the telephone for campaign purposes.
Pages: 125–26, 266–69

26) **THEODORE ROOSEVELT**
Born: October 27, 1858, New York, New York
Political Party: Republican
State Represented: New York

Vice President: Charles W. Fairbanks
First Lady: Edith Kermit Carow Roosevelt
Term of Office: 1901–1909 (one partial term and one full term)
Died: January 6, 1919, aged 60, Oyster Bay, New York
Distinctions: First president to win the Nobel Peace Prize. Youngest man to become president. First to ride in a car and airplane.
Pages: 79–85, 285

27) WILLIAM HOWARD TAFT
Born: September 15, 1857, Cincinnati, Ohio
Political Party: Republican
State Represented: Ohio
Vice President: James S. Sherman
First Lady: Helen Herron Taft
Term of Office: 1909–1913 (one term)
Died: March 8, 1930, aged 72, Washington, D.C.
Distinctions: Fattest president (300–332 lbs.). Only president to become chief justice of the U.S. Supreme Court. First to open the baseball season by pitching the first ball.
Pages: 79–85, 127–28

28) WOODROW WILSON
Born: December 29, 1856, Staunton, Virginia
Political Party: Democratic
State Represented: New Jersey
Vice President: Thomas R. Marshall
First Lady: (1) Ellen Louise Axson Wilson, (2) Edith Bolling Galt Wilson
Term of Office: 1913–1921 (two terms)
Died: February 3, 1924, aged 67, Washington, D.C.
Distinctions: Only president to have been president of a major university (Princeton). First to earn a doctorate degree. First to hold a press conference. First to visit Europe while in office.
Pages: 129–30, 196, 198

29) WARREN G. HARDING
Born: November 2, 1865, Corsica, Ohio
Political Party: Republican
State Represented: Ohio

Vice President: Calvin Coolidge
First Lady: Florence Mabel Kling DeWolfe Harding
Term of Office: 1921–1923 (one partial term)
Died: August 2, 1923, aged 57, San Francisco, California
Distinctions: First president to be broadcast on radio. Only newspaper editor to become president.
Pages: 21–23, 203–6

30) CALVIN COOLIDGE
Born: July 14, 1872, Plymouth, Vermont
Political Party: Republican
State Represented: Massachusetts
Vice President: Charles C. Dawes
First Lady: Grace Goodhue Coolidge
Term of Office: 1923–1929 (one partial term and one full term)
Died: January 5, 1933, aged 60, Northampton, Massachusetts
Distinctions: Only president sworn in by his father.
Page: 116

31) HERBERT C. HOOVER
Born: August 10, 1874, West Branch, Iowa
Political Party: Republican
State Represented: California
Vice President: Charles Curtis
First Lady: Lou Henry Hoover
Term of Office: 1929–1933 (one term)
Died: October 20, 1964, aged 90, New York, New York
Distinctions: First president to appear on television (as secretary of commerce). First to have a telephone at his desk. First born west of the Mississippi. Longest lived after presidency (31 years).

32) FRANKLIN D. ROOSEVELT
Born: January 30, 1882, Hyde Park, New York
Political Party: Democratic
State Represented: New York
Vice President: John Nance Garner (first and second terms); Henry A. Wallace (third term); Harry S Truman (fourth term)
First Lady: (Anna) Eleanor Roosevelt Roosevelt
Term of Office: 1933–1945 (three full terms and one partial term)

Died: April 12, 1945, aged 63, Warm Springs, Georgia
Distinctions: Only president to be elected to a third and fourth term. First to appoint a woman to cabinet. First to appear on television (as president).
Pages: 24–27, 86–92

33) **HARRY S TRUMAN**
Born: May 10, 1884, Lamar, Missouri
Political Party: Democratic
State Represented: Missouri
Vice President: Alben W. Barkley
First Lady: Bess (Elizabeth Virginia) Wallace Truman
Term of Office: 1945–1953 (one partial term and one full term)
Died: December 26, 1972, aged 88, Independence, Missouri
Distinctions: First president to travel in a submarine. First to be telecast from White House.
Pages: 93–99, 209–11

34) **DWIGHT D. EISENHOWER**
Born: October 4, 1890, Denison, Texas
Political Party: Republican
State Represented: New York
Vice President: Richard M. Nixon
First Lady: Mamie (Marie) Geneva Doud Eisenhower
Term of Office: 1953–1961 (two terms)
Died: March 28, 1969, aged 78, Washington, D.C.
Distinctions: First president to serve a constitutionally limited term (per Twenty-second Amendment). First televised press conference. First telecast in color.
Pages: 211–12

35) **JOHN F. KENNEDY**
Born: May 29, 1917, Brookline, Massachusetts
Political Party: Democratic
State Represented: Massachusetts
Vice President: Lyndon B. Johnson
First Lady: Jacqueline Lee Bouvier Kennedy
Term of Office: 1961–1963 (one partial term)
Died: November 22, 1963, aged 46, Dallas, Texas (assassinated)

Distinctions: First president born in the twentieth century. Only Roman Catholic president. Only one survived by both parents.
Pages: 28, 30–31, 100–111

36) **LYNDON B. JOHNSON**
Born: August 27, 1908, near Stonewall, Texas
Political Party: Democratic
State Represented: Texas
Vice President: Hubert H. Humphrey
First Lady: Lady Bird (Claudia Alta) Taylor Johnson
Term of Office: 1963–1969 (one partial term and one full term)
Died: January 22, 1973, aged 64, San Antonio, Texas
Distinctions: First president to take oath of office in an airplane. First to be sworn in by a woman.
Pages: 33, 100–111

37) **RICHARD M. NIXON**
Born: January 9, 1913, Yorba Linda, California
Political Party: Republican
State Represented: New York
Vice President: Spiro T. Agnew (first and second terms); Gerald R. Ford (second term)
First Lady: Thelma Catherine (Patricia) Ryan Nixon
Term of Office: 1969–1974 (one full term and one partial term)
Died: April 22, 1994, aged 81, New York, New York
Distinctions: Only president to resign. Only one to be pardoned by his successor. First to visit China.
Pages: 222–27

38) **GERALD R. FORD**
Born: July 14, 1913, Omaha, Nebraska
Political Party: Republican
State Represented: Michigan
Vice President: Nelson A. Rockefeller
First Lady: Elizabeth (Betty) Bloomer Warren Ford
Term of Office: 1974–1977 (one partial term)
Distinctions: Only president to hold nation's top two offices without being elected to either. First president whose parents were divorced.

39) **JAMES EARL CARTER**
Born: October 1, 1924, Plains, Georgia
Political Party: Democratic
State Represented: Georgia
Vice President: Walter F. Mondale
First Lady: Rosalynn Smith Carter
Term of Office: 1977–1981 (one term)
Distinctions: Only president to be sworn in using his nickname. First born in a hospital.

40) **RONALD W. REAGAN**
Born: February 6, 1911, Tampico, Illinois
Political Party: Republican
State Represented: California
Vice President: George H.W. Bush
First Lady: Nancy Davis Reagan
Term of Office: 1981–1989 (two terms)
Distinctions: Only divorced president. Oldest at first election (69). Longest-lived. Only president to have been an actor.

41) **GEORGE H. W. BUSH**
Born: June 12, 1924, Milton, Massachusetts
Political Party: Republican
State Represented: Texas
Vice President: J. Danforth Quayle
First Lady: Barbara Pierce Bush
Term of Office: 1989–1993 (one term)
Distinctions: Only president to have been chairman of his political party, ambassador to U.N., and director of CIA.

42) **WILLIAM J. CLINTON**
Born: August 19, 1946, Hope, Arkansas
Political Party: Democratic
State Represented: Arkansas
Vice President: Albert Gore Jr.
First Lady: Hillary Rodham Clinton
Term of Office: 1993–2001 (two terms)
Distinctions: Only president to both be sued for sexual misconduct and

forced to give a deposition while in office. Only president to have been a Rhodes Scholar. Only president to be elected twice without receiving at least 50% of the popular vote (43% in 1992 and 49% in 1996).

43) **GEORGE W. BUSH**
Born: July 6, 1946, New Haven, Connecticut
Political Party: Republican
State Represented: Texas
Vice President: Richard B. Cheney
First Lady: Laura Welch Bush
Term of Office: 2001–present
Distinctions: Only president to have been a general managing partner of a professional baseball team (Texas Rangers).

Appendix II

A Brief History of the United States (through 1980)

(Events covered in this book are italicized.)

c. 1000—Viking explorer Leif Ericson leads what is probably the first European expedition to North America.

1492—Christopher Columbus stumbles upon America while searching for an alternative sea passage to Asia. Of the natives he first encounters in San Salvador, Columbus reports to the Spanish monarchs Ferdinand and Isabella: "With fifty men all can be kept in subjugation and made to do whatever you desire."

1513—Spanish explorer Ponce de León begins his search for the fountain of youth in Florida.

1565—Spain establishes the first permanent settlement in the present-day United States at St. Augustine, Florida.

1579—Sir Francis Drake rounds Cape Horn and sails up the Pacific coast, possibly as far as the present state of Washington.

1607—Jamestown, Virginia, becomes the first permanent British settlement in North America. (An earlier English colony off the coast of North Carolina, known as "the Lost Colony of Roanoke," failed and all its inhabitants mysteriously vanished.)

1608—Captain John Smith writes what is regarded as the first American book, *A True Relation of . . . Virginia,* which describes the settlement of Jamestown.

1619—The House of Burgesses, the first representative legislative body in colonial America, convenes at Jamestown, then Virginia's capital.

1620—Seeking freedom of religion, a band of English separatists, known as Pilgrims, set sail aboard the *Mayflower* and establish the Plymouth Colony in Massachusetts. The following year, the colonists and their Indian allies celebrate the first Thanksgiving.

1636—Harvard College (now University) becomes the first institution of higher learning in the American colonies.

1649—The first religious toleration act in America grants freedom of worship to both Protestants and Catholics in Maryland.

1692—A group of young girls initiate a savage witch hunt in Salem Village, Massachusetts. Twenty people are executed, and many more imprisoned. Pages: 229–46.

1702—Edward Hyde, Lord Cornbury, becomes the royal governor of New York and reportedly takes to dressing like the British monarch he represents—Queen Anne. Pages: 247–48.

1733—Benjamin Franklin's *Poor Richard's Almanack* is first published.

1763—Britain defeats France in the French and Indian War, gaining all French territory east of the Mississippi River except New Orleans. It is an expensive victory, with unexpected consequences in the relationship between Britain and her colonies. Historian Carl Van Doren later writes, "The French and Indian War, which made the British government think of the colonies as important enough to be taxed, had made the Americans think of themselves as important enough to say how they should be taxed."

1765—The British Parliament passes the Stamp Act, imposing a tax on newspapers, legal documents, and other printed material. The act is bitterly opposed in the colonies, giving rise to organized resistance and the slogan, "No taxation without representation." The act is repealed the following year, but Parliament reasserts its right to tax the colonies.

1770—British soldiers stationed in Boston fire into a crowd of agitated colonists, killing three and wounding eight (two of whom later succumb to their injuries). The event, which colonial leaders call the Boston Massacre, is used to rally Americans against oppressive British policies.

1771—Patrick Henry's wife, Sarah, apparently suffering from extreme psychosis, is confined to the basement of the family home, sometimes in a straitjacket. Page: 249.

1773—Protesting the British importation of duty-free tea, American colonists dressed as Indians stage the Boston Tea Party, raiding three ships in Boston Harbor and dumping 342 chests of tea into the water.

1774—The First Continental Congress, a convention of delegates from all the American colonies (except Georgia), meets in Philadelphia to address British injustices. These include what became known as the Intolerable Acts, which Parliament imposed as punishment for the Boston Tea Party. The Congress adopts a Declaration of Rights, establishing the colonial position on taxation and trade. Britain ignores it.

1775—The Revolutionary War begins when British soldiers and Massachusetts minutemen clash at Lexington and Concord. The Second Continental Congress appoints George Washington as commander-in-chief of the colonial army, and makes a final, futile appeal to Britain to right matters without additional fighting.

1776—The United States of America becomes a new nation when the Second Continental Congress adopts the Declaration of Independence, written by Thomas Jefferson. Britain offers a reward to learn the names of the Declaration's signers, asserting that the act constitutes high treason punishable by death.

1776—Benjamin Franklin arranges for the harsh imprisonment of his only son, William, in retaliation for his remaining loyal to Britain. Pages: 3–6.

1777—American forces defeat the British at Saratoga, New York, turning the tide of the Revolutionary War and convincing France to form a military alliance with the new nation.

1778—John Adams joins Ben Franklin in Paris, and develops an intense dislike for him. Pages: 39–41.

1779—Benedict Arnold turns traitor. Pages: 171–76.

1781—British forces are defeated at Yorktown, Virginia, in the last major battle of the Revolutionary War.

1781—Mary Ball Washington humiliates son George by complaining of his financial neglect to the Virginia House of Delegates. Pages: 7–8.

1783—In what has been called the greatest diplomatic feat in American history, the United States and Britain sign the Treaty of Paris, officially ending the war between them and establishing the new nation's borders. U.S. territory is extended west to the Mississippi River, north to Canada, and south to Florida.

1787—The Founding Fathers write the Constitution, establishing a unique system of government that survives to this day. "Our Constitution is so simple and practical that it is possible to meet extraordinary needs by changes in emphasis and arrangement without loss of essential form," Franklin D. Roosevelt later states at his first inauguration. "That is why our constitutional system has proved itself the most superbly enduring political mechanism the modern world has produced."

1789—The Electoral College unanimously chooses George Washington to serve as the first president of the United States. Washington and his wife move into the first presidential home at No. 1 Cherry Street in New York City, the nation's first capital.

1789—John Adams becomes George Washington's vice president, taking a back seat, once again, to George Washington—and not liking it one bit. "I am vice president," he says. "In this I am nothing." Pages: 37–39.

1791—The Bill of Rights is added to the Constitution, guaranteeing freedom of speech, religion, the press, and the rights, among others, to trial by jury and peaceful assembly.

1793—Eli Whitney invents the cotton gin, allowing for a quicker, more economical means of separating cottonseeds from fiber. The invention helps make the fledgling United States the world's leading cotton producer, but "King Cotton" also leads to a greater dependence on slavery in the South.

1794—President Washington sends in federal troops to quash the Whiskey Rebellion, a violent protest by whiskey producers in Pennsylvania against the federal tax on their product. The president's action establishes the federal government's authority to enforce its laws within the states.

1796—John Adams and Thomas Jefferson clash in the first real presidential campaign, and in the second, four years later. Pages: 41–46, 155–58.

1798—Congress passes the Alien and Sedition Acts, designed to silence opposition to an expected war with France. The widely unpopular measures, which, among other things, make it a crime to criticize the president, contribute to the eventual demise of the Federalist Party.

1798—Representative Matthew Lyon of Vermont spits in the face of Connecticut's Roger Griswold, starting the first recorded congressional brawl. Page: 135.

1800—Washington, D.C., carved out of Maryland and Virginia, becomes the nation's capital. First Lady Abigail Adams describes the mostly undeveloped federal city as "romantic but wild, a wilderness at present."

1801—John Marshall is appointed chief justice of the U.S. Supreme Court by President John Adams. During his tenure of thirty-four years (the longest in court history), Marshall raises the Supreme Court to a level of importance equal to that of the executive and judicial branches of government. This is accomplished through such landmark decisions as *Marbury v. Madison* (1803), in which the court's authority to declare laws unconstitutional is established.

1803—The Louisiana Purchase from France doubles the size of the United States, extending its western border to the Rocky Mountains. Part or all of fifteen states are later formed from the vast acquisition. In making the deal with Napoleon of France, President Jefferson later admits that he "stretched the Constitution until it cracked."

1804—Meriwether Lewis and William Clark embark upon their epic trek across the continent to explore the lands recently acquired in the Louisiana Purchase and beyond to the Pacific Ocean. They are introduced to many Native American tribes, as well as to previously unknown plant and animal species. "It seemed," Lewis wrote, "as if those seens [sic] of visionary enchantment would never have an end."

1804—Aaron Burr kills Alexander Hamilton in a duel, then embarks on his potentially treasonous trek through the American West a year later. Pages: 47–51, 175–82.

1806—Andrew Jackson kills Charles Dickinson in a duel, one of many in which the violent future president engaged. Pages: 58–63.

1807—Robert Fulton's *Clermont* becomes the first financially successful steamboat, traveling up the Hudson River from New York City to Albany in about thirty hours. "Some imagined it to be a sea monster," a witness of the first voyage later recalls, "while others did not hesitate to express their belief that it was a sign of the approaching judgement."

1809—Famed explorer Meriwether Lewis kills himself in Tennessee. Pages: 250–53.

1809—Body of Revolutionary War hero "Mad" Anthony Wayne is exhumed; his corpse is boiled to separate flesh from bone. Pages: 273–74.

1811—A confederation of Indian tribes led by the charismatic Shawnee chief Tecumseh resists the westward movement of white settlers. Tecumseh's brother Tenskwatawa leads an attack on the forces of William Henry Harrison, governor of the Indiana Territory, and is defeated in the Battle of Tippecanoe. "The implicit obedience and respect which the followers of Tecumseh pay to him is astonishing," writes Harrison, "and more than any other circumstance bespeaks him one of those uncommon geniuses which spring up occasionally to produce revolutions, and overturn the established order of things."

1811—Construction begins on what becomes known as the National Road, linking the East with the Midwest.

1812—The War of 1812 begins after years of British interference with American shipping and other degradations.

1814—British forces capture the nation's capital, burning the President's House, the U.S. Capitol, and other government buildings. "Few thought of going to bed," a Washington resident later writes of the destruction. "They spent the night in gazing on the fires and lamenting the disgrace of the city." The British are subsequently repelled after attacking Baltimore, prompting Francis Scott Key to compose "The Star-Spangled Banner."

1817—Thomas Paine's corpse is removed from its grave in the United States and taken on an unsuccessful tour of Britain. Pages: 275–77.

1819—Spain cedes Florida to the United States.

1820—With the issue of slavery creating deep divisions within the nation, the Missouri Compromise is reached. Under its terms, Missouri is admitted to the Union as a slave state and Maine as a free state, thus maintaining the balance of slave and free states in the U.S. Senate. The Compromise also bans slavery from the Louisiana Purchase north of the southern boundary of Missouri, except in Missouri itself. "If the Union must be dissolved, slavery is precisely the question upon which it ought to break," writes John Quincy Adams. "For the present, however, this contest is laid asleep."

1820—James Barron kills Stephen Decatur in a duel, one of many that take place at the "Dark and Bloody Grounds" just outside Washington. Pages: 52–55.

1823—The Monroe Doctrine warns European nations against interfering in the affairs of the Western Hemisphere and declares that the North and South American continents are "henceforth not to be considered as subjects for future colonization by any European powers."

1828—Andrew Jackson blames his political foes for the death of his beloved wife, Rachael. Pages: 159–61.

1828—"The Eaton Malaria" spreads across official Washington, resulting in mass resignations from President Andrew Jackson's cabinet. Pages: 64–71.

1829—John Quincy Adams's eldest son George hurls himself into Long Island Sound rather than face his father's wrath. Pages: 9–11.

1829—Sam Houston and Eliza Allen marry, and immediately separate. Pages: 12–14.

1830—President Andrew Jackson signs the Indian Removal Act, requiring eastern Indians to be resettled west of the Mississippi River. During the forced exodus that follows, known as "The Trail of Tears," thousands die. "At this very moment a low sound of distant thunder fell on my ear," a witness to the first drive later recalls. "In almost an exact western direction a dark spiral cloud was rising above the horizon and sent forth a murmur I almost fancied a voice of divine indignation for the wrongs of my poor and unhappy countrymen, driven by brutal power from all they loved and cherished in the land of their fathers, to gratify the cravings of avarice."

1831—Nat Turner, a black preacher in Virginia, leads a violent slave revolt in which fifty-four whites are killed. During the manhunt that follows, at least one hundred blacks are killed, while Turner and twenty others are later hanged.

1836—Three thousand Mexican troops under Santa Anna storm the Alamo, a fortified mission in San Antonio, Texas. It is defended by 182 Texans and Tennessean Davy Crockett, under the command of Colonels William B. Travis and James Bowie. The garrison is overpowered within an hour and all the defenders killed.

1844—On a test line of his telegraph between Washington, D.C., and Baltimore, Samuel F. B. Morse taps the famous line, "What hath God wrought!"

1845—The Republic of Texas becomes the nation's twenty-eighth state.

1845—Frederick Douglass's autobiography, *Narrative of the Life of Frederick Douglass,* is published.

1845—Edgar Allan Poe's *The Raven* is published.

1846—At the request of President Polk, Congress declares war on Mexico. The United States quickly defeats its weaker southern neighbor and gains a vast stretch of territory, from Texas west to the Pacific Ocean and north to Oregon.

1846—Britain cedes the southern portion of its Oregon Territory below Vancouver to the United States.

1846—After Joseph Smith is killed by a mob, Brigham Young leads a mass exodus of Mormons from Illinois to Utah.

1848—Lucretia Mott and Elizabeth Cady Stanton organize the first U.S. women's rights convention in Seneca Falls, New York. The convention adopts a Declaration of Sentiments, which calls for women to receive "all the rights and privileges which belong to them as citizens of the United States." "The proceedings [of the convention] were extensively published, unsparingly ridiculed by the press, and denounced from the pulpit, much to the surprise and chagrin of the leaders," the convention's organizers later write. "Being deeply in earnest, and believing their demands preeminently wise and just, they were wholly unprepared to find themselves the target for the jibes and jeers of the nation."

1848—James Marshall discovers gold at Sutter's Mill in California, triggering the greatest gold rush in American history.

1850—The Compromise of 1850 temporarily simmers the growing strife over slavery by admitting California to the Union as a free state, and allowing the territories of New Mexico and Utah to decide the issue for themselves. The Compromise also abolishes the slave trade in the District of Columbia, while providing a stricter federal law for the return of runaway slaves.

1850—Nathaniel Hawthorne's *The Scarlet Letter* is published.

1851—Isaac Singer devises the first continuous-stitch sewing machine, the first major home appliance.

1851—Herman Melville's *Moby-Dick* is published.

1852—Harriet Beecher Stowe's antislavery novel *Uncle Tom's Cabin* becomes a best-seller and further inflames the agitation over slavery. When Stowe is introduced to President Lincoln a decade later during the Civil War, he greets her with the question, "Is this the little woman whose book made such a great war?"

1854—Congress passes the Kansas-Nebraska Act, allowing the people of the two territories to decide for themselves whether or not to allow slavery. President Franklin Pierce signs the bill into law, despite the fact that Kansas and Nebraska are in that part of the country where slavery had been "forever prohibited" under the Missouri Compromise of 1820. The bitter and violent reaction to the new law offers a preview of the Civil War to come.

1854—The Republican Party is formed in Ripon, Wisconsin, by antislavery groups opposed to the Kansas-Nebraska Act.

1854—Henry David Thoreau's *Walden* is published.

1855—Walt Whitman publishes at his own expense his first volume of poetry, *Leaves of Grass,* prompting one reviewer to call him "the dirtiest beast of his age."

1856—Charles Sumner, an abolitionist senator from Massachusetts, is beaten senseless by Representative Preston S. Brooks of South Carolina after delivering his "Crimes Against Kansas" speech. *Pages: 137–39.*

1857—Elisha G. Otis installs the first passenger elevator, in New York City.

1857—Chief Justice Roger Taney delivers the infamous Dred Scott *decision.* *Pages: 185–90.*

1859—The first commercially productive oil well is drilled near Titusville, Pennsylvania.

1859—Representative Daniel Sickles of New York kills friend Philip Barton Key, son of "Star-Spangled Banner" composer Francis Scott Key, in front of the White House after discovering Key's affair with his wife. Pages: 254–61.

1860—The Pony Express begins delivering mail from St. Louis, Missouri, then the western terminus of the American railroad system, to Sacramento, California. It closes the next year upon completion of the transcontinental telegraph.

1860—Abraham Lincoln is sharply abused and vilified in his quest for the presidency, and again four years later when he seeks reelection. Pages: 160–62.

1861—Ten Southern states follow South Carolina out of the Union and form the Confederate States of America. The Civil War begins on April 12, when Southern troops fire on Fort Sumter in Charleston Harbor.

1862—The Homestead Act grants free/cheap public land to frontier settlers.

1862—The nation's first federal income tax is levied to help pay for the Civil War. It ends in 1872, but becomes a permanent fixture in American life in 1913.

1862—President Lincoln fires General George B. McClellan for, among other things, his chronic "slows." Pages: 72–78.

1863—President Lincoln issues the Emancipation Proclamation, calling it "a fit and necessary war measure." Although the Proclamation does not actually free a single slave (because it applies only to those areas under Confederate control), it does formally establish the abolition of slavery as a goal of the war, and strengthens the Northern war effort by providing for the incorporation of blacks into the Union army and navy.

1863—In the greatest battle ever fought on the American continent, Union forces defeat invading Confederates at Gettysburg after three days. The decisive victory, occurring simultaneously with the Confederate surrender at Vicksburg, marks the turning point in the Civil War. Later that year, President Lincoln delivers his Gettysburg Address, declaring that the men who died on the battlefield gave their lives so "that this nation, under God, shall have a new birth of freedom—and that government of the people, by the people, for the people, shall not perish from the earth."

1863—The U.S. Capitol dome is completed and capped with the Statue of Freedom.

1865—General Robert E. Lee, commander of the Confederate Army, surrenders to Union commander Ulysses S. Grant at Appomattox Courthouse in Virginia on April 9. The last Confederate troops surrender a month later, ending the Civil War. The human cost of the four-year struggle is staggering, with approximately 620,000 Union and Confederate soldiers losing their lives.

1865—President Abraham Lincoln is assassinated in Washington, D.C., by Southern sympathizer John Wilkes Booth.

1865—The Thirteenth Amendment to the Constitution outlaws slavery throughout the United States. It is followed in 1868 by the Fourteenth Amendment confirming the citizenship of blacks, and the Fifteenth Amendment in 1870, which makes it illegal to deny voting rights based on race.

1865—Henry Wirz is executed for war crimes allegedly committed while commandant of the South's infamous Andersonville Prison. Pages: 191–95.

1866—The transatlantic cable is completed.

1866—The Ku Klux Klan is formed to terrorize liberated blacks in the South.

1867—Secretary of State William H. Seward negotiates the purchase of Alaska from Russia for $7,200,000 (or about 2 cents per acre). Opponents of the purchase deride it as "Seward's Folly."

1867—Christopher Latham Sholes, with assistance from Carlos Glidden and Samuel Soulé, make the first practical typewriter.

1868—President Andrew Johnson, an opponent of harsh measures against the South during Reconstruction, is impeached in the U.S. House of Representatives due largely to the efforts of radical Republicans. He is acquitted in the Senate by one vote.

1868—Louisa May Alcott's *Little Women* is published.

1869—A silver sledge hammering a golden spike into a railroad tie at Promontory Point, Utah, marks the completion of the world's first transcontinental railroad. Built in just over three years by 20,000 workmen, it has 1,775 miles of track.

1870—John D. Rockefeller founds Standard Oil.

1871—The Great Fire of Chicago leaves over 100,000 people homeless and destroys 17,500 buildings. "Nobody could see it all," Chicago *Tribune* editor Horace White later writes, "no more than one man could see the whole of the Battle of Gettysburg. It was too vast, too swift, too full of smoke, too full of danger, for anybody to see it all."

1871—Showman P. T. Barnum opens his circus, modestly dubbing it "The Greatest Show on Earth."

1872—In Rochester, New York, suffragist Susan B. Anthony illegally votes in the presidential election, and is arrested and fined. At her trial she declares, "Resistance to tyranny is obedience to God," which becomes a slogan of the suffragist movement.

1872—Congress establishes Yellowstone as the first national park.

1875—Congress passes a Civil Rights Act, giving blacks equal rights in public accommodations and access to jury duty. The U.S. Supreme Court declares the law unconstitutional in 1883.

1875—Robert Lincoln, eldest son of the late president, arranges for his mother's commitment to an insane asylum. Pages: 15–19.

1875—Texas governor James Stephen Hogg names his daughter Ima. Page: 20.

1876—Alexander Graham Bell transmits human speech for the first time while developing the telephone. His words are, "Mr. Watson, come here. I want you!" spoken to his assistant after spilling battery acid on himself. Bell demonstrates the telephone in Philadelphia as the United States celebrates its 100th birthday.

1876—General George A. Custer and 264 soldiers of the Seventh Cavalry die in the "Last Stand" battle at the Little Bighorn River during the war with the Sioux Indians. "Where the last stand was made," Sitting Bull later recalled, "the Long Hair [Custer] stood like a sheaf of corn with all the ears fallen around him."

1876—Grave robbers attempt to steal the body of Abraham Lincoln and hold it for ransom. Pages: 278–80.

1877—Reconstruction officially ends when the last federal troops are withdrawn from the South.

1877—The first commercial telephone line is installed in Massachusetts.

1878—A woman suffrage amendment is first introduced in Congress. It fails to pass, but is reintroduced in every session of Congress for the next forty years.

1878—The stolen corpse of Representative John Scott Harrison of Ohio is discovered hanging by the neck at the Ohio Medical College. Pages: 281–82.

1879—Thomas Edison, "The Wizard of Menlo Park," produces the first practical lightbulb. It his perhaps the greatest of his numerous accomplishments, including the invention of the phonograph and improvements to the telephone, telegraph, and motion pictures. "We sat and looked and the lamp continued to burn and the longer it burned the more fascinated we were," Edison writes. "None of us could go to bed and there was no sleep for over forty hours; we sat and just watched it with anxiety growing into elation."

1879—California Electric Light Co. begins operating the world's first central power plant selling electricity to private customers.

1880—New York streets are lit by electricity.

1880—Senator William Sharon of Nevada commences an ill-fated affair with Althea Hill, a liaison that eventually results in three different U.S. Supreme Court decisions. Pages: 141–47.

1881—Clara Barton organizes the Red Cross.

1881—Henry James's *Portrait of a Lady* is published.

1881—President James A. Garfield is assassinated in Washington by Charles Julius Guiteau, a mentally unbalanced drifter. Pages: 262–66.

1882—The United States bans Chinese immigration for ten years in reaction to simmering resentment over Chinese laborers.

1883—The Brooklyn Bridge is completed and hailed as the "Eighth Wonder of the World."

1883—William Frederick "Buffalo Bill" Cody organizes his Wild West show.

1884—Construction begins in Chicago on the Home Insurance Building, the world's first skyscraper.

1884—"Ma! Ma! Where's my Pa?" becomes the Republican campaign chant after it is revealed that Democratic candidate Grover Cleveland had sired an illegitimate son during his youth. Pages: 165–67.

1885—Mark Twain's *Huckleberry Finn* is published.

1886—The Statue of Liberty, a gift from the people of France, is dedicated in New York Harbor and becomes the first view of America for many in the growing "nation of immigrants."

1888—George Eastman perfects the "Kodak" box camera, the first designed for mass production and amateur use.

1889—Herman Hollerith's punched-card tabulating machine is the first successful computer, and is used to tabulate the results of the 1890 census.

1889—A dam on the Conemaugh River in Pennsylvania breaks, causing the great Johnstown Flood in which 2,200 are killed. "The water seemed to leap, scarcely touching the ground," a witness recalls. "It bounded down the valley, crashing and roaring, carrying everything before it. For a mile its front seemed like a solid wall twenty feet high."

1890—The Battle of Wounded Knee in South Dakota, which begins after the federal government bans the Sioux's Ghost Dance (a religious ceremony), is the last major conflict between Native Americans and U.S. troops. It ends with the slaughter of over 200 Lakota Sioux.

1890—The electric chair is used for the first time in the execution of convicted murderer William Kemmler. It is not a success. "The first execution by electricity has been a horror," writes an anonymous New York *World* reporter. "Physicians who might make a jest out of the dissecting room, officials who have seen many a man's neck wrenched by rope, surgeons who have lived in hospitals and knelt beside the dead and dying on bloody fields, held their breaths with a gasp, and those unaccustomed to such sights turned away in dread."

1890—The census bureau announces that so many people have filled in pockets throughout the West that it is no longer meaningful to talk about a "frontier line." The frontier is officially declared closed.

1891—Warren G. Harding and Florence Kling DeWolfe, aka "The Duchess," embark on one of American history's most miserable marriages. Pages: 21–23.

1891—James Naismith invents basketball.

1893—Henry Ford builds his first successful gasoline engine.

1893—Representative William Campbell Preston Breckinridge of Kentucky, a frequent lecturer on the evils of fornication, is sued for child support by his teenage mistress. Pages: 140–41.

1894—Thomas Edison markets the kinetoscope, an early form of movie in which a viewer peers through a magnifying lens at moving images illuminated by an electric light.

1895—Charles and Franklin Duryea establish the first American company for manufacturing gasoline-powered automobiles.

1895—Stephen Crane's *The Red Badge of Courage* is published.

1895—The first professional football game is played in Latrobe, Pennsylvania.

1897—The first American subway opens in Boston with 1.5 miles of track.

1898—In what U.S. ambassador to Britain John Hay calls "a splendid little war," the U.S. fights Spain over the independence of Cuba. The April to August hostilities, in which Spain is easily defeated, marks the emergence of the United States as a world power and results in the possession of Guam, Puerto Rico, and the Philippine Islands. The war also makes Theodore Roosevelt's Rough Riders national heroes.

1901—President William McKinley is assassinated in Buffalo, New York, by anarchist Leon Czolgosz. Pages: 266–69.

1903—Wilbur and Orville Wright design and build the first successful airplane. The first flight, near Kitty Hawk, North Carolina, goes 120 feet and lasts about 12 seconds. Man has at last taken wing, yet the feat barely makes a ripple in the nation's newspapers.

1903—*The Great Train Robbery,* an eleven-minute Western film, is the first major motion picture. It is a sensation, giving birth to the "Hollywood Dream Factory."

1903—The first World Series is held. Boston defeats Pittsburgh five games to three.

1905—Eleanor Roosevelt marries Franklin D. Roosevelt, acquiring in the process a most troublesome mother-in-law. Pages: 24–27.

1905—The body of naval hero John Paul Jones, buried in a long-lost cemetery outside Paris, is finally recovered and brought back to the United States. Pages: 283–86.

1906—San Francisco suffers one of the worst disasters in American history when a massive earthquake strikes, followed by a conflagration that consumes much of the city. "San Francisco is gone!" reports novelist Jack London. "Nothing remains of it but memories and a fringe of dwelling houses on the outskirts." At least 3,000 people are killed and 250,000 lose their homes.

1906—Upton Sinclair's *The Jungle* is published.

1906—Senator Arthur Brown of Utah is shot dead by his scorned mistress, Anna Addison Bradley. Pages: 147–49.

1908—President Theodore Roosevelt settles on William Howard Taft as his successor, resulting in a shattered friendship between the two men. Pages: 79–85.

1909—Robert E. Peary reaches the North Pole. (Frederick A. Cook's claim that he had reached the Pole a year earlier is later discredited after a congressional investigation.)

1911—Under the provisions of the Sherman Antitrust Act, the U.S. Supreme Court orders the Standard Oil Company, one of the richest and most powerful businesses in the world, to dissolve into a number of separate entities.

1912—The *Titanic* sinks on her maiden voyage, killing 1,517 people, including many Americans.

1913—Ford Company engineers develop the assembly line, making the manufacture of automobiles cheaper and more efficient. "We now have two general principles in all operations," writes Henry Ford, "that a man shall never have to take more than one step, if possibly it can be avoided, and that no man need ever stoop over." With automobiles more readily available to the masses, America takes to the road.

1914—The Panama Canal is completed, opening a passage between the Atlantic and Pacific Oceans in one of the world's greatest feats of engineering.

1915—A German submarine sinks the passenger ship *Lusitania,* killing over half of the nearly 2,000 people on board, including more than 100 Americans. "Remember the *Lusitania*" becomes a rallying cry when the United States enters World War I two years later.

1917—The United States enters World War I when Congress declares war on Germany. Over 116,000 Americans die in the conflict, which ends the following year, and more than 234,000 are wounded.

1918—An influenza epidemic sweeps the world, killing an estimated 20 million people, including about 600,000 in the United States.

1919—Attorney General A. Mitchell Palmer's "Red Raids" begin as the Bill of Rights takes a back seat. *Pages: 196–202.*

1920—Women are given the right to vote under the Nineteenth Amendment, which states, "The right of citizens of the United States to vote shall not be denied or abridged by the United States or by any state on account of sex."

1920—Prohibition begins following ratification of the Eighteenth Amendment outlawing liquor for all citizens. The ban ushers in an era of bootlegging and violent gang crime.

1920—The U.S. Senate rejects American participation in the League of Nations.

1923—President Warren G. Harding dies, mercifully spared full knowledge of his "God-damn friends'" treachery in Teapot Dome and other great scandals of his disastrous administration. *Pages: 203–6.*

1925—F. Scott Fitzgerald's *The Great Gatsby* is published.

1926—The first liquid-propelled rocket is launched using technology developed by aerospace pioneer Robert Goddard. "It looked almost magical as it rose," Goddard writes, "without any appreciably greater noise or flame, as if it said 'I've been here long enough; I think I'll be going somewhere else, if you don't mind.'"

1927—Charles Lindbergh becomes the first aviator to make a solo nonstop flight across the Atlantic Ocean. "I'm flying along dreamily when it catches my eye," Lindbergh later writes in his autobiography, *The Spirit of St. Louis,* "that black speck on the water two or three miles southeast. Seconds pass before my mind takes in the full impact of what my eyes are seeing . . . fishing boats! The coast, the European coast, can't be far away!"

1927—Television, later to dominate the American cultural landscape, makes a rather humble debut with the broadcast image of Secretary of Commerce (and later President) Herbert Hoover on two screens.

1929—The Roaring Twenties come to an abrupt end when the stock market crashes and the nation is plunged into the Great Depression. "It came with a speed and ferocity that left men dazed," the *New York Times* reports of the collapse. "The bottom simply fell out of the market."

1929—Robert Byrd becomes the first person to fly over the South Pole.

1929—Gangland violence in Chicago reaches its peak during Prohibition with the St. Valentine's Day Massacre.

1929—William Faulkner's *The Sound and the Fury* is published.

1930—U.S. astronomers announce the discovery of Pluto, the ninth planet in the solar system. They initially believe the diminutive planet to be even bigger than Jupiter.

1932—Amelia Earhart becomes the first woman to fly solo across the Atlantic Ocean.

1932—Franklin D. Roosevelt is elected president, to the eternal chagrin of Theodore Roosevelt's children, his distant relatives. Pages: 86–92.

1933—As the nation suffers through the Great Depression, with many believing that democracy itself is in danger of collapse, President Franklin Roosevelt declares at his inauguration, "The only thing we have to fear is fear itself." The new president immediately launches a massive recovery program known as the New Deal.

1933—Prohibition is repealed with the Twenty-first Amendment.

1936—Margaret Mitchell's *Gone With the Wind* is a best-seller, surpassing in six months sales of the previous best-seller in American history, *Uncle Tom's Cabin*.

1939—John Steinbeck's *The Grapes of Wrath* is published.

1940—"Democracy is all done . . . ," Joseph P. Kennedy declares after resigning as ambassador to Great Britain. "Democracy is finished in England. It may be here." (Democracy survived. Kennedy's political career did not.) Pages: 28–31.

1941—On December 7, "a date," President Franklin Roosevelt declares, "which will live in infamy," a surprise attack by Japan on Pearl Harbor devastates the U.S. Pacific fleet and propels the nation into World War II.

1942—President Roosevelt signs into law Executive Order No. 9006, which allows the military to move 112,000 Japanese-Americans from their homes on the West Coast to inland concentration camps.

1944—Allied forces invade Normandy, France, with over 150,000 troops on five beachheads. "We will accept nothing except full victory," declares Supreme Allied Commander Dwight D. Eisenhower. Thousands of soldiers are killed and wounded, but Europe, and possibly the world, is saved from Axis domination.

1945—Germany surrenders on May 7, ending the war in Europe. On August 6, an American B-29 bomber, the *Enola Gay,* drops the first atomic bomb used in warfare on Hiroshima, Japan. The explosion immediately kills an estimated 70,000–100,000 people and destroys an area of about five square miles. "The giant purple mushroom [cloud] . . . was still boiling upward like something terribly alive," *Enola Gay* pilot Colonel Paul W. Tibbets Jr. later writes. "It was a frightening sight, and even though we were several miles away, it gave the appearance of something that was about to engulf us." Another, larger atomic bomb is dropped on Nagasaki three days later, after which Japan surrenders and World War II ends.

1946—During the first session of the newly formed United Nations, the General Assembly agrees that the organization's headquarters should be in the United States.

1946—ENIAC becomes the first general-purpose electronic digital computer. The enormous machine, designed by J. Presper Eckert and John William Mauchly, occupies more than 1,500 square feet of floor space.

1947—Air Force Captain Charles Yeager, flying the Bell X-1, exceeds the speed of sound and becomes the world's first supersonic flyer.

1948—Under the European Recovery Program, better known as the Marshall Plan, the U.S. delivers billions of dollars in aid to war-ravaged Europe. The program helps stave off Soviet domination of the sixteen democratic nations participating in it.

1949—The United States signs the North Atlantic Treaty Organization—or NATO—pact, pledging to join Canada and ten West European nations in mutual resistance of armed attack on any member nation.

1950—The Korean War begins when North Korean forces cross the thirty-eighth parallel in an invasion of South Korea.

1950—Senator Joseph McCarthy launches his anticommunist campaign in Wheeling, West Virginia, producing a fabricated list of subversives in the State Department. *Pages: 207–14.*

1951—J. D. Salinger's *The Catcher in the Rye* is published.

1951—President Truman fires that "son of a bitch" General Douglas MacArthur. *Pages: 93–99.*

1952—Ernest Hemingway's *The Old Man and the Sea* is published.

1953—Ethel and Julius Rosenberg become the first U.S. civilians executed for espionage after being convicted of passing atomic secrets to the Soviet Union.

1954—In *Brown v. Topeka Board of Education,* the U.S. Supreme Court declares that racially segregated schools are unconstitutional, as is the long-standing legal precept of "separate but equal."

1954—The commissioning of the atomic submarine U.S.S. *Nautilus* marks the world's first full-scale use of controlled nuclear energy.

1955—Dr. Jonas Salk's polio vaccine is approved, beginning the end of a dreaded disease that often left its victims—mostly children—dead or paralyzed for life.

1959—The epic feud between Lyndon Johnson and Robert Kennedy takes root. Pages: 100–111.

1961—The first two U.S. military companies, including 32 helicopters and 4,000 men, arrive in South Vietnam as directed by the Kennedy administration.

1961—FBI director J. Edgar Hoover begins his campaign against "that burrhead," Martin Luther King Jr. Pages: 215–21.

1962—Publication of Rachel Carson's *Silent Spring,* an exposé of the widespread damage to life caused by pesticides, marks the beginning of the modern environmental movement.

1963—The Reverend Martin Luther King Jr. delivers his "I Have a Dream" speech during a civil rights march in Washington. "Now is the time to rise from the dark and desolate valley of segregation to the sunlit path of racial justice . . . ," King proclaims. "There will be neither rest nor tranquility in America until the Negro is granted his citizenship rights. . . . No, we are not satisfied and we will not be satisfied until justice rolls down like water and righteousness like a mighty stream."

1963—President John F. Kennedy is assassinated in Dallas, Texas, by Lee Harvey Oswald.

1964—President Lyndon Johnson signs the most comprehensive civil rights act in American history, integrating public accommodations and prohibiting job discrimination. The act also has provisions on voting, education, and federal funding.

1964—The U.S. Surgeon General releases the first report on the health dangers of smoking.

1964—The Beatles storm the nation on their first U.S. tour.

1968—Martin Luther King Jr. is assassinated in April in Memphis, Tennessee, prompting riots in many U.S. cities. Senator Robert F. Kennedy is assassinated two months later in Los Angeles.

1969—The seemingly impossible dream of landing a man on the moon and returning him safely to Earth is realized. "That's one small step for man," declares pioneer astronaut Neil Armstrong upon first stepping on the lunar surface, "one giant leap for mankind."

1969—About 500,000 people gather on a farm near Woodstock, New York, for a three-day music and arts festival.

1969—President Johnson's brother Sam publishes My Brother Lyndon, *a most unflattering account of his famous sibling. Page: 33.*

1970—National Guardsmen kill four students at Kent State University in Ohio after a campus protest against the U.S. invasion of Cambodia.

1971—Recording equipment is installed in the White House, preserving forever some colorful chitchat by President Nixon. Pages: 222–27.

1972—U.S. relations with China, almost nonexistent since the Korean War and made even worse by the conflict in Vietnam, begin to thaw after President Nixon makes an historic visit there.

1972—Five men are apprehended after burglarizing the Democratic National Committee's headquarters in the Watergate building complex in Washington, D.C. The event eventually brings down the presidency of Richard Nixon.

1972—An historic respite from the Cold War is achieved when the United States and the U.S.S.R. sign the Strategic Arms Limitations Treaty, better known as the SALT treaty.

1972—In the longest decision in U.S. Supreme Court history (and the shortest-lived), the death penalty is declared unconstitutional under the Eighth Amendment that bars "cruel and unusual punishment." It is restored four years later.

1973—The last U.S. ground troops leave Vietnam. Saigon falls two years later, officially ending the Vietnam War.

1973—The U.S. Supreme Court rules that state laws cannot forbid a woman from having an abortion in the first trimester of pregnancy, and can only regulate abortions during the second trimester to protect the woman's health.

1974—Facing certain impeachment and conviction arising from the Watergate scandal, Richard M. Nixon resigns as the thirty-seventh president of the United States. "By taking this action," he announces to the nation in a televised address, "I hope that I will have hastened the start of the process of healing which is so desperately needed in America." Vice President Gerald R. Ford assumes the presidency and pardons Nixon for any crimes he may have committed as chief executive.

1974—Stripper Fanne Foxe, a "friend" of Representative Wilbur Mills of Arkansas, takes her famous leap into the Tidal Basin. Pages: 149–50.

1976—The United States of America celebrates its 200th birthday.

1976—Elizabeth Ray, secretary and mistress of Representative Wayne Hays of Ohio, proclaims to the world: "I can't type. I can't file. I can't even answer the phone." Pages: 149–51.

1979—Radical Iranian students seize American diplomats and embassy employees in Tehran. They are not released until President Jimmy Carter's last day in office fourteen months later.

1980—A Senate subcommittee investigates Billy Carter's special relationship with Libya. Page: 33.

Select Bibliography

Books

Ambrose, Stephen E. *Eisenhower: Volume One.* New York: Simon & Schuster, 1983.

———. *Eisenhower: Volume Two.* New York: Simon & Schuster, 1984.

———. *Undaunted Courage: Meriwether Lewis, Thomas Jefferson, and the Opening of the American West.* New York: Simon & Schuster, 1996.

Baker, Jean H. *Mary Todd Lincoln: A Biography.* New York and London: W.W. Norton & Co., 1987.

Bartlett, Irving H. *John Calhoun: A Biography.* New York and London: W.W. Norton & Co., 1993.

Boller, Paul F. *Presidential Campaigns.* New York: Oxford University Press, 1996.

Bonomi, Patricia U. *The Lord Cornbury Scandal: The Politics of Reputation in British America.* Chapel Hill and London: University of North Carolina Press, 1998.

Brandt, Nat. *The Congressman Who Got Away With Murder.* Syracuse, New York: Syracuse University Press, 1991.

Collier, Peter (with Horowitz, David). *The Roosevelts: An American Saga.* New York: Simon & Schuster, 1994.

Cook, Blanche Wiesen. *Eleanor Roosevelt: Volume One, 1884–1933.* New York: Viking, 1992.

———. *Eleanor Roosevelt: Volume Two, 1933–1938.* New York: Viking, 1999.

Davis, Burke. *Old Hickory: A Life of Andrew Jackson.* New York: Dial Press, 1977.

De Bruhl, Marshall. *Sword of San Jacinto: A Life of Sam Houston.* New York: Random House, 1993.

Donald, David H. *Lincoln.* New York: Simon & Schuster, 1995.

Ellis, Joseph J. *Passionate Sage: The Character and Legacy of John Adams.* New York and London: W.W. Norton & Co., 1993.

Ferling, John. *John Adams: A Life.* Knoxville: University of Tennessee Press, 1992.

Foner, Eric. *Tom Paine and Revolutionary America.* New York: Oxford University Press, 1976.

Garrow, David J. *The FBI and Martin Luther King, Jr.* New York: Penguin Books, 1981.

———. *Bearing the Cross: Martin Luther King, Jr., and the Southern Christian Leadership Conference.* New York: Wm. Morrow & Co., 1986.

Goodwin, Doris Kearns. *The Fitzgeralds and the Kennedys.* New York: Simon & Schuster, 1987.

Hamby, Alonzo L. *Man of the People: A Life of Harry S Truman.* New York and London: Oxford University Press, 1995.

Herman, Arthur. *Joseph McCarthy: Reexamining the Life and Legacy of America's Most Hated Senator.* New York: Free Press, 2000.

Kane, Joseph N. *Facts About the Presidents: A Compilation of Biographical and Historical Information.* New York: H.W. Wilson Company, 1989.

Koskoff, David E. *Joseph P. Kennedy: A Life and Times.* Englewood Cliffs, NJ: Prentice-Hall, 1974.

Lash, Joseph P. *Eleanor and Franklin: The Story of Their Relationship Based on Eleanor Roosevelt's Private Papers.* New York and London: W.W. Norton & Co., 1971.

Lomask, Milton. *Aaron Burr: The Conspiracy and Years of Exile, 1805–1836.* New York: Farrar, Straus, 1982.

Lynn, John W. *800 Paces to Hell: Andersonville.* Fredericksburg, Virginia: Sergeant Kirkland's Museum and Historical Society, 1999.

Malone, Dumas. *Jefferson the President: Second Term, 1805–1809.* Boston: Little, Brown, 1974.

Marszalek, John F. *The Petticoat Affair: Manners, Mutiny, and Sex in Andrew Jackson's White House.* New York: Free Press, 1997.

Marvel, William. *Andersonville: The Last Depot.* Chapel Hill and London: University of North Carolina Press, 1994.

McCullough, David. *Truman.* New York: Simon & Schuster, 1992.

———. *John Adams.* New York: Simon & Schuster, 2001.

Middlekauff, Robert. *Benjamin Franklin and His Enemies.* London: University of California Press, 1996.

Morison, Samuel E. *John Paul Jones: A Sailor's Biography.* Boston and Toronto: Atlantic–Little Brown, 1959.

Murphy, Edwin. *After the Funeral: The Posthumous Adventures of Famous Corpses.* New York: Citadel Press/Carol, 1995.

Nagel, Paul C. *Descent from Glory: Four Generations of the John Adams Family.* New York and Oxford: Oxford University Press, 1983.

Perret, Geoffrey. *Old Soldiers Never Die: The Life of Douglas MacArthur.* New York: Random House, 1996.

Powers, Richard G. *Secrecy and Power: The Life of J. Edgar Hoover.* New York: Free Press, 1987.

Randall, Willard S. *A Little Revenge: Benjamin Franklin and His Son.* Boston and Toronto: Little, Brown, 1984.

Reeves, Thomas C. *A Question of Character: A Life of John F. Kennedy.* New York: Free Press, 1991.

Rehnquist, William H. *The Supreme Court.* New York: Alfred A. Knopf, new edition, 1987/2001.

Remini, Robert. *Andrew Jackson and the Course of the American Empire, 1767–1821.* New York: Harper and Row, 1977.

Rogow, Arnold A. *A Fatal Friendship: Alexander Hamilton and Aaron Burr.* New York: Hill and Wang, 1998.

Rovere, Richard H. *Senator Joe McCarthy.* New York: Harcourt, Brace, 1959.

Sears, Stephen W. *George B. McClellan: The Young Napoleon.* New York: Ticknor & Fields, 1990.

Shesol, Jeff. *Mutual Contempt: Lyndon Johnson, Robert Kennedy, and the Feud that Defined a Decade.* New York and London: W.W. Norton & Co., 1997.

Stampp, Kenneth M. *America In 1857: A Nation on the Brink.* New York and Oxford: Oxford University Press, 1990.

Starkey, Marion L. *The Devil in Massachusetts: A Modern Inquiry into the Salem Witch Trials.* New York: Anchor Books, 1949.

Theoharis, Athan G., and Cox, John Stuart. *The Boss: J. Edgar Hoover and the Great American Inquisition.* Philadelphia: Temple University Press, 1988.

Turner, Justin G., and Turner, Linda Levitt. *Mary Todd Lincoln: Her Life and Letters.* New York: Alfred A. Knopf, 1972.

Periodicals

Damon, Allan L. "The Great Red Scare." *American Heritage.* February 1968.

McCracken, Brooks W. "Althea and the Judges." *American Heritage.* June 1967.

Acknowledgments

I want to thank, as always, my wonderfully supportive family and friends; my agent, Jenny Bent; my editor, Caroline White, and the folks at Penguin; my guru, Ann Marie Lynch; and a good man named Joe McLellan.

I also appreciate the assistance of some fine historians, especially Thomas J. Dodd and Jack D. Warren. Finally, I thank Gene Weingarten of the *Washington Post* for everything.

FOR THE BEST IN PAPERBACKS, LOOK FOR THE 

In every corner of the world, on every subject under the sun, Penguin represents quality and variety—the very best in publishing today.

For complete information about books available from Penguin—including Penguin Classics, Penguin Compass, and Puffins—and how to order them, write to us at the appropriate address below. Please note that for copyright reasons the selection of books varies from country to country.

In the United States: Please write to *Penguin Group (USA), P.O. Box 12289 Dept. B, Newark, New Jersey 07101-5289* or call 1-800-788-6262.

In the United Kingdom: Please write to *Dept. EP, Penguin Books Ltd, Bath Road, Harmondsworth, West Drayton, Middlesex UB7 0DA.*

In Canada: Please write to *Penguin Books Canada Ltd, 10 Alcorn Avenue, Suite 300, Toronto, Ontario M4V 3B2.*

In Australia: Please write to *Penguin Books Australia Ltd, P.O. Box 257, Ringwood, Victoria 3134.*

In New Zealand: Please write to *Penguin Books (NZ) Ltd, Private Bag 102902, North Shore Mail Centre, Auckland 10.*

In India: Please write to *Penguin Books India Pvt Ltd, 11 Panchsheel Shopping Centre, Panchsheel Park, New Delhi 110 017.*

In the Netherlands: Please write to *Penguin Books Netherlands bv, Postbus 3507, NL-1001 AH Amsterdam.*

In Germany: Please write to *Penguin Books Deutschland GmbH, Metzlerstrasse 26, 60594 Frankfurt am Main.*

In Spain: Please write to *Penguin Books S. A., Bravo Murillo 19, 1° B, 28015 Madrid.*

In Italy: Please write to *Penguin Italia s.r.l., Via Benedetto Croce 2, 20094 Corsico, Milano.*

In France: Please write to *Penguin France, Le Carré Wilson, 62 rue Benjamin Baillaud, 31500 Toulouse.*

In Japan: Please write to *Penguin Books Japan Ltd, Kaneko Building, 2-3-25 Koraku, Bunkyo-Ku, Tokyo 112.*

In South Africa: Please write to *Penguin Books South Africa (Pty) Ltd, Private Bag X14, Parkview, 2122 Johannesburg.*